MOON

T0043902

BEST OF
COSTA RICA

Nikki Solano

CONTENTS

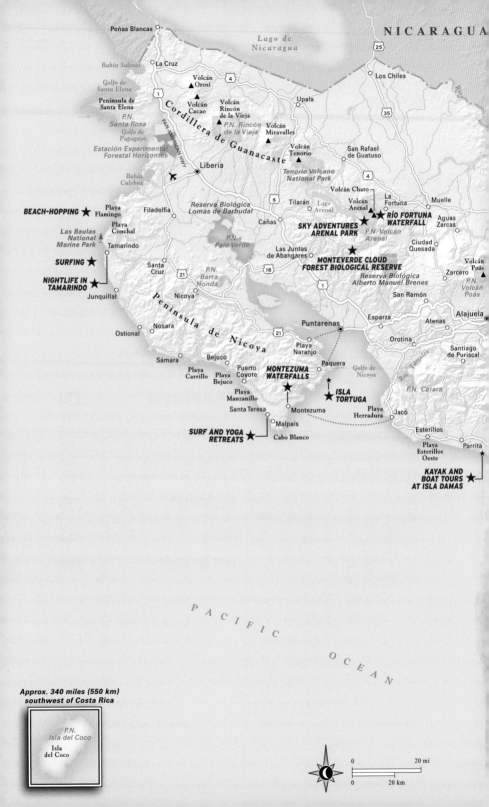

COSTA RICA

Barra del Colorado

San Juan

R.N. Silvestre
Barra del Colorado

Caribbean

Tortuguero

P.N.
Tortuguero

Puerto Viejo
de Sarapiquí

Río Chirripó

Sea

La
Virgen

Las
Horquetas

Parismina

4

Guácimo

Volcán
Barva ▲

Guápiles

Río

P.N.
Braulio
Carrillo

Volcán
Turrialba ▲

Siquirres

Matina

32

Moín

10

Limón

32

Heredia ◉

Volcán
Irazú ▲

P.N. Volcán
Turrialba

WHITE-WATER
RAFTING
RÍO PACUARE ★

✈ SAN JOSÉ

P.N. Volcán
Irazú

Turrialba

Cartago

Paraíso

Lago
Cachí

CAHUITA ★
NATIONAL PARK

San Ignacio
de Acosta

Orosi

Reserva
Biológica
Hitoy Cerere

Cahuita

Puerto Viejo
de Talamanca

2

Río Parrita

Cañon

Río Estrella

Bribrí

Manzanillo

Río Naranjo

P.N. Los
Quetzales

P.N.
Chirripó

Río Sixaola

Sixaola

Cerro de
la Muerte ▲

Cerro
Chirripó ▲

Parque
Internacional
La Amistad

Manuel
Antonio

NAUYACA
WATERFALLS

Cordillera

Cerro Durika ▲

Savegre

San Isidro de
El General

Cerro
Kamúk ▲

Playa
Savegre

de

★ MANUEL ANTONIO
NATIONAL PARK

Dominical

Río

Buenos Aires

Talamanca

Uvita

General

Marino Ballena
National Park

Ojochal

Costa Ballena

Palmar

2

Sierpe

PAN-AMERICAN HWY

Isla del Caño
Biological
Reserve

Bahía
Drake

Península
de Osa

San Vito

PANAMÁ

ISLA DEL
CAÑO ★

Isla del
Caño

*Golfo
Dulce*

Golfito

NIGHT TOUR WITH
THE BUG LADY ★

Zancudo

Ciudad
Neily

Puerto
Jiménez

Playa
Preciosa

Carate

CORCOVADO ★
NATIONAL PARK

Pavones

Cabo
Matapalo

Península
de
Burica

Punta
Burica

© MOON.COM

Playa Arrecife

WELCOME TO
COSTA RICA

Costa Rica will amaze you. Opportunities for immersion in nature are everywhere, so seize them. Boat safaris wind through rivers, mangroves, and canals teeming with wildlife. Treetop excursions provide panoramic forest, volcano, and ocean views. Nature trails showcase reptiles, amphibians, insects, and plants. Parks, reserves, and refuges span more than a quarter of the country's landmass, protecting the immense biodiversity that makes Costa Rica unique.

Prefer to be thrilled? Ride a zip line through the cloud forest, raft over raging rapids, rappel down waterfalls, and surf world-class breaks. To reenergize, pamper yourself with hot springs, mud baths, yoga, and wellness retreats.

Costa Rica's laid-back *pura vida* attitude will also change you. Travel mindfully and you'll reap bountiful rewards from this tiny corner of the world where people greet one another with a smile. In Costa Rica, magic is real—and within arm's reach.

toucan

CHOOSE YOUR BEST WEEK IN
COSTA RICA

Costa Rica's best experiences encompass nature exploration, adventure recreation, wildlife and marine life encounters, cultural immersion, and beach relaxation. Your level of interest in these activities will determine where you go and how much time you spend in each place.

You'll need at least two days in each region to fit in the very best experiences, plus extra time to travel within and between regions. With five or six days in Costa Rica, combine two of the mini-itineraries that follow to explore two distinct regions. If you have more time, stay longer in each region or combine three regional mini-itineraries to extend your vacation's reach.

LA FORTUNA AND MONTEVERDE

DAY 1

Immerse yourself in the verdant rain forest on the outskirts of La Fortuna. Ride an aerial tram, go zip-lining, and tour hanging bridges at the **Sky Adventures Arenal Park.** Afterward, check out the striking **Río Fortuna Waterfall,** then head to the **hot springs** for a luxurious soak.

DAY 2

Strap on a harness and spend a few hours rappelling rock walls on a thrilling **canyoneering tour.** After lunch, make the scenic trip from La Fortuna to Monteverde—blessed with views of Volcán Arenal—by traveling either around or across **Lago Arenal.**

DAY 3

Hike through clouds on a morning spent exploring the mystical **Monteverde Cloud Forest Biological Reserve.** In the afternoon, see butterflies, hummingbirds, reptiles, amphibians, and sloths at **Selvatura Park.**

For five days in La Fortuna and Monteverde, see page 44.

CARIBBEAN COAST

DAY 1

Brave the wild rapids of **Río Pacuare**—Costa Rica's top river for **white-water rafting**—on a full-day tour taken from Cahuita or Puerto Viejo de Talamanca. This unmissable attraction is perfect for thrill seekers, but beginners can join in the fun too.

DAY 2

Rise early to explore the nature trails and beaches inside **Cahuita National Park.** Spend the rest of the day tasting **Caribbean foods** at beloved establishments in or around Puerto Viejo de Talamanca. Order traditional dishes for lunch and dinner and catch the afternoon **Caribeans Chocolate Tour** between the two meals.

For five days on the Caribbean Coast, see page 94.

TAMARINDO

DAY 1

Embrace Tamarindo's vibrant **surf culture** by hitting the water and riding epic waves. No matter your experience level, there's a surf site for you. **Witch's Rock** and **Ollie's Point** deliver the biggest thrills. Breaks off **Playa Tamarindo, Playa Avellanas,** and **Playa Negra** are perfect for developing surf skills.

DAY 2

Swim, sunbathe, or simply take in the view while **beach-hopping** from **Playa Flamingo** to **Playa Conchal** to **Playa Puerto Viejo.** In the evening, explore Tamarindo's crowd-pleasing **nightlife.**

For five days in Tamarindo, see page 126.

SANTA TERESA AND MONTEZUMA

DAY 1

Nourish your body and mind with a day spent **surfing** and practicing **yoga** in serene Santa Teresa. Surf lessons and yoga classes are available. Set aside a few hours to pop over to **Playa Los Suecos** in nearby Mal País for a soothing soak in the pools that form at low tide.

DAY 2

Ease into a day of relaxation in Montezuma with a morning visit to the **Montezuma Waterfalls.** Then head to the sleek **Playa Las Manchas** for a lazy afternoon of sunbathing.

For five days in Santa Teresa and Montezuma, see page 152.

MANUEL ANTONIO AND COSTA BALLENA

DAY 1

Dedicate a full day to encountering **wildlife** in in two distinct ecosystems in Manuel Antonio. Hike in **Manuel Antonio National Park** in the morning. In the afternoon, take a guided **boat or kayak tour** around the **Isla Damas** mangroves to see and hear the flora and fauna.

DAY 2

Hop on a horse and head into the forest that envelops the picturesque **Nauyaca Waterfalls** near Dominical. Spend a few hours swimming in the waterfall's pool. For the afternoon, trade the forest setting for seaside relaxation at either **Playa Espadilla Norte** or **Playa Ventanas.**

For five days in Manuel Antonio and Costa Ballena, see page 184.

BAHÍA DRAKE

DAY 1

Climb aboard a boat from Bahía Drake and cruise to the biodiverse **Corcovado National Park.** Spend the day **hiking** in remote wilderness and searching for **wildlife,** including rare varieties like jaguars and tapirs, alongside an experienced tour guide.

DAY 2

Embark on a **scuba diving** or **snorkeling** excursion destined for the pristine **Isla del Caño Biological Reserve.** Search for whales, sharks, sea turtles, and rays around the island's protected, sun-kissed waters before returning to Bahía Drake.

For five days in Bahía Drake, see page 224.

ITINERARY TIPS

- Plan on spending **2-3 days in each region,** depending on the time you have.

- Add **extra time to travel** within and between regions.

- Visit action-packed **La Fortuna and Monteverde** at the start of your trip, regardless of whether you fly into San José or Liberia, so you can jump into fast-paced, tightly scheduled days before settling into a more relaxed pace on either coast. It's easy to travel from La Fortuna to any other region covered here.

- In a **rental vehicle,** you can drive to most of the regions covered in this guide. If you'd rather not drive, use convenient **shared shuttle services** or **private transfer services** to get around.

- **Organized tours** that offer **complimentary transportation** between regions (like the popular Pacuare River Rafting Tour that can be used to connect San José, La Fortuna, and beach towns on the Caribbean coast) not only make travel between destinations easy but are also time- and cost-efficient.

- While **public transportation** has a lower impact on the environment, it is not always efficient or possible.

Isla Tortuga

IF YOU'RE LOOKING FOR...

- **WILDLIFE:** Visit **Manuel Antonio, Bahía Drake,** or the **Caribbean coast.**

- **ZIP-LINING:** Visit **La Fortuna** or **Monteverde.**

- **CANYONEERING:** Visit **La Fortuna** or **Manuel Antonio.**

- **HIKING:** Explore challenging trails in **Corcovado National Park** on the Osa Peninsula.

- **WHITE-WATER RAFTING:** Plan a tour on the **Río Pacuare,** accessible from La Fortuna or the Caribbean coast.

- **SURFING:** Find the best breaks around **Tamarindo** and **Santa Teresa.**

- **DIVING:** Visit **Isla del Caño** off Bahía Drake.

- **YOGA RETREATS:** Visit **Santa Teresa.**

- **HOT SPRINGS:** Visit **La Fortuna.**

- **NIGHTLIFE:** Visit **Tamarindo, Manuel Antonio,** or **Puerto Viejo de Talamanca.**

Playa Tamarindo

TRANSPORTATION TIMES

DESTINATION	DRIVING FROM SAN JOSÉ	FLYING FROM SAN JOSÉ AIRPORT	PUBLIC TRANSIT FROM SAN JOSÉ (LOWEST ENVIRONMENTAL IMPACT)
LA FORTUNA AND MONTEVERDE			
La Fortuna	3 hours	30 minutes	4 hours
Monteverde	3 hours	N/A	4 hours
CARIBBEAN COAST			
Río Pacuare	2 hours	N/A	No access by bus
Cahuita	4 hours	45-minute flight to Limón; 45-minute drive to Cahuita	4 hours
Puerto Viejo de Talamanca	4.25 hours	45-minute flight to Limón; 1-hour drive to Puerto Viejo de Talamanca	4.5 hours
TAMARINDO			
Tamarindo	4.5 hours	50 minutes	5.5 hours

DRIVING FROM LIBERIA	FLYING FROM LIBERIA AIRPORT	PUBLIC TRANSIT FROM LIBERIA (LOWEST ENVIRONMENTAL IMPACT)
2.75 hours	1 hour and 20 minutes via two flights: Liberia to San José, then San José to La Fortuna	Better to avoid by bus
2 hours	N/A	Better to avoid by bus
5.25 hours	N/A	No access by bus
7 hours	1 hour and 35 minutes via two flights: Liberia to San José, then San José to Limón; 45-minute drive to Cahuita	Better to avoid by bus
7.25 hours	1 hour and 35 minutes via two flights: Liberia to San José, then San José to Limón; 1-hour drive to Puerto Viejo de Talamanca	Better to avoid by bus
1.25 hours	N/A	2.5 hours

TRANSPORTATION TIMES

DESTINATION	DRIVING FROM SAN JOSÉ	FLYING FROM SAN JOSÉ AIRPORT	PUBLIC TRANSIT FROM SAN JOSÉ (LOWEST ENVIRONMENTAL IMPACT)
SANTA TERESA AND MONTEZUMA			
Santa Teresa	4.5 hours (includes 1-hour ferry crossing)	30-minute flight to Tambor; 1-hour drive to Santa Teresa	6 hours (includes 1-hour ferry crossing)
Montezuma	4 hours (includes 1-hour ferry crossing)	30-minute flight to Tambor; 35-minute drive to Montezuma	5.5 hours (includes 1-hour ferry crossing)
MANUEL ANTONIO AND COSTA BALLENA			
Manuel Antonio	3 hours	30-minute flight to Quepos; 25-minute drive to Manuel Antonio	4 hours
Costa Ballena	3.5-4 hours	30-minute flight to Quepos; 30- to 60-minute drive to Costa Ballena	5-5.75 hours
BAHÍA DRAKE			
Bahía Drake	5.5 hours (includes 1-hour boat ride)	50 minutes	6 hours

DRIVING FROM LIBERIA	FLYING FROM LIBERIA AIRPORT	PUBLIC TRANSIT FROM LIBERIA (LOWEST ENVIRONMENTAL IMPACT)
4.5 hours	35-minute flight to Tambor; 1-hour drive to Santa Teresa	Better to avoid by bus
4 hours	35-minute flight to Tambor; 35-minute drive to Montezuma	Better to avoid by bus
4 hours	1 hour and 20 minutes via two flights: Liberia to San José, then San José to Quepos; 25-minute drive to Manuel Antonio	Better to avoid by bus
4.5-5 hours	1 hour and 20 minutes via two flights: Liberia to San José, then San José to Quepos; 30- to 60-minute drive to Costa Ballena	Better to avoid by bus
6.5 hours (includes 1-hour boat ride)	1 hour and 40 minutes via two flights: Liberia to San José, then San José to Bahía Drake; 15-minute drive to Agujitas	No access by bus

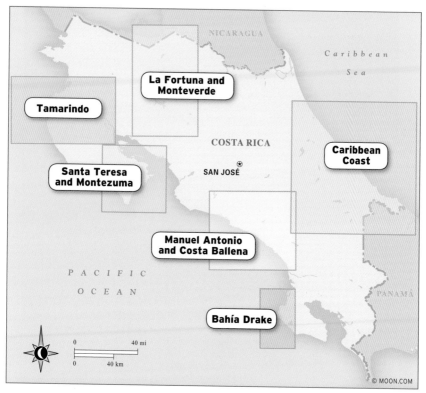

The map shows regions of Costa Rica:
- Tamarindo
- La Fortuna and Monteverde
- Santa Teresa and Montezuma
- Caribbean Coast
- Manuel Antonio and Costa Ballena
- Bahía Drake
- COSTA RICA — SAN JOSÉ

NICARAGUA
Caribbean Sea
PACIFIC OCEAN
PANAMÁ

0   40 mi
0   40 km

© MOON.COM

SEASONS OF COSTA RICA

HIGH SEASON

Generally, the high season runs from **mid-December to the end of April.** It begins no later than January 1 and ends no sooner than Easter. During the season, reservations for hotels, tours, and transportation can be tight, prices are high (notably for accommodations), and **crowds** are common at popular attractions. High season aligns with Costa Rica's **summer** and is also known as the **dry season.** The biggest draw is **favorable weather,** including sunny skies, warm temperatures, and little rain. The most expensive time to travel to Costa Rica is during brief **peak periods** around Christmas, New Year's, and Easter, when accommodation prices are hugely inflated.

TEMPERATURES: 75-85°F

LOW SEASON

The low season runs from the **beginning of May to mid-December.** Sometimes, it can begin immediately after Easter and last until December 31. The low season offers **quiet trails, smaller tour groups,** and **cheaper prices.** Since most tour operators require a minimum of two people to run tours, solo travelers can find it a challenge to travel at this time of year. Some businesses close or

NEED TO KNOW

- **Entry Requirements:** A valid **passport** and **proof of exit intent,** in the form of a ticket to travel to another country, are required to enter Costa Rica. Most stamps expire within 90 days of issuance.

- **Vaccinations:** Costa Rica doesn't require North American travelers to provide proof of vaccination. Nationals and recent travelers to Africa and South America are required to show proof of yellow fever vaccination.

- **Airports:** The **Aeropuerto Internacional Juan Santamaría** (Juan Santamaría International Airport, SJO) in the capital city of San Jose offers access to most of the country. If you plan to focus on Tamarindo, take advantage of **Aeropuerto Internacional Daniel Oduber Quirós** (Daniel Oduber Quirós International Airport, LIR) in the city of Liberia.

- **Ground Transportation:** Tourist-geared **shared shuttle services** and **private transfer services** are plentiful and convenient. Some tour outfitters provide **post-tour onward transportation,** allowing you to travel between destinations while experiencing an adventure along the way. **Taxis** and rented **golf carts, ATVs,** and **bikes** facilitate travel within towns. **Public buses** are reliable in most parts of the country.

- **Car Rentals:** Renting your own vehicle gives you more freedom and more responsibility for your travels. A **4x4 vehicle** is required in many areas and recommended in most others.

- **Other Modes of Transportation:** Domestic **flights, water taxis,** and **ferries** connect several destinations and help save travel time.

- **Advance Reservations:** Reserve tours, accommodations, and transportation services in advance. In high season, spaces fill quickly. Take advantage of **early-booking discounts** and handle payment from home. Many businesses have **flexible cancellation policies.**

- **Taxes:** A **value-added tax (VAT)** of up to 13 percent is charged on tourism services. Some tour operators, hotels, and transportation service providers include the VAT in their rates, but others do not. Confirm directly with the company to see whether the tax is included.

undergo renovations between September and November.

Low season aligns with the **green season** (colloquially referred to as the **wet season**), which is considered Costa Rica's **winter. Heavy rain,** occasional **thunderstorms,** and whipping **winds** at high elevations can cause landslides, traffic delays, flooding, road closures (typically only in back-road areas), and **last-minute tour cancellations.**

TEMPERATURES: 68–78°F

Playa Avellanas

BEST OF THE BEST
COSTA RICA

BEST WILDLIFE EXPERIENCES

MANUEL ANTONIO NATIONAL PARK

Manuel Antonio and Costa Ballena, page 187

If your ideal day in Costa Rica combines beach relaxation and wildlife encounters, this is the place for you. **Monkeys** are known to fraternize with people on this region's beautiful crescent beaches. Beyond the sand are forested trails where sightings of **sloths** (both two-toed and three-toed varieties) are guaranteed. Hire a guide who can provide spotting scopes, trained eyes, and years of experience.

CORCOVADO NATIONAL PARK

Bahía Drake, page 228

With nearly 400 species of **birds,** more than 70 varieties of reptiles, 45 types of amphibians, and a whopping 8,000 species of insects, this park is a wonderland of biodiversity, where you may encounter some of the rarest wildlife species in Costa Rica—and the world. **Sea turtles** nest on the shores of the park's perimeter. **Bull sharks** and **crocodiles** invade the area's rivers and swamps. Tapirs, monkeys, peccaries, anteaters, agoutis, ever-elusive jungle cats, and other mammals roam freely.

MONTEVERDE CLOUD FOREST BIOLOGICAL RESERVE

La Fortuna and Monteverde, page 70

Book a 6am guided tour for fantastic **bird-watching.** You're likely to hear the **three-wattled bellbird** and might even spot the **resplendent quetzal,** a brightly colored and sometimes long-tailed trogon. More encounters can be had along the aptly named **Cloud Forest Trail.**

monkeys at Playa Manuel Antonio (top); Monteverde Cloud Forest Biological Reserve (bottom)

CAÑO NEGRO WILDLIFE REFUGE

La Fortuna and Monteverde, page 53

The Caño Negro Wildlife Refuge is home to diverse wildlife, including **monkeys, iguanas,** and **caimans.** Avid **birders** shouldn't miss it, especially in February and March, its peak bird-watching period. The best way to experience the refuge is by boat tour.

ISLA DEL CAÑO BIOLOGICAL RESERVE

Bahía Drake, page 227

Abundant marine life congregates in the waters surrounding this tiny island off the coast of Bahía Drake. Snorkelers can explore offshore reefs while open-water divers spot **sharks, rays, sea turtles,** and **dolphins.**

caiman in the Caño Negro Wildlife Refuge

There's a good chance you'll see **humpback whales** playing in the waves while en route to the island from December to March and July to October.

boats bound for Isla del Caño Biological Reserve

BEST WATERFALLS

RÍO FORTUNA WATERFALL

La Fortuna and Monteverde, page 48

Imagine a rain forest scene of vivid lime and emerald greens sliced by a stark white cascade spilling into a pool 70 meters below. You can capture photos of this dramatic scene, as well as explore an on-site **Orchid Garden,** from just beyond the entrance to **Río Fortuna Waterfall.** A 517-step staircase leads to the waterfall's churning base. Calmer waters perfect for swimming are slightly downstream.

NAUYACA WATERFALLS

Manuel Antonio and Costa Ballena, page 209

These stunning cascades are tucked amid dense rainforest and scenic rolling hills. From the **upper falls,** water flows to the **lower falls.** Here, you'll find a quiet space, fresh water, bright green flora, and few distractions.

RÍO CELESTE WATERFALL

La Fortuna and Monteverde, page 52

In Tenorio Volcano National Park, hiking along Río Celeste takes you to a mountain *mirador,* the calm **Laguna Azul,** and **Los Teñideros,** where the color of the water transforms from crystal clear into a celestial blue. The highlight of the hike is the **waterfall** that spills out of the rainforest and into an aquamarine pool. You can get relatively close via a steep, 250-step staircase.

bottom tier of the Nauyaca Waterfalls

BEST BEACHES

PLAYA CONCHAL
Tamarindo, page 134

Much of **Playa Conchal** is composed of millions of tiny shell fragments. Polished like sea glass, the shells are soft enough to walk on barefoot. Craggy headlands frame the coast to the north and south. The less-crowded west end of the beach shifts into fine white sand lapped by aquamarine waters.

PLAYA LOS SUECOS
Santa Teresa and Montezuma, page 157

The cove at Playa Los Suecos has nearly white sand and almost teal waters. At high tide, it's great for **snorkeling** among marine life visiting from the nearby Cabo Blanco Absolute Nature Reserve. At low tide, soak in the naturally formed pools or wade into the water to visit **Punta Murciélago,** whose massive crevice is home to hundreds of bats.

PLAYA TROPICAL
Santa Teresa and Montezuma, page 169

Uninhabited **Isla Tortuga** is a vision of paradise: lush vegetation, snow-white sand, and calm turquoise waters. Its stunning beauty attracts crowds of day-trippers. An escape to solitude is possible at heavenly Playa Tropical, separated from the crowds by a rocky headland.

PLAYA BLANCA
Caribbean Coast, page 101

Cahuita National Park protects the region's coral reef. Its main attraction is this undeveloped stretch of white sand—one of the prettiest beaches on the Caribbean coast. Couple your visit to the beach with a snorkeling tour to nearby Punta Cahuita for a chance to spot local marine life.

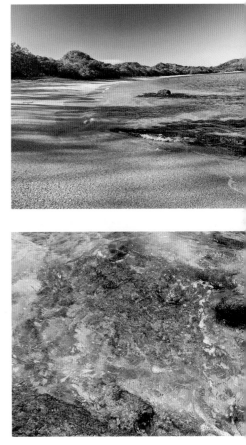

Playa Conchal (top); tide pools at Playa Los Suecos (bottom)

BEST SURFING

WITCH'S ROCK AND OLLIE'S POINT
Tamarindo, page 129

Two of Costa Rica's top surf spots neighbor each other up the coast from Tamarindo. Witch's Rock, just off the coast at Playa Naranjo, offers both left and right wave breaks. At

Playa Potrero Grande and accessible only by boat is Ollie's Point, which has sharp walls and long rights. Both sites are for advanced surfers only.

PLAYA GRANDE, PLAYA AVELLANAS, AND PLAYA NEGRA
Tamarindo, page 129

The year-round waves just up and down the coast from Tamarindo provide stellar surf. Playa Grande is a great spot for surf schools, camps, and tours. Experienced local instructors know how to maneuver the swells but also how to keep surfers safe. At Playa Avellanas, beginner-to-intermediate surfers congregate around the breaks **La Purruja, El Parqueo, Las Olas, El Palo** (or **Palo Seco**), and **El Estero**. Barrels await the pros at the north end of the beach. To the south at Playa Negra is a notorious, consistent reef break. Less intimidating surf can be found at **Callejones,** a beach break just down the coast.

SURF AND YOGA RETREATS
Santa Teresa and Montezuma, page 155

Peaceful retreats at remote **Santa Teresa** welcome you into a community developed around the practices of both surfing and yoga. Come ready to learn how to surf, have fun, and meet new friends. Options include empowering **women-only retreats** for "surf sisters" and a handful of camps designed for youths who use wheelchairs.

sunset at Playa Grande (top); surfing on a beach in Santa Teresa

BEST ADVENTURE EXPERIENCES

ZIP-LINING AT THE SKY ADVENTURES ARENAL PARK

La Fortuna and Monteverde, page 50

La Fortuna is a microcosm of Costa Rica's adventures, and Sky Adventures Arenal Park is one of its largest and most modern attractions. The thrilling Sky Trek Canopy Tour takes you on a zip-lining adventure high above the rainforest canopy.

WHITE-WATER RAFTING ON RÍO PACUARE

Caribbean Coast, page 97

Float past towering mountains, rocky canyons, and green forests. Look for iguanas, sloths, and exotic birds. Along with calm moments to connect with nature, you'll get the adrenaline rush of the raging Class III and IV rapids. Rafting down Río Pacuare isn't just a thrill ride, it's an opportunity to experience Costa Rica's wild jungle from within.

rafting down Río Pacuare

verdant forest in Monteverde

LA FORTUNA AND MONTEVERDE

La Fortuna and Monteverde illustrate much of Costa Rica's appeal. Lush rain forest and cloud forest cover the majority of the region, keeping it green, gorgeous, and replete with wildlife year-round. Among the area's memorable features are deep valleys, rich agricultural plains, an idyllic lake sunken amid rolling hills, and a conical stratovolcano that never fails to make jaws drop. Hundreds of guided excursions are available day and night, immersing travelers in rich biodiversity and providing many of the country's most thrilling adventures.

This northern inland area is undeniably touristy, but even adamant off-the-beaten-path travelers shouldn't miss it. Quite simply, it encompasses too many worthwhile experiences to skip. It's telling that both La Fortuna and Monteverde remain favorites among return visitors—faithful lovers of the land who cannot seem to get their fill of adrenaline-inducing activities, nature expeditions, and community tourism.

Monteverde Cloud Forest Biological Reserve

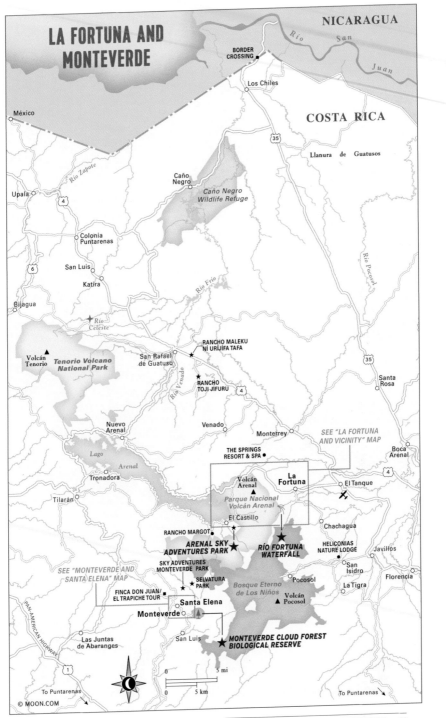

LA FORTUNA AND MONTEVERDE

NICARAGUA

Río San Juan

BORDER CROSSING

Los Chiles

COSTA RICA

México

Río Zapote

Llanura de Guatusos

Caño Negro

Caño Negro Wildlife Refuge

Upala

Colonia Puntarenas

San Luis

Katira

Río Frío

Bijagua

Río Celeste

Río Pacuar

Volcán Tenorio

Tenorio Volcano National Park

San Rafael de Guatuso

RANCHO MALEKU NÍ URIJIFA TAFA

Santa Rosa

RANCHO TOJI JIFURU

Río Venado

Nuevo Arenal

Venado

Monterrey

SEE "LA FORTUNA AND VICINITY" MAP

Boca Arenal

Lago Arenal

THE SPRINGS RESORT & SPA

Tronadora

Volcán Arenal

La Fortuna

El Tanque

Tilarán

Parque Nacional Volcán Arenal

El Castillo

Chachagua

RANCHO MARGOT

ARENAL SKY ADVENTURES PARK

RÍO FORTUNA WATERFALL

HELICONIAS NATURE LODGE

Javillos

SEE "MONTEVERDE AND SANTA ELENA" MAP

SKY ADVENTURES MONTEVERDE PARK

SELVATURA PARK

Bosque Eterno de Los Niños

Pocosol

San Isidro

La Tigra

Florencia

FINCA DON JUAN/ EL TRAPICHE TOUR

Santa Elena

Monteverde

Volcán Pocosol

PAN-AMERICAN HIGHWAY

Las Juntas de Abaranges

San Luis

MONTEVERDE CLOUD FOREST BIOLOGICAL RESERVE

0   5 mi

0   5 km

To Puntarenas

To Puntarenas

© MOON.COM

TOP 3

★ **1. RÍO FORTUNA WATERFALL:** Capture postcard-worthy snapshots of the falls rushing into crystalline waters (page 48).

★ **2. SKY ADVENTURES ARENAL PARK:** Zip-line around a volcano (page 50).

★ **3. MONTEVERDE CLOUD FOREST BIOLOGICAL RESERVE:** Hike through the clouds in this nearly 26,000-acre reserve, a bastion of biodiversity (page 70).

BEST 5 DAYS IN
LA FORTUNA AND MONTEVERDE

DAY 1

Explore **La Fortuna**'s rain forest in the morning on a guided **hanging bridges tour** at **Místico Arenal Hanging Bridges Park.** Afterward, grab lunch at **Soda Víquez** or **Orgánico Fortuna** in downtown La Fortuna, then head to the picturesque **Río Fortuna Waterfall.** Give yourself a few hours to swim in the river, snap photos, and take in the waterfall views. Later, enjoy dinner at **Restaurante Nene's.**

DAY 2

Set out in the early morning to Tenorio Volcano National Park to lay your eyes on the striking blue **Río Celeste,** or join a **bird-watching** expedition to **Caño Negro Wildlife Refuge.** Both attractions lie outside La Fortuna; plan to return to town in the late afternoon. Spend a relaxing evening at one of La Fortuna's famous hot springs, such as **Tabacón** or **The Springs Resort & Spa,** soaking in thermal pools and enjoying dinner.

DAY 3

Kick off an action-packed day in La Fortuna on a **canyoneering tour,** where you'll rappel down rock walls beside rushing waterfalls. Keep the adrenaline flowing throughout the afternoon while **zip-lining** above the treetops at the **Sky Adventures Arenal Park.** On your final evening in La Fortuna, treat yourself to dinner at the **Don Rufino Restaurante.**

DAY 4

Give yourself the morning to travel from La Fortuna to **Monteverde.** After settling in, eat lunch at **Café Orquídeas,** then spend a few hours learning about the production of coffee and chocolate on a tour of **Finca Don Juan.** Cap off the day with a late dinner at the charming **Ristorante e Pizzeria Tramonti.**

DAY 5

Rise early and head for the **Monteverde Cloud Forest Biological Reserve** soon after it opens to increase your chances of seeing birds and other wildlife—and to give yourself ample time to hike the reserve's extensive trail system. On the way back from the reserve, stop at **Restaurante Sabor Tico** for lunch. Check out the butterfly garden, hummingbird garden, and sloth sanctuary at **Selvatura Park** in the afternoon, then finish the day with a sunset dinner at **Restaurante Morpho's.**

resplendent quetzal at Monteverde Cloud Forest Biological Reserve

PLANNING YOUR TIME

Reservations

Secure reservations for accommodations, transportation, and activities **3-6 months in advance** if you will be in the country between the end of **December** and **April.** (Book even earlier if your visit coincides with Christmas, New Year's, or Easter.) Reserving a few weeks prior to your trip is sufficient if you plan to travel between May and mid-December. **Early bookings** mean discounted prices, which can help offset the area's tourism-inflated costs.

Best Bases

Geographically, La Fortuna and Monteverde are near each other, but Lago Arenal and dense forest block direct access between the two destinations. If you intend to split your time in the region between La Fortuna and Monteverde, treat each destination as a separate home base. It takes 3-3.5 hours to travel between La Fortuna and Monteverde, so give yourself a half day to get from one base to the next.

When visiting **La Fortuna,** station yourself in downtown La Fortuna if you have an interest in strolling around the commercial core. Pick a lodging on the outskirts west or south of La Fortuna if you'd prefer to be close to the best attractions and adventure parks.

In the **Monteverde area,** choose either the town of Santa Elena (Monteverde's developed core) or the nearby community of Cerro Plano (one kilometer east of Santa Elena) as your home base if you want to be within walking distance of restaurants and shops. If you prefer a quieter spot, stay in the more remote community of Monteverde (2.5 kilometers southeast of Santa Elena), neighbor to the cloud forest reserve of the same name.

Weather

The region's climate conditions vary between La Fortuna and Monteverde. In lowland **La Fortuna, hot, sunny,** and **muggy** days are common, especially from **January to April.** Rain showers are frequent throughout the year, but heavier and longer-lasting **downpours** are more likely between **September and November.** There is a noticeable temperature drop in **Monteverde,** which has a **higher elevation** than La Fortuna. Although Monteverde receives less rainfall than La Fortuna, it sometimes has **whipping winds** between **May and December.** Be prepared to encounter **fog** on the roads, which can reduce visibility. It's a good idea to rent a **4x4 vehicle;** the extra traction and stability will make driving to and around mountainous Monteverde safer and more comfortable.

Connect with...

La Fortuna is the hub of the country's tourism wheel. The town is centrally located between the international airports in **San José** and **Liberia,** as well as the **Caribbean** and **Pacific coasts,** so it's relatively easy to travel onward to the country's other major destinations.

A number of organized adventure tours include **post-tour onward transportation,** a time- and cost-efficient way of connecting visits to other regions.

The Río Pacuare rafting tour from Exploradores Outdoors includes transportation from La Fortuna, and will drop you in Puerto Viejo de Talamanca or Cahuita in the Caribbean region at the end of the day.

The Springs Resort & Spa

LA FORTUNA AND ARENAL

The area's biggest draw is adventure tourism, which is unrivaled elsewhere in the country. Several **adventure parks** and a seemingly endless list of stand-alone **day tours** provide a variety of activities, from leisurely aerial tram rides to thrilling zip-line glides. Most of La Fortuna's experiences are family friendly, but some outfitters enforce a minimum age requirement.

The town of La Fortuna de San Carlos ("La Fortuna" for short) is geographically small but packed with restaurants, shops, and tourism offices. At the town's core is the **central park,** bordered to the west by the **central church.** From downtown La Fortuna, Road 142 (the main drag)

departs west toward Volcán Arenal. It skirts north around the volcano and passes by countless hotels, hot springs, and other attractions before arriving at the Lago Arenal Dam. Most activity centers and accommodations that fall between La Fortuna's center and the dam are considered La Fortuna operations. The region at large is colloquially referred to as "Arenal."

West of La Fortuna, a handful of small towns—El Castillo, Nuevo Arenal, and Tilarán—are scattered around Lago Arenal, which is nearly 30 kilometers long from west to east. In all three towns, you'll find privacy, peace, and a respite from tourist traps.

HIGHLIGHTS

★ RÍO FORTUNA WATERFALL

Road 142, tel. 506/2479-9515, www. cataratalafortuna.com, 7am-5pm daily, last entry 4pm, $18 pp 8 years and older

Imagine a rain forest scene so leafy and lush that it looks soft enough to snuggle in, a picture of vivid lime and emerald greens with a view that fills your gaze as far as your eyes can see. Now envision a stark white cascade slicing through and spilling into a river pool 70 meters below. Most people who visit the **Río Fortuna Waterfall,** also known as **La Fortuna Waterfall,** have fun swimming in its waters and exploring its on-site **Orchid Garden.** I love admiring the waterfall at a distance

from the **viewpoint** just beyond the entrance.

You can catch an equally impressive view of the powerful waterfall from its base. The trail of 517 steps that leads down to the waterfall from the entrance is daunting (especially knowing that you'll have to return uphill), but worth every ounce of effort. Most visitors, including children, make the trek without a problem, and benches provide a break along the way. I don't recommend swimming in the waterfall's pool, as the current here is strong. It's better to wade in the calmer waters slightly downstream.

Although nearly every operator in town offers guided hikes to the waterfall for roughly $50 per person,

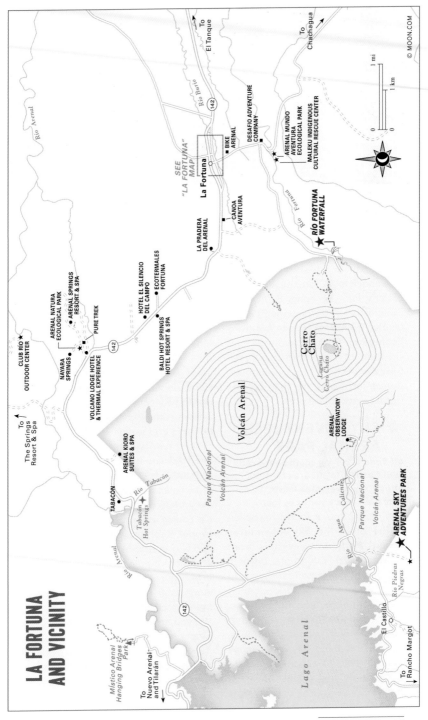

LA FORTUNA AND VICINITY

To Nuevo Arenal and Tilarán

Místico Arenal Hanging Bridges Park

Río Arenal

The Springs Resort & Spa

To Tabacón

TABACÓN

Tabacón Hot Springs

Río Tabacón

CLUB RÍO OUTDOOR CENTER

ARENAL NATURA ECOLOGICAL PARK

ARENAL SPRINGS RESORT & SPA

PURE TREK

NAYARA SPRINGS

VOLCANO LODGE HOTEL & THERMAL EXPERIENCE

BALDI HOT SPRINGS HOTEL RESORT & SPA

HOTEL EL SILENCIO DEL CAMPO

ECOTERMALES FORTUNA

ARENAL KIORO SUITES & SPA

Parque Nacional Volcán Arenal

Volcán Arenal

Cerro Chato

Laguna Cerro Chato

ARENAL OBSERVATORY LODGE

Río Agua Caliente

Parque Nacional Volcán Arenal

ARENAL SKY ADVENTURES PARK

Río Piedras Negras

El Castillo

To Rancho Margot

Lago Arenal

LA PRADERA DEL ARENAL

CANOA AVENTURA

SEE "LA FORTUNA" MAP

La Fortuna

BIKE ARENAL

DESAFIO ADVENTURE COMPANY

ARENAL MUNDO AVENTURA ECOLOGICAL PARK

MALEKU INDIGENOUS CULTURAL RESCUE CENTER

Río Fortuna

RÍO FORTUNA WATERFALL

Río Burío

To El Tanque

To Chachagua

© MOON.COM

1 mi

1 km

Sky Tram at Sky Adventures Arenal Park (left); Río Fortuna Waterfall (right)

the attraction is one you can easily navigate and explore on your own. Another option is to visit via a **guided horseback tour** (8am, 10:30am, and 1:30pm daily, 3.5 hours, $70 adults, $53 children 7-12, min. age 7) coordinated by **Arenal Mundo Aventura Ecological Park** (Road 702, 1.5 km south of the central church, tel. 506/2479-9762, www.arenalmundoaventura.com); the tour departs from the adventure park.

★ SKY ADVENTURES ARENAL PARK

off Road 142, 7 km south on the road to El Castillo, tel. 506/2479-4100, https://skyadventures.travel, 7am-9pm daily, price varies by tour

The most popular tourist attraction in the area, the **Sky Adventures Arenal Park** draws visitors from downtown La Fortuna and beyond. It is one of the region's largest and most modern theme parks, offering a plethora of recreational activities. The guided **Sky Tram** (multiple times 8am-3pm daily, 1 hour, $48 adults, $33 children 0-12), **Sky Trek canopy tour** (multiple times 8am-4pm daily, 2-2.5 hours, $84 adults, $58 children 5-12, min. age 5), and **Sky Walk**

hanging bridges tour (multiple times 7am-2pm daily, 3 hours, $41 adults, $28 children 0-12, self-guided tour $27 adults, $19 children 6-12)—known as "the classics"—are the most popular park offerings. If you opt for the three-activity **combo tour** (multiple times 7am-1pm daily, 5 hours, $104 adults, $72 children 5-12, min. age 5), you'll glide amid the rain forest on a tram ride, zip back and forth above it during your canopy tour, and explore it from within while traversing five hanging bridges, all in a day's work.

My favorite feature is the **Sky Limit Adrenaline Challenge** (9am, 10:30am, 11:30am, 1pm, and 2pm, 3-3.5 hours, $84 pp, min. age 15, min. height 1.35 meters). This fun obstacle course incorporates zip lines, a rappel, a Tarzan swing, a superman cable, a ladder bridge, high ropes, and other hurdles. Give it a go solo to test your own abilities, or else challenge your travel mates for some friendly competition.

If you drive to the park, you'll find ample free parking out front. Alternately, Sky Adventures can provide round-trip transportation ($17 pp) between the park and La Fortuna hotels.

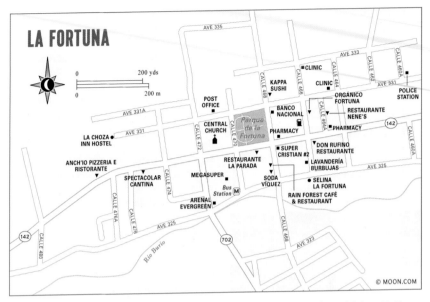

HANGING BRIDGES AT MÍSTICO PARK

2.5 km north of Road 142 just beyond the Lago Arenal Dam, tel. 506/2479-8282, www.misticopark. com, 6am-4:30pm daily, last entry 3:50pm, advance reservations required, $26 adults, $16 children 11-18

Amid the tourist boom that sounds throughout La Fortuna, I seek respite at **Místico Park.** It's one of the area's busiest attractions, yet it remains a peaceful place where you can hear a symphony of birdsong, cicada buzzes, and monkey howls. Visitors flock to the park to traverse its **trail system** comprising 16 **bridges,** 6 of which are suspended among the treetops and allow you to hover in midair over deep rain forest valleys.

The park is home to insects, birds, and the occasional monkey or sloth; the best way to experience it is alongside a **guide** who is trained to spot wildlife. The park offers the **Natural History Guided Tour** (8am, 9am, 10am, noon, 1pm, and 2pm, 2.5

hours, $40 adults, $30 children 11-18, $14 children 6-10). However, most tour operators in La Fortuna offer the same guided walk through the park, often bundling the experience with other area activities. Exploring without a guide is allowed, but all visits require **advance reservations** (via the park's website or by telephone, or through a third-party tour operator), as strict capacity limits are enforced. The park prohibits sandals and hiking shoes that expose sections of skin.

The **main trail** is an oval circuit of over three kilometers, consisting of uphill and downhill sections. By completing the full loop, you'll cross all the bridges, pass through a tunnel, and be able to access the **Morpho Azul Waterfall.** The steep steps that lead down to the waterfall are easy to miss; look for them to your right after the Keel-Billed Toucan Bridge but before the Ant Hill Bridge. When hiked nonstop, the course takes roughly 90 minutes to complete. The park's **accessible trail** explores the first 1,500 meters of the park; guests with limited mobility can check out this 30-minute mini loop that features seven bridges (including one suspension bridge) and only slight trail inclines and declines.

DAY TRIP TO RÍO CELESTE

Travel time: 1.5 hours from La Fortuna
Tenorio Volcano National Park (Parque Nacional Volcán Tenorio), tel.

hanging bridge at Místico Park (top); a bridge over Río Celeste (bottom)

506/2206-5369, www.sinac.go.cr, 8am-4pm daily, last entry 2pm, $12 adults, $5 children 2-12
Covering more than 30,000 acres, **Tenorio Volcano National Park** spans much of the land northwest of Lago Arenal, between the towns of Guatuso (to the east) and Bijagua (to the west). From a distance, the lush, dense, forest-filled and stream-strewn park resembles a mountain. It conceals Volcán Tenorio, whose crater is inaccessible to the public. **Río Celeste,** the jaw-dropping bright blue river that weaves its way throughout the park, is the foremost draw. You can witness the river change from a clear, colorless stream to a cloudy azure waterway. Most vibrant in color during the high season (when rainfall that can diminish the potency of the river's hue is minimal), Río Celeste is a natural phenomenon you must see for yourself. Note that swimming in the river anywhere inside the park is not allowed.

The park amazes with the picturesque, 30-meter-tall **Río Celeste Waterfall,** which spills out of the rain forest and into an aquamarine pool. You can get relatively close via a steep, 250-step staircase that branches off from the main trail and leads down to the waterfall's base. Swimming is not allowed. You'll approach the staircase to the waterfall on your left, roughly halfway (1.5 km) into the hike.

Hiking the park's main trail takes you to the river's other noteworthy features: a mountain *mirador* (lookout); the calm blue pool known as **Laguna Azul;** piping-hot riverside gas vents that create the Jacuzzi-like **Borbollones** ("gushing waters" or "bubbling waters"); and **Los Teñideros** (The Dyers)—the area where the color of the river's water transforms from a crystal-clear silver to an opaque, celestial blue. Operators all over the country offer guided tours to the park. Tours typically start and end in La Fortuna ($95-136 pp) or at destinations in Guanacaste ($132-168 pp). The main trail can be hiked independently.

The park's main entrance is via **El Pilón ranger station** (9.5 km east of Bijagua, 23 km west of Guatuso) on the north side of the park. A lesser-known, unofficial entrance exists on the west side of the park via the private **Heliconias Lodge and Rainforest** (off Hwy. 6, 300 m southeast of Bijagua, tel. 506/2466-8483, www.heliconiascr.com). This entrance doesn't provide access to Río Celeste.

Getting There

To reach the park from La Fortuna, first head to Guatuso. Guatuso is a 45-kilometer, 50-minute drive east on Road 142 and northwest on Highway 4 from La Fortuna. From Highway 4, at the north end of Guatuso, the unnamed road that the park is on will be on your left (south), just beyond the bridge over Río Frío. Look for the sign for the Río Celeste Hideaway Hotel. The total drive is 68 kilometers and takes about 1.5 hours.

There's no direct bus service to the park. Instead, you can take the **La Fortuna to Río Celeste Shuttle** (departs La Fortuna 7:30am daily, departs park 2pm daily, 1.5 hours, $50 pp round-trip) provided by tour outfitter **Arenal Evergreen** (tel. 506/2479-8712, www.arenal-evergreen.com). Reservations are required.

DAY TRIP TO CAÑO NEGRO WILDLIFE REFUGE

Travel time: 2 hours from La Fortuna tel. 506/2471-1309, www.sinac.go.cr, 8am-4pm daily, free

Ornithologists and avid birders shouldn't miss the **Caño Negro National Wildlife Refuge** (Refugio Nacional de Vida Silvestre Mixto), a 25,000-acre protected area approximately 60 kilometers north of Muelle, sandwiched between Highway 4 and Highway 35. The grassy and marshy swamps here provide some of the country's best **bird-watching** opportunities, especially from December to April (the peak bird-watching period spans Feb.-Mar.), when North American waterfowl migrate to the refuge to escape the chilly north. Home to a slew of other wildlife, including monkeys, iguanas, and lizards, the refuge's most obvious inhabitants are the hundreds of caimans that lurk in its waters and nap on its shores.

The most popular way to explore the area is to take a **boat tour** on **Río Frío,** the river that borders the refuge. Guided excursions advertised throughout the country as

Anhingas are a common sight in Caño Negro Wildlife Refuge.

Caño Negro tours are almost always of this kind, unless specified otherwise. Most depart from La Fortuna, although tours to the river can also be arranged from San José or Guanacaste.

Tour operator **Canoa Aventura** (tel. 506/2479-8200, www.canoa-aventura.com) runs three similar, slow-moving **Río Frío float tours** (7:30am, 8.5 hours) from La Fortuna daily, on which you can spot birds and other wildlife around the peaceful refuge. The **Unique Caño Negro tour** ($69 adults, $40 children 4-11) traverses the river in a covered pontoon boat that can protect you from the sun or rain. Alternatively, you can float down the river in a motorized raft during the **Caño Negro Eco Safari** ($112 pp, min. age 3). For a rare opportunity to go canoeing in Costa Rica, treat yourself to the **Caño Negro canoe tour** ($112 pp, min. age 5)—it's Canoa Aventura's specialty. Each tour option includes a typical Costa Rican lunch served at Canoa Aventura's own restaurant, El Caimán.

Bird-watching during boat tours is the foremost activity. The list of bird species that call the refuge home is far too long to detail, but sightings of cormorants, herons, owls, anhingas, egrets, ibises, and Costa Rica's tallest bird, the **jabiru stork,** are definite draws. The brilliant-pink **roseate spoonbills,** which I have been fortunate enough to spy in great numbers at the refuge, are always dazzling.

Contained within the refuge is the small community of **Caño Negro.** To explore the refuge on land, head to **El Sitio,** a visitors center in the southwest end of Caño Negro. It has a long boardwalk that extends out over the water and provides a 360-degree view of the refuge. Though wheelchair-accessible, the boardwalk has a steep incline and decline. A gazebo at the end of the pathway provides seating so you can enjoy the quiet, natural surroundings in comfort.

Getting There

Most Río Frío tours depart from La Fortuna. If you opt to drive yourself to the refuge from La Fortuna, it's a 110-kilometer, two-hour drive north on Road 142, Highway 4, Highway 35, and Route 138 to the community of Caño Negro. You'll pass through the community of Muelle on this drive. A 4x4 vehicle is not required but is good to have on the bumpy Route 138. There is no direct bus service to Caño Negro from La Fortuna.

HOT SPRINGS

La Fortuna's hot springs offer one of the country's top experiences for visitors. Hot springs complexes are everywhere you look around Arenal, and competition between them is fierce. All provide an opportunity to reap the therapeutic benefits of soaking in thermal water. The properties vary in size, design, luxury, day-pass duration and price, child-friendliness, and pool variety.

Most complexes have a restaurant on-site and do not allow guests to enter with food or drinks purchased elsewhere. Many offer the option to include lunch or dinner in the cost of their visitors pass. The restaurants offer everything from full table service to a buffet. The food is typically

Costa Rican and international cuisine. Tabacón and The Springs Resort & Spa provide the finest dining experiences. Many complexes also have on-site accommodations.

TABACÓN

Road 142, 11 km west of the central church, tel. 506/2479-2000, www.tabacon.com, half-day sessions 10am-2pm or 6pm-10pm daily, visitors pass $70 adults, $28 children 6-11

Tabacón is renowned for the natural, swift-moving, thermal-water river that flows throughout the property and for the beautiful gardens that create a relaxing, romantic atmosphere. Step into the riverbed (water shoes are recommended) or one of five pools for a rejuvenating soak. Although newer luxury developments around Arenal give Tabacón—La Fortuna's oldest hot springs attraction—a run for its money, this classic site remains a hit among couples and honeymooners. The visitors pass here includes lunch or dinner. Two open-air restaurants adjacent to gardens and the hot springs operate as buffets and provide à la carte options. Reservations are required. The on-site accommodations ($345 s/d) are liked for the classy rooms and fancy bathrooms.

THE SPRINGS RESORT & SPA

4 km north of Road 142, tel. 506/2401-3313, www.thesprings-costarica.com, Cascadas Calientes 8am-10pm daily, Los Perdidos Hot Springs 10am-10pm daily, visitors pass $70 pp 4 years and older

I love the combination of luxury and lush surroundings at **The Springs Resort & Spa.** The five-story open-air resort offers a panoramic view of Volcán Arenal from every level,

multitiered hot springs with waterfalls and swim-up bars, and a waterslide that is as much fun for adults as it is for kids.

This is the largest hot springs attraction in the region. On the property you'll find 12 pools, known as the **Cascadas Calientes,** near the resort's main building, and seven secluded lagoons, referred to as **Los Perdidos,** a brief walk away down a paved path. Visit during the day when

Tabacón (top); The Springs Resort & Spa (bottom)

INDIGENOUS PEOPLE OF COSTA RICA: THE MALEKU

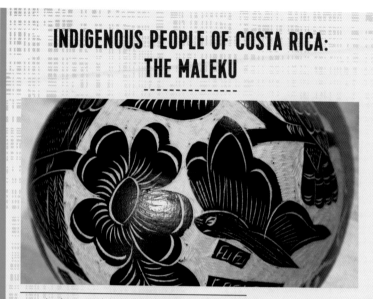

a carving by a member of the Maleku Indigenous group

Though the Maleku people represent Costa Rica's smallest Indigenous group with roughly 600 members, they're a tight-knit unit that's actively trying to protect their cultural heritage. Tourism is viewed by many group members as a means to this end. Some individuals and families invite non-Indigenous Costa Ricans and foreign visitors onto their land to learn about the Maleku way of life through organized tours and cultural presentations.

MALEKU INDIGENOUS CULTURAL RESCUE CENTER
Inside the Arenal Mundo Aventura Ecological Park in La Fortuna, the **Maleku Indigenous Cultural Rescue Center** invites visitors to learn about the culture of the Maleku people. The guided **Maleku Indian**

you can admire the beauty of the resort's architecture and heliconia gardens or during the evening when the mood is idyllic and romantic. Advance reservations are required during peak periods (Christmas, New Year's, and Easter). At the four open-air restaurants in the resort's main building, enjoy Costa Rican and international food and drinks, along with fabulous service. Each one is sophisticated but comfortable, and overlooks the rain forest canopy. The on-site accommodations perfectly fuse rustic decor with luxury.

The resort's on-site adventure park, **Club Río Outdoor Center** (9am-4:30pm daily by guided tour only), has additional hot springs and a restaurant.

Village Tour (7am-5pm daily, 2.5 hours, $36 adults, $20 children 4-12) offers a peek into Maleku life. You'll witness ceremonial rituals performed in cultural dress, learn about the use of food and medicinal plants, and listen to Maleku people speak Jaíca (sometimes spelled Jaíka or Ihaíca)—their traditional language. My favorite part of the experience is when group members explain how birds and other wildlife symbolize virtues such as love, power, and fidelity. The symbols are common throughout Maleku artwork, most notably in fruit, seed, and wood carvings. You can purchase many of these works at the end of the tour.

RESERVA INDÍGENA MALEKU

North of La Fortuna, Highway 4 cuts through the region. It passes through the small farming community of San Rafael de Guatuso (simply "Guatuso" to locals), home to the highest concentration of the Indigenous Maleku people.

Guatuso is home to **Margarita, Tonjibe,** and **El Sol,** the three primary *palenques* (communities) that make up the village **Reserva Indígena Maleku** (Maleku Indigenous Reserve).

An assortment of Maleku cultural centers cluster around Highway 4, a few kilometers southeast of Guatuso. At the **Rancho Toji Jifuru** (Palenque Tonjibe, 4 km south of Hwy. 4 at Margarita, 4 km southeast of Guatuso, tel. 506/6060-8874, www.malekuindiansco-starica.com, 9am daily by guided tour only, 3-4 hours, $65 pp), you can learn about the history of the Maleku people and the importance of their medicinal gardens on a guided walk through the group's reforestation project. At **Rancho Maleku Ní Uríjífa Tafa** (Hwy. 4, 3 km southeast of Guatuso, tel. 506/8559-1767, 9am-5pm daily by guided tour only, 2.5 hours, $40 pp), you can attend a cultural *charla* (talk) about the importance of dress, plants, and art to the Maleku people. Both locales offer demonstrations of traditional ceremonies (advance reservations are required by telephone or through Facebook) and sell original Maleku artwork.

ECOTERMALES FORTUNA

Road 142, 4.5 km west of the central church, tel. 506/2479-8787, www. ecotermalesfortuna.cr, half-day sessions 9am-4pm or 4pm-9:30pm daily, visitors pass $44 adults, $30 children 5-11

If you prefer nature over novelty, consider **EcoTermales Fortuna.** The property's five contiguous waterfall-fed hot springs and an additional non-thermal-water pool flow into one another, creating an illusion that you're swimming in a river. Natural stone and tropical foliage border the springs, which hide amid a forest clearing. Sip a cocktail poolside or while relaxing on a chaise lounge under swaying palms. Visit between May and November when there's more availability at this small, sought-after property. Advance reservations are required due to the 150-person capacity for each session. Two on-site restaurants serve Costa Rican fare; one is a buffet.

BALDI HOT SPRINGS HOTEL RESORT AND SPA

Road 142, 4.5 km west of the central church, tel. 506/2479-2190, www.baldihotsprings.cr, 9am-10pm daily, visitors pass $41 adults, $20.50 children 6-10

The **Baldi Hot Springs Hotel Resort and Spa** is the most popular middle-of-the-road option. It is also one of the area's largest properties, with 25 thermal-water pools that rarely feel crowded. Baldi appeals to a wide range of travel groups. Pools with music and bars draw in social groups; quieter, more intimate swimming spaces attract couples; and the water activity park at the back of the property is perfect for young children. Despite the grandeur of the entrance, the grounds don't feel elegant, but the spa, swim-up bars, and steam room up the level of sophistication. There are two restaurants on-site. A buffet restaurant serves traditional Costa Rican food and an Italian restaurant provides à la carte options. Baldi also has a standard hotel on-site, offering basic rooms ($248 s/d) with balconies and terraces.

WILDLIFE TOURS

MÍSTICO PARK

2.5 km north of Road 142 just beyond the Lago Arenal Dam, tel. 506/2479-8282, www.misticopark.com, 6pm daily, 2.5 hours, $49 adults, $39 children 11-18, $23 children 10, min. age 10

A variety of nocturnal specimens—including amphibians, reptiles, insects, and night-blooming flowers—enliven La Fortuna after dark. Try your luck at seeing them in the wild via the guided **Místico Night Walk.** A tour guide will explain how the rain forest changes at night while you explore the same three-kilometer trail system and hanging bridges that day visitors travel. Reservations are required.

ARENAL MUNDO AVENTURA ECOLOGICAL PARK

Road 702, 1.5 km south of the central church, tel. 506/2479-9762, www.arenalmundoaventura.com, 5:30am daily, 2-4 hours, $53 adults, $38 children 4-12

The Arenal Mundo Aventura Ecological Park offers **bird-watching tours** of its own quiet private land, so you're bound to see and hear more birds here than if you opted to explore a public area or a more popular hiking trail in the region. Tours begin before the park opens to the public and reservations are required. Tour guides provide spotting equipment, but you're welcome to bring your own.

CANYONEERING

PURE TREK

across from Arenal Natura Ecological Park, tel. 506/2479-1313, www.pure trek.com, 7am-5pm daily

Some of the country's best canyon descents lurk in the crevasses and gullies that surround La Fortuna. The **Canyoning Tour** (7am and noon daily, 4 hours, $105 pp, min. age 5) run by **Pure Trek** feels like a jungle obstacle course. There are four rappel descents (three of which parallel waterfalls), a brief rock ascent, and a rappel and zip-line cable combo coined the "Monkey Drop." It's loads of fun to complete, especially for kids. Tour guides prioritize safety throughout.

DESAFIO ADVENTURE COMPANY

Road 702, 1.5 km south of Road 142, tel. 506/2479-0020, www.desafiocostarica.com, 8am-4pm Mon.-Sat.

The **Canyoning in the Lost Canyon Tour** (7am, 10am, and 1pm daily, 4 hours, $99 pp, min. age 13) is for adults looking to be challenged. This activity is one of the best offered by canyoning pioneers **Desafio Adventure Company**. After being shuttled from your La Fortuna hotel to the canyon in a 4x4 nicknamed the Jungle Limo, you'll rappel down waterfalls, pause for a photo op in a canyon amid a river's rush, and throw caution to the wind during a secure and exhilarating freefall. The tour ends with a tough 15-minute uphill hike and a well-deserved buffet meal of home-style eats.

FOOD

STANDOUTS
Soda Víquez
Calle 468, 60 m south of the central park, tel. 506/2479-8772, 8am-10pm daily, $5-11

To sample a variety of Costa Rican foods, don't miss the small and homey **Soda Víquez**. The restaurant is a favorite among locals for its flavorful food and fair prices. In addition to ordering entrées from the menu, you can visit the small buffet at the back of the restaurant. The buffet features side dishes like *ensalada rusa* (Russian salad; a combination of beets, potatoes, eggs, and mayonnaise),

Soda Víquez

LA FORTUNA AND ARENAL FOOD

NAME	LOCATION
★ Soda Víquez	Calle 468, 60 m south of the central park, La Fortuna
★ Restaurante Nene's	50 m north of the pharmacy on Road 142, La Fortuna
★ Don Rufino Restaurante	corner of Road 142 and Calle 466, La Fortuna
★ Orgánico Fortuna	Calle 466, immediately south of Banco San José, La Fortuna
Spectacolar Cantina	250 m west of the central church, La Fortuna
Restaurante La Parada	Road 142, across from the central park, La Fortuna
Anch'io Pizzeria e Ristorante	Road 142, 350 m west of the central church, La Fortuna
Kappa Sushi	Calle 468, 50 m north of the central park, La Fortuna
Rain Forest Café & Restaurant	Calle 468, 50 m south of the central park, La Fortuna
La Ventanita Café	500 m south of the El Castillo school, El Castillo

yuca frita (fried cassava; similar in taste and appearance to thick french fries), and other preparations you may never have tried before. If a number of these catch your eye, skip the menu and ask the waitstaff for a custom plate composed entirely of side dishes.

Restaurante Nene's
50 m north of the pharmacy on Road 142, tel. 506/2479-9192, www.nenes cr.com, 11am-10pm daily, $9-28
For a more elegant dining experience than what is typical in La Fortuna, plan a dinner out on the town at **Restaurante Nene's.** The small establishment provides soft lighting, quiet music, and attentive service yet maintains a rustic charm with its wood decor. A broad selection of seafood and meat preparations

is offered (filet mignon is hard to come by elsewhere), as are impressive flambéed dishes, but the diverse lineup of red and white wines is the standout here.

Don Rufino Restaurante
corner of Road 142 and Calle 466, tel. 506/2479-9997, http://donrufino. com, 11:30am-9:45pm daily, $19-34
The classiest restaurant in downtown La Fortuna is **Don Rufino Restaurante,** an American steak house. It is a bit pretentious but deserves its accolades, especially with respect to food presentation and service. Choose from above-average meat, seafood, pasta, and sandwich offerings that pay attention to detail. The pottery serving pieces created specifically for the restaurant by artisans in Santa Ana are a nice touch.

CONTACT INFO	FOOD	PRICE
tel. 506/2479-8772	Costa Rican	$5-11
tel. 506/2479-9192, www.nenescr.com	Costa Rican	$9-28
tel. 506/2479-9997, http://donrufino.com	American steakhouse	$19-34
tel. 506/2572-2115	vegetarian and vegan	$5-18
tel. 506/8569-7676	Mexican	$5-7
tel. 506/2479-9119, www.restaurantelaparada.com	Costa Rican	$4-12
tel. 506/2479-7024	Italian	$9-19
tel. 506/2479-1639	sushi	$7-13
tel. 506/2479-7239	café	under $5
tel. 506/2479-1735	Mexican	$3-6

Orgánico Fortuna
Calle 466, immediately south of Banco San José, tel. 506/2572-2115, 9am-9pm Mon.-Sat., $5-18
Orgánico Fortuna is an organic market and restaurant in one. Its style is hippie-ish, its food is healthy, and the variety of vegetarian, vegan, and gluten-free options (all easily identifiable on the menu) will make you happy. Salads, sandwiches, breads, smoothies, and organic coffee are abundant, as are signs and slogans that preach peace and love. If you have a craving for health food, satisfy it in the eatery's small but cozy space.

LODGING

Many of the hot springs attractions in the vicinity of La Fortuna also have on-site accommodations. (For more information on these attractions, see the *Hot Springs* section on page 54.)

STANDOUTS
La Pradera Del Arenal
Road 142, 2.4 km west of the central church, tel. 506/2479-9597, www.lapraderadelarenal.com, room $85 s/d, bungalow $105 s/d
The best-value hotel in the region is

LA FORTUNA AND ARENAL LODGING

NAME	LOCATION
★ La Pradera Del Arenal	Road 142, 2.4 km west of the central church, La Fortuna
★ Arenal Springs Resort & Spa	7 km west of the central church, 1 km east off Road 142, La Fortuna
★ Tabacón	Road 142, 11 km west of the central church, La Fortuna
★ Nayara Springs	7 km west of the central church, 1 km east off Road 142, La Fortuna
★ Arenal Observatory Lodge	off Road 142, 8.5 km south on the road to El Castillo
★ Rancho Margot	4.5 km southwest of the El Castillo school, El Castillo
Selina La Fortuna	Avenida 325 at Calle 466, La Fortuna
Volcano Lodge Hotel & Thermal Experience	Road 142, 7 km west of the central church, La Fortuna
Hotel El Silencio del Campo	Road 142, 5 km west of the central church, La Fortuna

La Pradera Del Arenal. Opt for one of the 25 quaint and quiet rooms or try one of the eight bungalows; both sleep 1-4 people. Both the rooms and the bungalows offer standard amenities, a volcano view, and a hearty breakfast for a fair price. The clean property has a pool, hot tub, and game room. High-quality stays around Arenal aren't usually this cheap.

Arenal Springs Resort & Spa
7 km west of the central church, 1 km east off Road 142, tel. 506/2479-1212, www.hotelarenalspring.com, $275 s/d
I'm partial to the **Arenal Springs Resort & Spa,** with its aura of sophistication and friendly, accommodating staff. People love this vast resort, which has 90 rooms within 45 bungalow-style duplexes, especially for its adjoining rooms (perfect for families), two upscale restaurants, and property-wide volcano views. The resort's best features include a yoga deck, vegetable garden, spa, and swim-up sushi bar, as well as hot springs and bird-watching gardens (pick up a free bird booklet at reception). There are even rooms designed for guests with asthma and seasonal allergies.

Tabacón
Road 142, 11 km west of the central church, tel. 506/2479-2000, www.tabacon.com, $345 s/d
Tabacón has a fresh and luxurious contemporary look that's every bit as inviting as its hot springs. At the 103-room resort, you'll be treated

CONTACT INFO	OPTIONS	PRICE
tel. 506/2479-9597, www.lapraderadelarenal.com	hotel rooms, bungalows	$85-105
tel. 506/2479-1212, www.hotelarenalspring.com	adjoining rooms in bungalow dupexes	$275
tel. 506/2479-2000, www.tabacon.com	resort rooms and suites	$345
tel. 506/2479-1600, www.nayarasprings.com	luxury villas, adults only	$775
tel. 506/2290-7011, www.arenalobservatorylodge.com	lodge rooms, two-story villas	$170 s/d, $550-700 villas
tel. 506/8302-7318, www.ranchomargot.com	private bunkhouse rooms, bungalows	private room $110-190, bungalow $159-249
tel. 506/2479-7259, www.selina.com	dorm rooms, private rooms, tepee-style huts	$15 dorm, $98 tepee, $113 private
tel. 506/2479-7055, www.volcanolodge.com	rooms in motel-style buildings, upgraded option has private pool	$180
tel. 506/2479-7055, www.hotelsilenciodelcampo.com	stand-alone villas	$216

to ever-attentive staff, valet parking, nightly turndown service, and a bountiful breakfast bar full of both decadent and health-conscious selections. A full-day pass to Tabacón's eponymous hot springs is also included; perks for hotel guests include early-morning access (8am-10am) and entry to the **Shangri-La Gardens,** an exclusive, adults-only area that has additional pools and private cabanas. Resort rooms (for 1-4 people) and suites (for 1-6 people) feature a mix of canopy beds, plush mattresses, garden or volcano views, and Jacuzzis; each one has a palatial shower that rejuvenates bathers with natural thermal water.

Nayara Springs
7 km west of the central church, 1 km east off Road 142, tel. 506/2479-1600, www.nayarasprings.com, $775 s/d

Nayara Springs is La Fortuna's sole adults-only accommodation. It comprises 35 individual luxury villas (each sleeps 1-3 people) with exquisite furnishings, including a canopy bed, a patio with a daybed, and a private pool fed with mineral water. Enclosed within a serene, rain forest-wrapped property further beautified by elegant tropical gardens, the lavish villas feel light-years away from La Fortuna, a mere 10-minute drive away. Stay here if you're looking for romance, relaxation, and ridiculously

thermal-water river at Tabacón

and clean rooms, all without televisions so you can hear the natural soundtrack of the nearby national park. Two fully equipped and furnished two-story villas (sleep 8 and 10 people, $550-700) are a one-kilometer walk from the hotel's main building. The quiet, remote lodge offers unobstructed views of Volcán Arenal as well as a volcano museum with a live seismometer. Coatimundis, oropendolas, and other wildlife inhabit the property, which has observation decks and nature trails of varying difficulties. Don't miss the **Danta Waterfall,** reached via a moderate hike along the Catarata Trail. Nonguests can visit the property with a day pass (5am-11pm daily, $10).

good food. The hotel has five top-notch restaurants and bars. Drink coffee at Mi Cafecito, experience a wine-pairing dinner at the **Nostalgia Wine & Tapas Bar,** and don't miss the boldly decorated **Amor Loco** for fine dining.

Arenal Observatory Lodge
off Road 142, 8.5 km south on the road to El Castillo, tel. 506/2290-7011, www.arenalobservatorylodge.com, $170 s/d
Stays at the **Arenal Observatory Lodge** are an unmatchable experience. The property has 48 spacious

Rancho Margot
4.5 km southwest of El Castillo school, tel. 506/8302-7318, www.ranchomargot.com, private room $110 s, $190 d, bungalow $159 s, $249 d
If you want to go off the grid, escape to **Rancho Margot.** The sustainable ranch, adorned with living roofs and furniture made from fallen wood, recycles everything imaginable: Who knew cooking oil could be reused as detergent and soap? As a guest, you'll swim in a pool built around a tree trunk, practice yoga twice a day, fish for *guapote* (rainbow bass), milk a cow, tour on-site trails, and enjoy three complimentary daily meals prepared with ingredients grown at the ranch. For privacy and comfort, choose one of the property's 19 bungalows (sleeps up to 5 people); each has its own hammock and terrace. The bunkhouse provides 20 private rooms (for 1-2 people) with bunk beds and communal bathrooms.

Arenal Springs Resort & Spa

Arenal Observatory Lodge

LA FORTUNA AND ARENAL TOUR OUTFITTERS

NAME	LOCATION
Desafio Adventure Company	Road 702, 1.5 km south of Road 142, La Fortuna
Canoa Aventura	Road 142, 1.5 km west of the central church, La Fortuna
Exploradores Outdoors	San José, Puerto Viejo de Talamanca
Pure Trek	across from the Arenal Natura Ecological Park, La Fortuna
Bike Arenal	corner of Road 142 and Avenida 319, La Fortuna

INFORMATION AND SERVICES

La Fortuna does not have a hospital, but two **clinics, Centro Medico Sanar La Fortuna** (corner of Avenida 331 and Calle 464, tel. 506/2479-9420, 7am-midnight Mon.-Sat., 8am-11pm Sun.) and **Ebais La Fortuna** (corner of Avenida 333 and Calle 466, tel. 506/2479-8565, 7am-3pm Mon.-Fri.), can attend to medical issues. Centro Medico Sanar La Fortuna tends to be less busy. A few **pharmacies** are scattered throughout the downtown core along the main drag; most are open 9am-9pm daily.

The town has a **police station** (corner of Avenida 331 and Calle 460A, tel. 506/2479-9689, 24 hours daily) and a **post office** (Avenida 331 across from the central church, tel. 506/2479-8070, 8am-5pm Mon.-Fri., 8am-noon Sat.).

The most well-stocked grocery stores are **Super Cristian #2** (corner of Road 142 and Calle 468) and **Megasuper** (100 Centro Comercial Adifort), beside the regional bus station.

There are a number of banks in town. The easiest to spot is **Banco Nacional** (on the corner of Avenida 331 and Calle 468, tel. 506/2479-9022, www. bncr.fi.cr, 8:30am-3:45pm Mon.-Fri., 8:30am-11:30am Sat.). It has an **ATM** (5am-11pm daily).

There's a **gas station** on the corner of Road 142 and Calle 466.

Many hotels in the area offer laundry services to guests. Otherwise, you can have your clothes washed at **Lavandería Burbujas** (Calle 466, 75 m south of Road 142, tel. 506/2479-7115, 8am-4pm daily).

TRANSPORTATION AND TOURS

Getting There

If you're heading to La Fortuna by way of San José or the Caribbean, you will enter town from either the east or the south. If you arrive via Guanacaste, access is from the west.

Air

The **Aeropuerto Arenal** (FON) is eight kilometers east of downtown La Fortuna, roughly a 10-minute drive. **SANSA Airlines** (tel. 506/2290-4100, www.flysansa. com) offers direct flights to La Fortuna from San José daily. The flight time from San José is approximately one hour.

There's no taxi stand at the airport. Call

CONTACT INFO	SERVICES AND SPECIALTIES	PRICE
tel. 506/2479-0020, www.desafiocostarica.com	adventure tours; onward transportation	rates vary by tour
tel. 506/2479-8200, www.canoa-aventura.com	nature tours, safari float tours, boating, canoeing	rates vary by tour
tel. 506/2222-6262, www.exploradoresoutdoors.com	adventure tours, onward transportation, white-water rafting	$99-224
tel. 506/2479-1313, www.puretrek.com	canyoneering	$105 pp
tel. 506/2479-9020, www.bikearenal.com	mountain biking	$53-118

the taxi dispatch line **Central de Taxis La Fortuna** (tel. 506/2479-9605, 6am-10pm daily) to request a taxi to pick you up from the airport to take you wherever you need to go. Expect to pay $15 to downtown La Fortuna, more to reach hotels on the outskirts of town.

Boat

If you plan to visit La Fortuna from the **Monteverde** vicinity, boat crossings over **Lago Arenal** save ground transportation time. The entire trip—which consists of ground transportation from Santa Elena (Monteverde) to the lake, a boat ride across the lake, and ground transportation on to La Fortuna—is known as the **van-boat-van service** (formerly called the jeep-boat-jeep service, sometimes referred to as the taxi-boat-taxi service, $32-45 pp) and takes approximately 3.5 hours to complete. A number of companies provide the service, typically twice daily, once in the morning and again in the afternoon. Those with the best reputations include **Aventuras Arenal** (Road 702, 750 m south of Road 142, tel. 506/2479-9133, www.aventurasarenal.com, 7am-8pm daily) and **Desafio Adventure Company**

(Road 702, 1.5 km south of Road 142, tel. 506/2479-0020, www.desafiocostarica. com, 8am-4pm Mon.-Sat.).

Car

Most people visit La Fortuna directly from **San José.** The most popular version of this drive is 130 kilometers and takes three hours via Highway 1 and Road 702, which passes through San Ramón. Another option is 140 kilometers and takes 3.5 hours via Highway 1 and Road 141, which goes through Ciudad Quesada.

Getting to La Fortuna from **Liberia** requires a 135-kilometer, 2.5-hour drive via Highway 1 and Road 142. From **Monteverde,** it's a 115-kilometer, 3.5-hour drive via Roads 606, 145, and 142.

From La Fortuna, **El Castillo** is a 25-kilometer, 40-minute drive west on Road 142 and south on the gravel road known as "the road to El Castillo." It's beneficial to have a **rental car** if you're staying in El Castillo. The community is a $30 taxi ride from La Fortuna center, and most La Fortuna tour operators charge transportation fees for pickups and drop-offs at El Castillo accommodations. You can avoid paying these if you drive yourself to and from La Fortuna, where most Arenal-area tours start and end.

The roads that lead to La Fortuna are generally paved, well maintained, and safely maneuvered by the average driver. Travel to La Fortuna from the west (along Road 142 between Tilarán and the Lago Arenal Dam) is curvy in many places but primarily flat. South of La Fortuna is rather mountainous. Each of these routes is easily passable with slow and cautious driving; aim to make the trip early in the day when fog cover is less of an issue. Access to La Fortuna from the east (via Highway 4 from Puerto Viejo de Sarapiquí) offers the fewest twists.

Bus

La Fortuna's regional **bus station** is on the corner of Calle 470 and Avenida 325. Public buses travel to La Fortuna daily. You can catch one from **San José** (5am, 6:15am, 8:40am, and 11:50am daily, 4 hours, $4) or **Tilarán** (7am, 12:15pm, and 3:30pm daily, 2 hours, $5), among other locales.

A local bus travels between La Fortuna and **El Castillo** ($2.50) once daily in each direction. The bus leaves El Castillo around 6:45am, stops in La Fortuna, and then continues to Ciudad Quesada. From Ciudad Quesada, the bus leaves at 3:30pm, stops in La Fortuna, and then continues to El Castillo.

Private Transfer Service

Most La Fortuna tour operators (and nearly all transportation service providers in the country) can get you to La Fortuna from any destination by way of a private transfer service. My votes go to **Desafío Adventure Company** (Road 702, 1.5 km south of Road 142, tel. 506/2479-0020, www.desafiocostarica.com, 8am-4pm Mon.-Sat.) and **Ride Costa Rica** (2.5 km southwest of Los Ángeles, 10 km east of La Fortuna on Road 141, tel. 506/2469-2020, www.ridecr.com, 7am-8pm Mon.-Sat.) for their free onboard Wi-Fi. Prices average around $160-174 from San José, $174-180 from Liberia, and $205-240 from Monteverde.

Shared Shuttle Service

Interbus (tel. 506/4100-0888, www.interbusonline.com), **Ride Costa Rica** (tel. 506/2469-2525, www.ridecr.com), and **Grayline Costa Rica** (tel. 506/2220-2126, www.graylinecostarica.com) can shuttle you to La Fortuna from many popular tourist towns. Morning and afternoon departures are available from most destinations daily. One-way services to La Fortuna cost $47-91 per person. Most of these eight-person shuttles offer drop-offs at La Fortuna hotels.

Local resident Arturo operates an inexpensive **shuttle service** (tel. 506/8887-9141) that commutes between La Fortuna and **El Castillo** three times daily (departs El Castillo 8am, noon, and 4pm; departs La Fortuna 9am, 1:30pm, and 6:30pm). It leaves from La Fortuna in front of Super Cristian #1 (Road 702, 125 m south of Road 142) and travels to most El Castillo hotels. The cost varies by drop-off location, but the most expensive ride (La Fortuna to Rancho Margot) is only $10 per person. Arturo also offers **private transfer services** between La Fortuna and El Castillo for $35 per group (1-4 people).

Organized Tour

A number of tour operators, such as **Desafio Adventure Company** (tel. 506/2479-0020, www.desafiocostarica. com) and **Exploradores Outdoors** (tel. 506/2222-6262, www.exploradoresoutdoors.com), offer **post-tour onward transportation** to La Fortuna from various cities around the country. A variety of adventure and nature tours ($85-224 pp), including **white-water rafting on the Río Pacuare,** can be arranged to include pickups at hotels in San José, Monteverde, Puerto Viejo de Talamanca, Cahuita, Manuel Antonio, and many Guanacaste beach towns, and drop-offs at hotels in La Fortuna.

Getting Around

Car and Taxi

Driving around downtown La Fortuna is generally easy. In the middle of town, Road 142 becomes a one-way street (traffic flows west) between Road 702 and Calle 464. Parking is available but limited; there are usually free spaces along the north side of the central church across the street from the post office.

Official **taxis** line up along Calle 468 between Road 142 and Avenida 331 on the east side of the central park; unlicensed taxi drivers station themselves along the park's south side.

Bicycle

Bike Arenal (on the corner of Road 142 and Avenida 319, tel. 506/2479-9020, www.bikearenal.com, 8am-5pm Mon.-Sat.) offers daylong bike rentals for $15. High-quality road bikes will run you closer to $55 per day. All bike rentals include a helmet and lock. If you want a bike for a shorter period, **Montaña de Fuego** (Road 142, 8.5 km west of the central church, tel. 506/2479-1220, www.montanadefuego.com) rents bikes by the hour ($8) or in four-hour periods ($15).

Shared Shuttle Service

La Choza Inn Hostel (Avenida 331, 300 m west of the post office, tel. 506/2479-9091, www.lachozainnhostel.com) operates the **Arenal Shuttle Pass** ($15 pp), which includes unlimited transportation on a preset pickup and drop-off schedule between their property in downtown La Fortuna and a number of noteworthy sights like the Río Fortuna Waterfall and Lago Arenal. The shuttle service departs from the central church in downtown La Fortuna (8:30am, 10am, 1pm, and 3:20pm daily), but you can also be picked up at any one of the attractions visited along the circuit.

MONTEVERDE AND SANTA ELENA

The Monteverde region is one of the best places in Costa Rica to experience a cloud forest ecosystem. Puffy clouds waft through the air, sometimes dense enough to swathe your surroundings in a blanket of white—but only for a moment. As quickly as the haze creeps up on you, it carries on down the road. Steady low-cloud cover keeps the area cool and refreshing, and the land moist. Myriad tree, lichen, flower, fern, and moss species flourish in the climate and create a rich environment for wildlife.

The region referred to as Monteverde is essentially three communities: **Santa Elena, Cerro Plano,** and **Monteverde.** The town of Santa Elena, the developed core of the region, has a cluster of restaurants, shops, and accommodations nestled within walking distance of one another. One kilometer east is Cerro Plano, a community with additional businesses that are spread out over several side roads. The community of Monteverde is the least developed. It is located 2.5 kilometers southeast of Santa Elena (1.5 kilometers southeast of Cerro Plano), not far from the entrance of the Monteverde Cloud Forest Reserve. Road 620 connects all three communities.

HIGHLIGHTS

- -

★ MONTEVERDE CLOUD FOREST

Road 620, 5.5 km southeast of Santa Elena, tel. 506/2645-5122, www. cloudforestmonteverde.com, 7am-4pm daily, last entry 2pm, $25 adults, $12 children 6-12

Several kilometers southeast of Santa Elena is the nearly 26,000-acre **Monteverde Cloud Forest Biological Reserve** (Reserva Biológica Bosque Nuboso de Monteverde), lush and jungle-like, with giant tree trunks, intertwining roots and branches, moist and sometimes musky air, and regular wafts of fog.

The protected land area is a beacon of biodiversity in Costa Rica. More than 100 species of reptiles, 60 species of amphibians, and 6 species of jungle cats (among other mammals, including monkeys, bats, peccaries, and tapirs) inhabit the reserve, along with an immeasurable number of insects and birds. Nonstop visitor flow during operating hours makes wildlife-watching a challenge, but certainly not impossible. Easier to see is the reserve's extraordinary collection of over 3,000 species of plants and trees.

The reserve is fantastic for **bird-watching,** especially from December to April, when migratory species come to visit. Rife with fruit and insects, the reserve pleases the **resplendent quetzal,** a brightly colored and sometimes long-tailed trogon (a type of tropical bird). More likely to be heard, however, is the **three-wattled bellbird.** Their tinny "bonk" is easily recognizable; it sounds throughout the reserve like a rusty swing.

The reserve boasts an impressive 13-kilometer **trail system** beyond the main visitors center. The **Cloud Forest Trail** (2 km one-way, 45 minutes, moderate) is one of the most frequented paths. It starts at the reserve's entrance and follows a jagged line that ascends to the east and ends near **La Ventana** (The Window), a lookout point over the Continental Divide. The trail is named "cloud forest" for a reason; the narrow path cuts through dense forest where the air is moist and usually cluttered with clouds. It is the prettiest trail in the park, and perfectly resembles the scene you probably envision when you think of a cloud forest.

Guided tours come in the form of the early-morning **bird-watching tour** (6am, 6 hours, $85 pp), the daytime **natural history walk** (7:30am, 11:30am, and 1:30pm, 2 hours, $20 pp), and the **night tour** (5:45pm, 2 hours, $23 pp). You can arrange tour guides directly through the reserve—which is managed by the Centro Científico Tropical (Tropical Science Center)—or through tour operators in town. Advance reservations for tours are required; they can be made via telephone or the reserve's website. The park's trails can also be explored without a guide. Advance reservations for unguided visits are recommended (but not required), especially if you plan to visit during the morning, when the reserve is the busiest. Because entry is restricted to 250 people at a time, those without a reservation may end up waiting at the entrance indefinitely.

Getting There

To drive to the reserve, exit Santa Elena to the east and take Road 620 as far as you can, roughly 5.5 kilometers. From downtown Santa Elena,

hummingbird

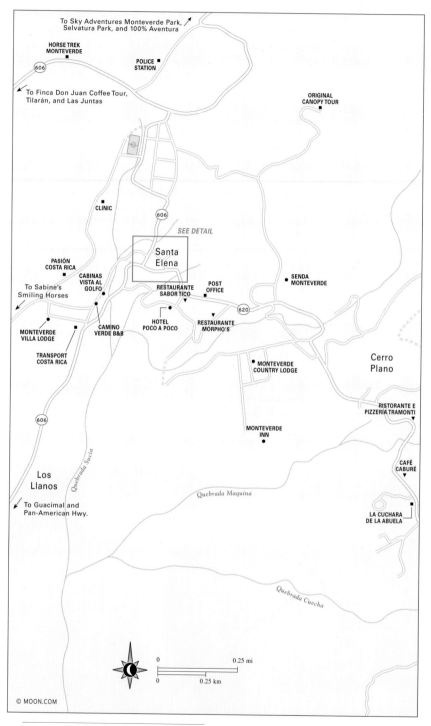

To Sky Adventures Monteverde Park,
Selvatura Park, and 100% Aventura

HORSE TREK
MONTEVERDE

POLICE
STATION

606

To Finca Don Juan Coffee Tour,
Tilarán, and Las Juntas

ORIGINAL
CANOPY TOUR

CLINIC

606

SEE DETAIL

Santa
Elena

PASIÓN
COSTA RICA

CABINAS
VISTA AL
GOLFO

SENDA
MONTEVERDE

To Sabine's
Smiling Horses

RESTAURANTE
SABOR TICO

POST
OFFICE

620

MONTEVERDE
VILLA LODGE

CAMINO
VERDE B&B

HOTEL
POCO A POCO

RESTAURANTE
MORPHO'S

TRANSPORT
COSTA RICA

MONTEVERDE
COUNTRY LODGE

Cerro
Plano

606

RISTORANTE E
PIZZERIA TRAMONTI

MONTEVERDE
INN

Los
Llanos

Quebrada Sucia

CAFÉ
CABURÉ

To Guacimal and
Pan-American Hwy.

Quebrada Maquina

LA CUCHARA
DE LA ABUELA

Quebrada Cuecha

0   0.25 mi

0   0.25 km

© MOON.COM

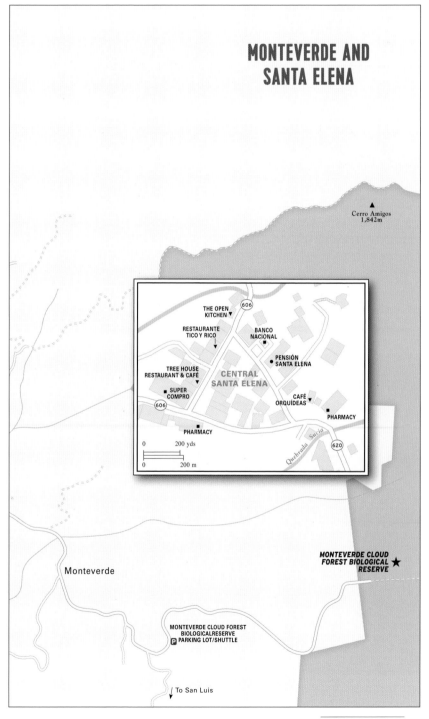

MONTEVERDE AND SANTA ELENA

Cerro Amigos
1,842m

THE OPEN
KITCHEN ▼

606

RESTAURANTE
TICO Y RICO ▼

BANCO
NACIONAL ■

PENSIÓN
SANTA ELENA ●

TREE HOUSE
RESTAURANT & CAFÉ ▼

CENTRAL
SANTA ELENA

■ SUPER
COMPRO

606

CAFÉ
ORQUÍDEAS ▼

PHARMACY ■

■ PHARMACY

0   200 yds

0   200 m

Quebrada Sucia

620

Monteverde

MONTEVERDE CLOUD
FOREST BIOLOGICAL ★
RESERVE

MONTEVERDE CLOUD FOREST
BIOLOGICALRESERVE
🅿 PARKING LOT/SHUTTLE

↓ To San Luis

Monteverde Cloud Forest Biological Reserve

the drive is 12 minutes. A 4x4 vehicle is recommended but not required.

The reserve's official parking lot, which is the only place to park in the vicinity (roadside parking is not permitted), is on the east side of Road 620, approximately 1.5 kilometers before the entrance to the reserve. Shuttles provide complimentary transportation to the entrance (and vice versa) every few minutes. The fee to park is $5. It's paid upon arrival at the entrance to the reserve, not at the parking lot. Hold onto the receipt you receive at the entrance; you'll need it to exit the parking lot.

You can hire an official taxi to take you to the reserve, or take the public bus that travels between downtown Santa Elena and the reserve (6:15am, 7:30am, and 1:15pm daily, departures to Santa Elena at 11am, 2pm, and 4pm daily, 20 minutes, $1.25). A one-way taxi trip from downtown Santa Elena costs about $10. If you're staying at an accommodation along Road 620, you can catch the bus as it travels between town and the reserve.

SKY ADVENTURES MONTEVERDE PARK

off Road 619, 3.5 km north of Santa Elena, tel. 506/2479-4100, https:// skyadventures.travel, 7am-9pm daily, prices vary by activity

If you want to maximize your experience in Monteverde and minimize precious travel time, no place in the area combines nature exploration with adventure excursions better than **Sky Adventures Monteverde Park.** The multifaceted operation is one of the best one-stop-shop adventure centers. Visited by hundreds of people a day, the famed theme park (a sibling of Sky Adventures Arenal Park) offers quintessential Monteverde experiences, including a guided tram ride, zip-line course, and hanging bridges tour.

You'll make eerie but thrilling zips across cables that speed through the clouds during the **Sky Trek canopy tour** (multiple times 8am-3pm daily, 2-2.5 hours, $84 adults, $58 children 5-12, min. age 5), and throw caution—and your body—to the wind during an adrenaline-inducing bungee jump called the "Vertigo Drop" (free with zip-lining tour). This is the only zip-line tour in the area that allows participants to brake with metal handlebars, as opposed to gripping the cables by hand using a thick leather glove. Included with the tour is a complimentary Sky Tram ride; the gondola takes you to the top of the forest, offering views of the lush landscape that go for miles.

During the **Sky Walk hanging bridges tour** (multiple times 8am-2pm daily, 2 hours, guided tour $41 adults, $28 children 6-12, self-guided tour $27 adults, $19 children 6-12), you'll cross a 236-meter hanging bridge, the longest in the area. You'll also encounter plant and animal species that contribute to the region's famed biodiversity.

The five-hour **combo tour** ($104 adults, $72 children 5-12) includes the Sky Tram, the canopy tour, and the hanging bridges tour. It runs multiple times between 8am and 1pm daily and allows you to maximize your time at the park.

Sky Adventures offers round-trip transportation ($10 pp) between the park and Santa Elena and Monteverde hotels.

SELVATURA PARK

off Road 619, 2 km north of Santa Elena, tel. 506/4001-7899, www. selvatura.com, 7am-4pm daily by

hanging bridge inside Sky Adventures Monteverde Park

three-toed sloth (top); snake on exhibit in Selvatura Park (middle); cacao pods at Finca Don Juan (bottom)

guided tour only, prices vary by activity

To admire some of Costa Rica's most cherished creatures, don't miss **Selvatura Park,** where you'll have the chance to check out hummingbirds, snakes, butterflies, and other species that contribute to the area's biodiversity. The park, which also offers zip-lining and hanging bridges tours, has four live animal exhibits (each one a short walk from the rest) that are only accessible by guided tour. You can visit any combination of the exhibits. Tour guides narrate at each, discussing topics such as species identification, behaviors, life cycles, and roles within the ecosystem. The exhibit tours occur every 15 minutes (8:30am-2:30pm daily).

The most immersive exhibits are those with creatures that fly: At the **Hummingbird Garden** (30-40 minutes, $6 pp), a small outdoor patio equipped with benches and tables, expect hummingbirds to whiz past your nose as they visit freestanding feeders. Inside the 2,500-square-meter, domed **Butterfly Garden** (45 minutes, $17 pp), don't be surprised if a shimmering blue morpho butterfly lands on your shoulder while you stroll around the humid enclosure's brick paths.

You can scare yourself silly at the sight of 30 different types of snakes and frogs living in glass terrariums at the **Reptile and Amphibian Exhibition** (45 minutes, $17 pp), including a fer de lance snake (one of Costa Rica's deadliest species), large boa constrictors, and tiny tree frogs. If you would rather gaze at adorable smiling sloths, check out the **Sloth Sanctuary** (45 minutes, $35 adults, $25 children 4-12), the park's newest exhibit, which opened in 2020. Rescued sloths unable to return to their natural habitat reside in a large, humidity-drenched dome. Inside, sloths roam freely and sluggishly around wooden structures and trees. Though the sanctuary was designed in a way that invites visitors to view sloths at a distance, due to an abundance of foliage all around, you may find yourself standing next to a sloth here. Maintain a safe distance at all times and don't try to touch or take selfies with the sloths to avoid frightening the already fragile creatures.

Adventure tours at the park include a zip-lining **canopy tour** (8:30am, 11am, 1pm, and 2:30pm, 2.5 hours, $55 adults, $38.50 children 4-12, min. age 4) and the **Treetop Walkways hanging bridges tour** (8:30am, 11am, 1pm, and 2:30pm, 2-2.5 hours, guided tour $55 adults, $38.50 children 4-12, self-guided tour $39 adults, $27.50 children 4-12).

ZIP-LINING

100% AVENTURA
Road 619, 3.5 km north of Santa Elena, tel. 506/2645-6388, www. aventuracanopytour.com, 7am-4pm daily

MONTEVERDE EXTREMO
off Road 606, 5.5 km north of Santa Elena, tel. 506/2645-6058, www. monteverdeextremo.com, 8am-5pm daily

Can't get enough of zip-lining? Leading the way in excitement and thrills are **100% Aventura** and **Monteverde Extremo.** If you want to experience a **superman cable**—a forward-facing zip line that allows you to fly through the air like Superman, no cape required—100% Aventura's **canopy tour** (8am, 11am, 1pm, and 3pm, 2 hours, $57 adults, $46 children 5-12, min. age 5) has the longest one in Latin America at more than 1,500 meters. To experience a superman cable in the dark, Monteverde Extremo's **canopy tour** (8am, 11am, and 2pm, 2.5-3 hours, $50 adults, $40 children 3-12, min. age 3) provides a **subterranean superman cable** that whizzes through a fabricated tunnel. Both outfitters' tours include a Tarzan swing and a rappel for added fun.

FOOD AND FARM TOURS

FINCA DON JUAN
Road 606, 2.5 km northwest of Santa Elena, tel. 506/2645-7100, www. donjuancr.com/monteverde, 8am-5pm daily

For a coffee education direct from the farm, I favor the operation at **Finca Don Juan,** where the charming Don Juan makes an effort to greet customers and is a pleasure to chat with. His jam-packed **Coffee, Chocolate, and Sugarcane Tour** (8am, 10am, 1pm, and 3pm daily, 2 hours, $37 adults, $11 children 6-12) provides great value by explaining the processing of three tasty products. During the tour you'll visit stations around the

MONTEVERDE AND SANTA ELENA FOOD

NAME	LOCATION
★ Restaurante Sabor Tico	Road 620, 250 m southeast of downtown Santa Elena
★ Ristorante e Pizzeria Tramonti	off Road 620, 2 km southeast of Santa Elena
★ Restaurante Morpho's	Morpho's Lane, 350 m southeast of Santa Elena
★ Café Orquídeas	Road 620, 25 m east of Road 606
Restaurante Tico y Rico	Road 606, 35 m north of the central church, downtown Santa Elena
Tree House Restaurant & Café	Road 606, 15 m south of the central church, downtown Santa Elena
The Open Kitchen	Road 606, 25 m north of downtown Santa Elena
La Cuchara de la Abuela	Road 620, 2.5 km southeast of Santa Elena
Café Caburé	Road 620, 2 km southeast of Santa Elena

farm to see coffee plant seedlings; the working coffee plantation; the coffee pulping, drying, and shelling processes; and the bean-roasting house. You'll also visit a station that explains how cacao is produced, as well as a station that demonstrates how sugarcane is processed. Samples of chocolate and sugarcane are provided during the tour, and you can try a complimentary cup of coffee upon tour completion. Lined with accessible trails, the farm offers an experience for the whole family.

EL TRAPICHE TOUR

Road 606, 3 km northwest of Santa Elena, tel. 506/2645-7650, www. eltrapichetour.com, 10am and 3pm Mon.-Sat., 3pm Sun., 2 hours, $35 adults, $13 children 6-12

El Trapiche Tour focuses on the production of sugarcane, though it also includes chocolate and coffee components. During your visit, you can ride around in an oxcart, see how three different types of sugarcane mills operate, and make your own sugarcane candy. Advance reservations are recommended.

CONTACT INFO	FOOD	PRICE
tel. 506/2645-5827, www.restaurantesabortico.com	Costa Rican	$5-12
tel. 506/2645-6120, www.tramonticr.com	Italian and pizza	$5-16
tel. 506/2645-7373	Costa Rican and American	$6-20
tel. 506/2645-6850, www.orchidcoffeecr.com	café with vegetarian and vegan options	$7-11
tel. 506/2645-5204, www.ticoyricomonteverde.com	Costa Rican	$7-15
tel. 506/2645-5751, www.treehouse.cr	American, Mexican, Peruvian	$6-22
tel. 506/2645-5775	vegetarian and vegan	$6-12
tel. 506/2645-5190	Costa Rican	$5-8
tel. 506/2645-5020, www.cabure.net	café with homemade chocolate	$5-15

FOOD

STANDOUTS
Restaurante Sabor Tico
Road 620, 250 m southeast of downtown Santa Elena, tel. 506/2645-5827, www.restaurante sabortico.com, 7am-10pm daily, $5-12

First-time visitors shouldn't miss **Restaurante Sabor Tico,** on the 2nd floor of Monteverde's principal commercial center. The restaurant showcases Costa Rican cuisine in an establishment with plenty of Tico pride, where traditional oxcart art and red, white, and blue banners are displayed. Nearly every authentic Costa Rican entrée, beverage, and dessert is served here, including mini corn tamales ($3), traditionally prepared and served wrapped in a banana leaf. Be forewarned: The large restaurant can get loud during busy periods, especially around dinner. Ask for a table on the balcony,

a traditional tamale at Restaurante Sabor Tico

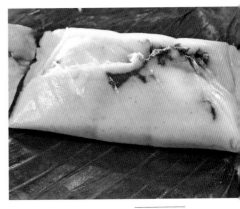

MONTEVERDE AND SANTA ELENA LODGING

NAME	LOCATION
★ Monteverde Villa Lodge	off Road 606, 750 m southwest of downtown Santa Elena
★ Monteverde Inn	off Road 620, 2 km southeast of Santa Elena
★ Hotel Poco a Poco	off Road 620, 500 m south of Santa Elena
Pensión Santa Elena	Road 606, 25 m south of Banco Nacional, downtown Santa Elena
Cabinas Vista al Golfo	off Road 606, 350 m southwest of downtown Santa Elena
Camino Verde B&B	off Road 606, 350 m southwest of downtown Santa Elena
Monteverde Country Lodge	off Road 620, 1.5 km southeast of Santa Elena
Senda Monteverde	off Road 620, 750 m southeast of Santa Elena

a quieter area that is perfectly positioned to take in the sunset and a delightful breeze.

Ristorante e Pizzeria Tramonti

off Road 620, 2 km southeast of Santa Elena, tel. 506/2645-6120, www.tramonticr.com, 11:30am-9:30pm daily, $5-16
Ristorante e Pizzeria Tramonti has fantastic Italian food and an even better view of the cloud forest from above the treetops. I'm a sucker for their wood-fired thin-crust pizzas. Twinkling lights and elegantly set tables keep this rustic, architecturally stunning restaurant classy, creating the perfect setting for a romantic or relaxing night out. As good as the entrées are, don't fill up on them; save room for tiramisu, panna cotta, or an ice cream off the dessert menu.

Restaurante Morpho's

Morpho's Lane, 350 m southeast of Santa Elena, tel. 506/2645-7373, 11am-9pm daily, $6-20
Monteverde's mountainous terrain provides plenty of places where you can take in a sunset, but the scene is particularly beautiful from **Restaurante Morpho's,** where an outdoor patio and floor-to-ceiling windows are perfectly positioned to capture the view. At its hilltop location, Morpho's offers a spruced-up menu full of classic Costa Rican dishes and American favorites like stacked burgers and sub sandwiches. Arrive by 4:30pm to get a table for dinner, or go one hour earlier for happy hour (3:30pm-5pm daily).

Café Orquídeas

Road 620, 25 m east of Road 606, tel. 506/2645-6850, www.orchid coffeecr.com, 7am-8pm daily, $7-11
At **Café Orquídeas,** choose from among plenty of breakfast selections

CONTACT INFO	OPTIONS	PRICE
tel. 506/2645-7283, www.monteverdevillalodge.com	hotel rooms, cabins, bungalow	$75-78
tel. 506/2645-5156, www.monteverdeinncr.com	economy and standard rooms	$140
tel. 506/2645-6000, www.hotelpocoapoco.com	hotel rooms	$185
tel. 506/2645-5051, www.pensionsantaelena.com	dorm rooms, private rooms in a motel-style pension	dorm $13, private room $32
tel. 506/2645-6321, www.cabinasvistaalgolfo.com	dorm rooms, private rooms	dorm $14, private room $38
tel. 506/2645-5641, www.hotelcaminoverde.com	private rooms, some with shared bath	$70
tel. 506/2645-7175, www.monteverdecountrylodge.com	lodge rooms	$123
tel. 506/4001-0421, www.sendamonteverde.com	private rooms in chalet-style duplexes	$360

(omelets, waffles, and crepes) and lunch options (soups, salads, and sandwiches). The restaurant is one of my favorites in Monteverde because of its laid-back vibe, homey ambience, friendly service, and delicious fresh food and drinks, including rich coffee and flavorful smoothies.

LODGING

STANDOUTS
Monteverde Villa Lodge
off Road 606, 750 m southwest of downtown Santa Elena, tel. 506/2645-7283, www.monteverde villalodge.com, $75 s, $78 d

The place I stay at most often in Santa Elena is the **Monteverde Villa Lodge.** It's easy to feel at home at this small, quiet hotel because the Costa Rican couple that owns it strives to make guests feel welcome. I love the four spacious cabins in particular (for 1-5 people). The four rooms (for 1-4 people) in the main building and the

Restaurante Morpho's

bungalow (for 1-5 people) are also worthy of a stay. All are immaculately kept, have a small kitchen area equipped with a microwave and mini fridge, and have natural mixed-wood decor; some have murals of rain forest scenes. Included with your stay is a delicious home-cooked breakfast. If you would like to join the chef in the kitchen and take part in meal preparation, inform the owners of your interest the day before.

Monteverde Inn
off Road 620, 2 km southeast of downtown Santa Elena, tel. 506/2645-5156, www.monteverde inncr.com, $140 s/d
Monteverde Inn, with 20 economy and standard rooms spread out over four one-story and two-story buildings, is a model of ecotourism in the area thanks to its commitment to permaculture. In addition to the hotel's numerous energy-saving and eco-friendly efforts, the owner operates an on-site permaculture farm (www.permaculturecr.com) where rainwater and gray water is collected and reused, compost and organic waste is repurposed as fertilizer, and guided tours and workshops explore sustainability in theory and practice.

Hotel Poco a Poco
off Road 620, 500 m south of Santa Elena, tel. 506/2645-6000, www. hotelpocoapoco.com, $185 s/d
The modern **Hotel Poco a Poco** brings a touch of elegance to the vicinity yet remains unpretentious. It has indoor fine dining, casual patio dining, and a spa, and each of the hotel's 34 rooms (for 1-4 people) features hypoallergenic bedding, blackout curtains, bathrobes, and contemporary bathroom finishes. Roofs and sunshades provide cover throughout the property, so when it rains, you can walk around, swim in the pool, or soak in the Jacuzzi without being bothered by a drop.

Monteverde Villa Lodge

INFORMATION AND SERVICES

The Monteverde region does not have a hospital, but there is a **clinic, Ebais Monteverde** (200 m southwest of the *fútbol* field, tel. 506/2645-5076, 6am-5pm daily), just outside of the downtown core. **Farmacia Vitosi** (Road 606, the southwestern side of Santa Elena's downtown triangle, tel. 506/2645-5004, 8am-8pm daily) and other **pharmacies** can be found in the heart of Santa Elena.

A **police station** (off Road 606, 500 m north of the *fútbol* field, tel. 506/2645-7074, 24 hours daily) and a **post office** (Road 620, 400 m southeast of Santa Elena center, tel. 506/2645-5042, 8am-5pm Mon.-Fri.) are on the outskirts of town.

The grocery store **Super Compro** (Road 606, 100 m west of Santa Elena center, tel. 506/7269-9337, 7am-9pm daily) is within walking distance of most establishments in downtown Santa Elena.

Money can be obtained from **Banco Nacional** (Road 606, the northeastern side of Santa Elena's downtown triangle, tel. 506/2645-5610, www.bncr.fi.cr, 8:30am-3:45pm Mon.-Fri.) or the **ATM** just up from the Super Compro.

There's a **gas station** on Road 620 roughly 2 kilometers southeast of Santa Elena, across from the administrative office for the Bosque Eterno de los Niños.

TRANSPORTATION AND TOURS

Boat

If you plan to visit the Monteverde vicinity from **La Fortuna,** one of the best ways to reach Santa Elena is by a boat crossing over **Lago Arenal.** The **van-boat-van** service (formerly called the jeep-boat-jeep service, sometimes referred to as the taxi-boat-taxi service, $32-45 pp) combines ground transportation from La Fortuna to the lake, a boat ride across the lake, and further ground transportation on to Santa Elena. The entire route takes approximately 3.5 hours to complete and typically operates twice daily—once in the morning and once in the afternoon. The two best service providers are **Aventuras Arenal** (Road 702, 750 m south of Road 142, La Fortuna, tel. 506/2479-9133, www.aventurasarenal.com, 7am-8pm daily) and **Desafío Adventure Company** (Road 702, 1.5 km south of Road 142, La Fortuna, tel. 506/2479-0020, www.desafiocostarica.com, 8am-4pm Mon.-Sat.).

Car and Taxi

From **San José** to Santa Elena, the 150-kilometer drive on Highway 1 and Road 606 takes about three hours. From **La Fortuna,** the 115-kilometer drive around Lago Arenal on Roads 142, 145, and 606 takes about 3.5 hours. From **Liberia,** the 110-kilometer drive on Highway 1, Road 145, and Road 606 takes around two hours.

There are **gas stations** on Highway 1 before the turnoff for Las Juntas de Abangares (coming from Liberia), at the main intersection in Tilarán (coming from La Fortuna), and on Road 606 on the outskirts of Santa Elena as you enter town (coming from San José).

The roads around Santa Elena are a mixed bag—some are freshly paved, and others are gravel and dirt paths that require driving at slow speeds. Prepare yourself for mountainous driving, including sharp turns, steep cliffs, and bumpy stretches. A 4x4 vehicle is recommended regardless of when you plan to visit, but is required during the low season when rainfall contributes to a messy drive. You're bound to encounter cloud cover as the drive increases in elevation, so avoid driving at night because darkness only worsens the hazard. However, the views of the rich landscape more than make up for the rough drive.

The smoothest route into town is via the southeast. Road 606 between Highway 1

MONTEVERDE AND SANTA ELENA TOUR OUTFITTERS

NAME	LOCATION
Pasión Costa Rica	150 m north of the Santa Elena cemetery, Santa Elena
Nasua Tours	Santa Elena
100% Aventura	Road 619, 3.5 km north of Santa Elena
Monteverde Extremo	off Road 606, 5.5 km north of Santa Elena
Horse Trek Monteverde	Road 606, 1.5 km north of Santa Elena
Sabine's Smiling Horses	off Road 606, 2 km west of Santa Elena
Finca Modelo Ecológica	off Road 606, 4.5 km northwest of Santa Elena, La Cruz

and Santa Elena is entirely paved. Other routes to Santa Elena, via the southwest and the northwest, also offer paved sections but require longer drives on poorer roads.

Driving around the center of Santa Elena is much easier; the roads are hilly but smooth. Note that Road 606—the main drag—takes the shape of a triangle, and all three sides are one-way streets where traffic flows counterclockwise. Parking spaces line the westernmost side of the triangle, which is also where **taxis** (up to $12) can be hailed; they can take you wherever you need to go.

Bus

The regional **bus station** is on Road 620, 250 meters southeast of Santa Elena's center. Public buses travel to Santa Elena daily. You can catch one from **San José** (6:30am and 2:30pm daily, 4 hours, $5) or **Tilarán** (3:50am, 9:30am, 12:30pm, and 4:30pm Mon.-Sat., 4am and 12:30pm Sun., 1.5-2 hours, $2.50), among other locales.

Private Transfer Service

Prices for private transfer services average around $165-170 from San José, $155-195 from Liberia, and $150-205 from La Fortuna.

Operating directly from Monteverde is **Transport Costa Rica** (Road 606, 500 m southwest of Santa Elena center, tel. 506/2645-6768, www.transportcostarica.com, 7am-8pm daily). They can get you to Santa Elena from virtually any destination countrywide.

CONTACT INFO	SERVICES AND SPECIALTIES	PRICE
tel. 506/6095-7472, www.pasioncostarica.com	tours of small nature reserves and cloud forests	from $67 pp half day, $125 pp full day
tel. 506/8313-6679, www.nasuatours.com	day and night tours; bird-watching	$25 pp half day, $220 per group full day
tel. 506/2645-6388, www.aventuracanopytour.com	zip-lining	$57 adults, $46 children 5-12
tel. 506/2645-6058, www.monteverdeextremo.com	zip-lining	$50 adults, $40 children 3-12
tel. 506/8359-3485, www.horsetrekmonteverde.com	horseback riding	$49-65 pp half day, $85 pp full day
tel. 506/8385-2424, www.horseback-riding-tour.com	horseback riding	$50-125 pp
tel. 506/2645-5581, www.familiabrenestours.com	tree-climbing tours	$45 pp

Shared Shuttle Service

Well-known service providers **Interbus** (tel. 506/4100-0888, www.interbusonline.com) and **Grayline Costa Rica** (tel. 506/2220-2126, www.graylinecostarica.com) can shuttle you to the Monteverde region from the country's most frequented areas, including La Fortuna, Manuel Antonio, San José, and many others. Daily morning and afternoon departures are available from most cities. Depending on the route, one-way services to Santa Elena range $47-97 per person. Most shuttles fit eight people with luggage and offer drop-offs at Monteverde-area hotels.

Organized Tour

A number of tour operators include **post-tour onward transportation** to the Monteverde vicinity from a variety of towns. Many adventure and nature tours ($85-150 pp) can arrange pickups at hotels in La Fortuna and several Guanacaste beach towns; you are dropped off afterward at hotels around Monteverde. **Tenorio Adventure Company** (Hwy. 1 at Río Corobicí, 5 km northwest of Cañas, tel. 506/2668-8203, www.tenorioadventurecompany.com) provides this service under the name **Adventure Connections.**

Playa Blanca, Cahuita National Park

CARIBBEAN COAST

The pace of life in the Caribe—the Caribbean—is gentler than in the rest of the country. It moves to reggae rhythms and calypso claps. Bright colors saturate the landscape, sultry breezes sway the palm branches, and the cuisine is rich and flavorful, something to be savored.

Culturally distinct from the rest of Costa Rica, the Caribbean coast is where Afro-Costa Rican, Indigenous, Chinese, and mestizo traditions and languages come together. It boasts an easygoing vibe and a no-frills approach to tourism. Amenities that are standard in other areas of the country (like air-conditioning, reliable Wi-Fi, potable water, and private parking) are considered luxuries here. Economy accommodations and outdoorsy lodges equipped with fans, screened windows, and mosquito nets are the norm. (So is drinking bottled water to minimize the chance of getting sick.) This is also where hammocks are heaven, bikes outnumber cars, and dollars—when compared to spending on the Pacific coast—can stretch for miles.

The Caribbean's most obvious draws are the beautiful and rapid-filled Río Pacuare, and the laze-inviting beach town of Puerto Viejo de Talamanca. But the region is also home to a handful of ecological habitats where some of Costa Rica's rarest wildlife resides. Possible sightings of jaguars, monkeys, and great green macaws delight visitors who flock to the region's verdant forests.

Puerto Viejo de Talamanca

CARIBBEAN COAST

Parque Nacional Tortuguero

Lomas de Sierpe

Parismina

Parismina

Caribbean

Sea

Río Pacuare

Reventazón

Barra de Matina Norte

EXPLORADORES OUTDOORS

Matina   Barra de Matina Sur

Siquirres

★ **WHITE-WATER RAFTING RÍO PACUARE**

32

Moín   Limón

● **PACUARE RIVER LODGE**

Liverpool   **AEROPUERTO INTERNACIONAL DE LIMÓN**

▲ Cerro Tigre

Westfalia

Tuis

▲ Cerro Matama

Valle de la Estrella   Bananito Sur

36

Chirripó de Atlántico

▲ Cerro Tsuitabeta

Fila de Matama

Reserva Biológica Hitoy Cerere

Penshurst

SEE "CAHUITA TO MANZANILLO" MAP

★ **CAHUITA NATIONAL PARK**

Punta Cahuita

Cahuita

Puerto Viejo de Talamanca

Hone Creek

Shiroles

Bribri

Manzanillo   **Gandoca-Manzanillo National Wildlife Refuge**

Parque Nacional Chirripó

Gandoca

Paraíso

Yorkin

Cordillera de Talamanca

▲ Cerro Chirripó

Fila Dúrika

Cerro Punibeta

Coén

Amubri

Parque Internacional La Amistad

Sixaola

Sixaola

▲ Cerro Amí

Parque Internacional La Amistad

Cerro Stutuk

Río Yorkin

Cerro Durika

Urén

PANAMÁ

© MOON.COM

0   10 mi

0   10 km

---

coral reef

TOP 3

★ **1. WHITE-WATER RAFTING:** The journey down the **Río Pacuare** isn't just an adventure, it's a chance to see, hear, and feel the wild jungle from within (page 97).

★ **2. CAHUITA NATIONAL PARK:** Enjoy the Caribbean's best stretch of sand while watching monkeys playing in the trees overhead (page 101).

★ **3. CARIBBEAN CUISINE:** Smoky jerk chicken, *patís*, ginger and lime cocktails . . . every meal at a home-style kitchen or roadside stand is another chance for a culinary treat (pages 112–113).

BEST 5 DAYS ON THE CARIBBEAN COAST

DAY 1

Ready yourself for a day of extreme adventure on **Río Pacuare,** Costa Rica's top river for **white-water rafting** (no previous experience is required). Brave thrilling Class III and Class IV rapids as you raft down the jungle-clad river amid a dramatic, secluded setting. A casual complimentary lunch prepared by rafting tour guides and served on the bank of the river adds to the fun.

DAY 2

Dedicate the morning to experiencing the **Cahuita National Park,** either on your own or as part of a guided tour. **Snorkel** around protected reefs and schools of tropical fish, hike the park's flat **nature trails,** or kick back on **Playa Blanca.** Exit the park midday and grab lunch at **Soda Kawe** up the street. Move down the coast from Cahuita to either **Playa Chiquita** or **Playa Arrecife** and spend the afternoon sunbathing or swimming at the beach. Be sure to dine at the beloved **Blanca y Selvin's Restaurante** for dinner.

DAY 3

Take a morning tour at the **Jaguar Rescue Center** to see rescued and rehabilitated wildlife and learn about wildlife preservation efforts. Afterward, relax at nearby **Playa Cocles,** ordering delicious street food from the **Take It Easy food cart** whenever hunger strikes. Enjoy more culinary delights at the midafternoon **Caribeans Chocolate Tour** (across from the beach) to see how chocolate is made at a cacao farm and chocolate factory. Enjoy the sunset back at Playa Cocles, and later, drinks at **Hot Rocks** in Puerto Viejo de Talamanca.

DAY 4

Take some time to get to know the **Bribri indigenous group** through cultural presentations demonstrated during a guided full- or half-day **community tour.** Depending on the tour you select, a traditional lunch prepared by group members using homegrown crops may be included. In the evening, head to **Lidia's Place** in Puerto Viejo de Talamanca and order a plateful of Caribbean-inspired foods for dinner.

DAY 5

Embrace the slow pace in the Caribbean by taking a day to wander around Puerto Viejo de Talamanca. Check out the town's shops and souvenir stands and eat lunch at **Bread and Chocolate.** If you like to surf, give yourself a couple of hours to ride the advanced break at **Salsa Brava** or to take a surf lesson. Spend the evening soaking up the region's reggae-inspired vibe at the waterfront **Salsa Brava Beach Restaurant and Bar.**

jaguar at the Jaguar Rescue Center

PLANNING YOUR TIME

Best Bases

With the exception of Río Pacuare, the top experiences can all be found within a 15-minute drive of the central hub **Puerto Viejo de Talamanca,** the most obvious choice for a home base. Choose **Cahuita** if you would rather stay in a smaller town with less vehicular and foot traffic. Since most of its visitors stick to the destination's eponymous national park, you'll encounter fewer travelers.

Weather

Weather patterns in the Caribbean are the opposite of those everywhere else in the country for part of the year. During **September and October,** when the majority of Costa Rica is either damp or waterlogged, much of the Caribbean basks in **tropical sun. February** and **March** too are notoriously sunny. The remaining months are splashed steadily with **rain.** Temperatures average 75-77°F.

Connect with...

The Caribbean coast is best visited before or after time spent in **La Fortuna and Monteverde.** The **Río Pacuare** rafting tour from Exploradores Outdoors includes transportation to Puerto Viejo de Talamanca and Cahuita from La Fortuna and San José, and vice versa, making it the perfect way to accomplish cross-country travel while having the time of your life. To avoid lengthy cross-country travel, don't plan connections between the Caribbean coast and the Pacific coast.

---

beach at Puerto Viejo de Talamanca (left); chocolate bars for sale on the Caribeans Chocolate Tour (right)

RÍO PACUARE

The stunning Río Pacuare is undoubtedly one of Costa Rica's most precious natural masterpieces. Set in the heart of virgin Costa Rican jungle, the 107-kilometer river is known for its lush mountainsides, rocky banks, tall waterfalls, and narrow canyons. Originating high in the Cordillera de Talamanca, south of the town of Turrialba, the river flows northeast down the mountains and empties into the Caribbean Sea, 35 kilometers northwest of Limón. Weaving through undeveloped land inhabited primarily by members of the Cabécar Indigenous group, the remote Río Pacuare outshines Costa Rica's other rivers with dramatic and breathtaking scenery.

★ WHITE-WATER RAFTING

To experience the river yourself, sign up for a **guided white-water rafting tour.** Different from other rafting excursions, trips down Río Pacuare aren't just thrilling adventure tours. They're rare invitations to see, hear, and feel Costa Rica's wild jungle from within. Massive mountains tower above both banks of the river. Overgrown, verdant forests blanket the steep slopes. You'll float past rocky canyons and steer around giant, moss-covered boulders. The setting is grandiose and secluded. During calm floats between rapids, only the occasional birdsong, monkey howl, and whistle of wind can be heard. These river trips reward rafters with fresh air, clean water, and an invigorating connection to nature. Add the adrenaline rush of a white-water rafting expedition, and a journey down the enchanting Río Pacuare is a singular experience. Although guided kayaking tours down the

white-water rafting on Río Pacuare

blue morpho butterfly (top); typical beachside food stand (middle); vibrant colors on the wheel of a Costa Rican oxcart (bottom)

river are also possible, these are for expert kayakers only.

Wildlife near Río Pacuare is abundant, but it can be difficult to spot. Look for iguanas and sloths in the trees that line the river. Herons, toucans, kingfishers, oropendolas, and other exotic birds make regular appearances. Swimming is permitted in the river's second canyon, where water flows quickly but calmly.

Beyond its unrivaled landscape, Río Pacuare's claim to fame is its raging rapids. Rafting the river's renowned Class III and IV rapids requires physical effort but no previous rafting experience. One-day rafting tours are **full-day excursions;** depending on water levels, group size, and traffic to and from the river, the experience lasts 8-13 hours, 3-4 of which are spent paddling intermittently.

Planning Tips

Most river put-ins (rafting tour starting locations) take place off Highway 10 to the east, roughly halfway between Siquirres and the town of Turrialba, but many tour outfitters provide **round-trip transportation.** Exploradores Outdoors was one of the first companies in Costa Rica to combine adventure tours with free **onward travel.** Choose to raft Río Pacuare with this company and you can be picked up and dropped off at accommodations in San José, Puerto Viejo de Talamanca, Cahuita, and La Fortuna, among other locales. All outfitters require advance reservations for rafting tours.

With a rental car, you can drive yourself to your chosen rafting tour outfitter's operation center and take their complimentary shuttle to the river. With this option, you can drive yourself to a new destination as soon as the rafting tour wraps up mid-afternoon. The rafting tour outfitters that I recommend have operation centers in Siquirres that provide free, secure parking. A few other rafting tour companies have operation centers in Turrialba.

The Class III and IV thrills are most aggressive from **November to December,** when rainfall in the area is significant. Be aware that substantial overnight rain can cause the river to flood to dangerous levels by morning, resulting in possible last-minute cancellations. If you prefer a tamer river trip, raft during February or March when rainfall is less significant and water levels are generally low.

Exploradores Outdoors
tel. 506/2222-6262 or 506/2750-2020, www.exploradoresoutdoors. com, $99 pp, min. age 12
I have rafted with **Exploradores Outdoors** more times than I can count. The company operates daily river trips from its modern, secure base, called the Exploration Center, 2.5 kilometers east of Siquirres. The center has bathrooms, showers, oversized lockers, and a restaurant. I prefer this reputable rafting tour operator for its long-standing river operations and spotless safety record. Owners Miguel and Yency Cabrera Chan are a Costa Rican brother-and-sister team, as well as avid rafters and kayakers. Their tour guides are a professional, well-trained group whose lighthearted humor and playful camaraderie make trips down the river comfortable and fun. Exploradores

Outdoors' tour includes a buffet breakfast before the river trip begins, as well as a buffet lunch served on the riverbank. Overnight trips are typically one-night packages ($239 s, $478 d, all-inclusive) that include two days of rafting and a stay at **Pacuare River Lodge,** which is more of a wilderness camp with 13 small, one-room (single or double occupancy) cabins; bathrooms are a short walk away in the lodge's main building. Set atop a mountain, the camp's overlooks have top-notch rainforest and river views. Reservations are required and meals are included. Longer stays are available upon request.

Aventuras Naturales
Avenida 5, 50 m east of Calle 33 and 300 m north of Hwy. 2, San José, tel. 506/2224-0505, all-inclusive 2-night package, min. stay 2 nights
Aventuras Naturales offers two-night packages that include a stay at the luxurious riverfront **Pacuare Lodge** (tel. 506/4033-0060, www. pacuarelodge.com, $1,198 s, $2,396 d, all-inclusive 2-night package, min. stay 2 nights). Its 20 spacious bedroom suites have soaking tubs, canopy beds, high-quality linens and mattresses, outdoor showers, and private terraces. The architecturally stunning property's peaked roofs, beautiful stonework, and well-kept gardens are impressive, as is the lodge's restaurant, which serves spectacular gourmet cuisine. The lodge can also be accessed by helicopter or via a combined 4x4 vehicle, cable-crossing, and electric car ride provided by the hotel.

CAHUITA TO MANZANILLO

Cahuita and Puerto Viejo de Tal-amanca are perfect examples of the strong Jamaican influence that sweeps Costa Rica's southern Caribbean coast. Inhabitants proud of their Afro-Costa Rican roots cook up Caribbean fare, play calypso and reggae music, paint images of legendary figures on business walls, and live by the unifying mantra "one love." The towns have a laid-back vibe and unapologetically slow pace. In Cahuita, the foremost attraction is the beach- and reef-filled Cahuita National Park at the east end of town. Southeast of Cahuita, Highway 36 leads to the popular beach town of Puerto Viejo de Talamanca, called Puerto Viejo for short.

Cahuita's main (unnamed) inter-section is just two blocks north of the more popular entrance to the national park. Road 256 is Puerto Viejo's main drag for roughly two kilometers, paralleling the Caribbean Sea much of the way before the road continues southeast along the coast toward the village of Manzanillo.

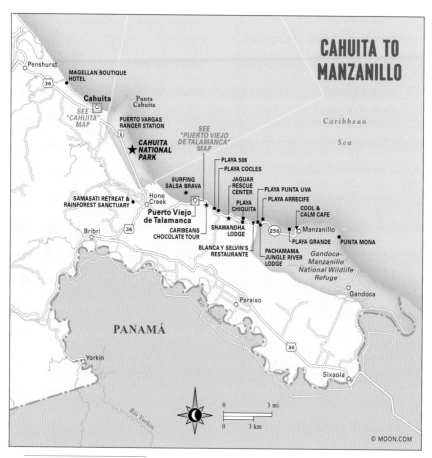

East of Puerto Viejo, splendid light-sand beaches stretch for 13 kilometers along the coast, from Playa Cocles and Playa Chiquita to Punta Uva, Playa Arrecife, and the village of Manzanillo. The southern Caribbean coast's highest-quality accommodations and restaurants, plus a handful of noteworthy attractions, line Road 256.

HIGHLIGHTS

★ CAHUITA NATIONAL PARK

tel. 506/2755-0302, www.sinac. go.cr, hours and admission vary by sector

The main attraction at **Cahuita National Park** (Parque Nacional Cahuita) is the light-sand **Playa Blanca,** one of the Caribbean coast's prettiest stretches of sand. Encompassing 57,550 acres of water, the park is primarily a marine attraction that protects the region's coral reef. Visitors can see the reef and its inhabitants for themselves by **snorkeling** at **Punta Cahuita.**

The park has two sectors: the **Playa Blanca Sector** (easternmost point of downtown Cahuita, 6am-5pm daily, donations accepted) and the **Puerto Vargas Sector** (east of Hwy. 36, 4.5 km southeast of downtown Cahuita, 8am-4pm daily, $5 pp). A **ranger station** marks the entrance to each. The Playa Blanca Sector is more popular, easier to access from town, and technically free to enter; however, a $5 per person donation is respectful.

If you're bound for Playa Blanca, enter via the Playa Blanca Sector, stroll along the sand-swept trail until you find a section of coastline you'd like to station yourself at, and enjoy

Cahuita National Park

your stay. Beware of skittish ghost crabs that burrow in the beach; they're harmless, but the little critters camouflage themselves with the sand and can be startling when they dart out in front of you.

Development along the beach is scarce (bathrooms are provided at the sector's entrance), except for a 180-meter wheelchair-accessible path. Built from recycled plastic, the eco-friendly path departs from the ranger station, briefly travels through the forest, crosses the sand, and nearly touches the water.

If you want relaxing hikes, you'll love touring this park. The flat **main trail** (8.5 km one-way, 3 hours, moderate) parallels the coast much of the way and has ample opportunities to rest along the beach or take a refreshing dip in the Caribbean Sea. The first several meters of the trail are wheelchair accessible, providing an opportunity to explore part of the forest and Playa Blanca. If you wish to tour the trail's entirety, you'll span the park's two sectors. The section of the main trail that passes through the Puerto Vargas Sector is the least visited and densest, providing your best chance for spotting **wildlife.** The tree-laden interior is home to **sloths, basilisks, birds,** and **monkeys** (look for howler monkeys near the entrance and capuchin monkeys

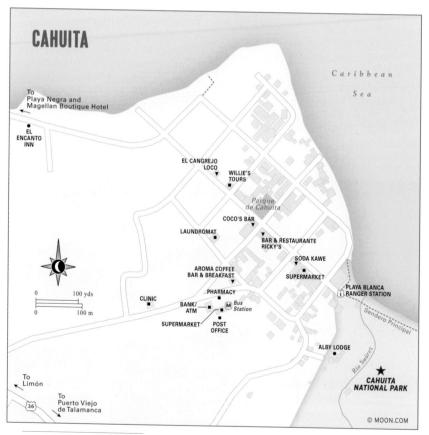

farther into the forest). Keep your eyes open for the mustard-yellow **snakes** (venomous eyelash vipers) that inhabit the park.

The park occupies the southeast end of Cahuita. The Playa Blanca Sector entrance is within walking distance of nearly everything in the village. The Puerto Vargas Sector is best accessed by car. The turn-off to the entrance is off Highway 36, 4.5 kilometers southeast of downtown Cahuita.

JAGUAR RESCUE CENTER

Road 256, 4 km southeast of Puerto Viejo de Talamanca at Playa Cocles, tel. 506/2750-0710, www.jaguar rescue.foundation, 9am-4pm daily, by guided tour only

One of the area's most notable attractions, the **Jaguar Rescue Center** is at the east end of Playa Cocles and the west end of Playa Chiquita. Named somewhat misleadingly, the site is commonly devoid of jaguars, although animal intake varies from day to day. Still, there are more than enough other kinds of wildlife here to feast your eyes on: The center usually has 130-200 temporary or permanent residents at any given time.

On average, the rescue center takes in 420-570 birds, reptiles, and mammals each year; slightly less than half of them are released back into the wild. Tour guides provide more information about the center's operations during the **Public Tour** (9:30am and 11:30am Mon.-Sat., 1.5 hours, $20 pp 10 years and older), a light walk around the property. During the experience, you'll have up-close but safe encounters with an ever-changing collection of species that usually includes monkeys, sloths, crocodiles, snakes, birds, and deer. Wildlife babies (many orphaned) are adorable, particularly the baby sloths. Though the center is a great place for kids, the stories behind each rescue—including electrocution, car accident, attack by other animals, and illegal trafficking—may upset some children.

The Jaguar Rescue Center may be the most popular privately owned attraction you can visit along the southern Caribbean coast, and crowds are common. Tours stick to a strict schedule, and multiple tour groups, each accompanied by a guide, are shuffled between wildlife exhibits in a timely manner. Although the structured tour feels a bit out of place in the slow-paced Caribbean, it's an experience worth having to help the region's wildlife. The center is not funded by the government; tour proceeds fuel the center. Visitors cannot pet, handle, or feed the animals here.

CARIBEANS CHOCOLATE TOUR

Road 256, just northwest of Playa Cocles, tel. 506/8341-2034, www. caribeanschocolate.com, 10am Mon., 10am and 2pm Tues. and Thurs.-Fri., 2pm Sat., 2.5-3 hours, $28 adults, $14 children 9-12

Some of Costa Rica's best chocolate comes from the Caribbean region. Taste it for yourself during the **Caribeans Chocolate Tour,** provided by the café and bakeshop of the same name. During the hands-on tour, you'll walk up the hill behind the shop to an operating cacao farm and chocolate factory, where a guide will explain how it's possible to get such smooth and rich dark chocolate from bumpy, bright yellow cacao pods. What sets this experience apart from other chocolate tours around the country is Caribbeans' focus on farming quality. You can literally taste differences across bars produced with cacao developed in different ways. The fact that fair wages are paid to local cacao farmers—and that an endless supply of organic chocolate samples are provided during the tour—is all the more reason to sign up; walk-ins are welcome. Don't forget to purchase a drink or dessert from the café before you leave.

BEACHES

South of Cahuita National Park are still more picturesque beaches. Few people know that much of this beautiful coastline is part of a national wildlife refuge, the Refugio Nacional de Vida Silvestre Gandoca-Manzanillo. No official refuge entrances exist and no access fees apply along this stretch, so treat the beaches here as you would any other. Be sure to pack out whatever you bring in to help keep the refuge free of debris.

There is little development on the beaches themselves, but restaurants and the occasional street vendor are spread along Road 256, just south of the coast. No matter which beach you choose, food, drinks, and bathrooms are nearby.

Each beach is accessible by car; however, there are no official, secure parking lots. There is space for a few cars at the back of each beach and along the beach access roads (most depart from Road 256). Don't leave any valuables in your rental car, and keep it locked at all times.

PLAYA COCLES

The area's best swimming and sunbathing beach, **Playa Cocles** is southeast of Puerto Viejo, within walking distance of town. You'll find a mix of swimmers and surfers here, with lifeguards keeping a watchful eye on both, plus beach volleyball nets and plenty of surfboards available to rent. Choose this beach if you wish to remain close to town or socialize with other beachgoers. Even though it's a popular choice, the long, light brown, sandy beach provides plenty of room to stretch out.

PLAYA CHIQUITA

East of Playa Cocles, **Playa Chiquita** is situated between the headlands of Punta Cocles and Punta Uva. This pristine cove, containing one of my favorite Caribbean beaches, boasts clear waters and sees few visitors. When you've had enough of the tropical sun or you tire of wading in the shallow waters, retreat to the line of leafy palms and *almendro* (almond) trees that backs the beach and provides cooling shade. I've had luck spotting great green macaws around this beach; look for them in the treetops.

PLAYA PUNTA UVA AND PLAYA ARRECIFE

The two crescent beaches that make up **Playa Punta Uva** are roughly 2.5 kilometers east of Playa Chiquita. The fine sand is lovely, but the coral reef offshore is even more beautiful. Swimming and snorkeling around the reef are permitted, provided you cause it no harm. A short **nature trail** climbs up and over the Punta Uva headland and connects the separate beach areas. Locals colloquially refer to the easternmost beach, arguably the most attractive stretch of the southern Caribbean coast, as **Playa Arrecife.**

PLAYA GRANDE

Fronting the village of Manzanillo (and aptly nicknamed **Playa Manzanillo**) is **Playa Grande.** On sunny days, the beach shimmers like gold, and the depths of the Caribbean Sea can be seen through turquoise waters. Don't expect to have the idyllic place to yourself, though, as it's the home beach of the area's residents. Stick to the east end of the beach if you wish to be close to the village and its handful of restaurants and supermarkets. Backed by a wall of dense vegetation, the west

Playa Grande in Manzanillo

end of the beach is farther away from development. Swimming is best during September and October, when favorable weather calms the sea.

SURFING

The Caribbean region isn't known for stupendous surf, but there are a handful of wicked waves. The best is **Salsa Brava,** a right-hand reef break that's a short paddle off the coast from Puerto Viejo. Best attempted by seasoned surfers, the powerful break (the name translates to "angry sauce") offers a full-speed, narrow, and gnarly ride. Besides common risks like riptides and undertows, the shallow break barrels over rocks and sharp coral reef. Surfers are spit out bloodied and bruised, yet the spot is one of the Caribbean coast's most crowded. Expect long lines and respect your fellow surfers by curbing your drop-ins; most are locals who have surfed the break for years and have earned priority. Novice participants should head 2.5 kilometers south to the beach break at Playa

Cocles, where less challenging surf awaits over a soft, sandy seabed.

Want to watch the pros from the shore? Seat yourself at a picnic table or in an Adirondack chair on the beach at the **Salsa Brava Beach Restaurant and Bar** (Road 256 just east of Avenida 69, tel. 506/8429-2929, noon-midnight Tues.-Sun.). The restaurant and bar offer a perfect view of the action.

CARIBBEAN SURF SCHOOL

Calle 217, 50 m northwest of Road 256, tel. 506/8357-7703, 9am-6pm Sun.-Fri., 2-hour lessons 8am and 3pm daily, group $55 pp, 2-3 students per instructor, private $60 pp, 1 student per instructor

Although local surfers offering up lessons are a dime a dozen in Puerto

INDIGENOUS PEOPLE OF COSTA RICA: THE BRIBRI

On the west side of Highway 36, 20 kilometers south of Cahuita and 13 kilometers southwest of Puerto Viejo de Talamanca, the small, inland village of Bribri serves as a gateway to several Indigenous communities. The majority of the Caribbean's Indigenous population, who are primarily members of the Bribri group, reside in reserves spread out around the foothills of the Cordillera de Talamanca. The hardworking, remote group is largely self-sufficient. They survive by hunting for meat and fish, growing their own food (mainly corn, beans, bananas, plantains, and cassava), and trading cacao to chocolatiers for cash. Their earnings help develop clinics, schools, and community centers, which in turn help sustain the communities themselves.

Many group members welcome the economic boost that tourism provides to Indigenous reserves. Families in several communities—among them Yorkin, Watsi, Shiroles, and Amubri—take turns working with local outfitters to host tour groups and provide cultural presentations that demonstrate the group's way of life. Tour experiences

Viejo, the go-to guys are Hershel Lewis Gordon and his crew at the **Caribbean Surf School.** They stand out with their patience, professionalism, and passion for surfing. Choose from group or private lessons. Each lesson includes the use of a surfboard and rash guard.

SNORKELING

In Cahuita National Park, find Costa Rica's best coral reef roughly 500 meters off **Punta Cahuita** (Cahuita Point). Snorkeling here provides a peek at live coral and two shipwrecks, plus an opportunity to be surrounded by schools of tropical fish. The point is a 3.5-kilometer hike from the entrance of the Playa Blanca Sector and a 5-kilometer hike from the entrance of the Puerto Vargas Sector.

Nearly every tour company operating from Limón to Manzanillo runs snorkeling tours to the site. In an effort to preserve the reef, snorkeling without a guide is not permitted. Most tours couple snorkeling with a guided nature walk through the park. The **Snorkeling and Hiking in Cahuita National Park Tour** (8:30am daily, 4.5-5.5 hours, $45 pp) is a best seller of well-known Cahuita tour operator **Willie's Tours** (main street Cahuita, 300 m northwest of the park entrance to the Playa Blanca Sector, tel. 506/2755-1024, www.williestourscostarica.com, 8am-7pm daily).

vary; you could see how cacao is processed, visit a local waterfall, give archery a go, take an Indigenous cooking class, learn about medicinal plants, or participate in a purification ceremony performed by one of the group's doctors. Most visits include a home-cooked meal prepared with crops grown on the reserve. All visits provide an opportunity to interact with the Bribri people on their beloved land.

Indigenous community visits require traveling to remote areas of the Caribbean, sometimes via a combination of ground and canoe transportation. Book your experience through an operator familiar with the logistics and known to local groups. In Puerto Viejo, the tourism company **Life Culture & Travel Costa Rica** (Calle 215 and Avenida 73, Puerto Viejo de Talamanca, tel. 506/2750-2158, www.lifeculture-travelcostarica.com), run by Bribri group member and passionate tour guide Tirza Morales Sanchez, offers 14 different day tours ($45-135 pp, 2-7 hours) that allow you to choose the experiences you want to have during your visit to an Indigenous community. Another option is the Cahuita-based tour operator **Willie's Tours** (1 block northwest of the main intersection, Cahuita, tel. 506/2755-1024, www.willie-stourscostarica.com), which offers two day tours ($59 pp, 5-7 hours) and two multiday tours ($165-215 pp, 2-3 days) that permit overnight stays on a reserve.

NIGHTLIFE

CAHUITA

Barhopping around small-scale Cahuita is easy and mostly safe to accomplish on foot. After dark, stick to bars along the main street, particularly Coco's and Ricky's, which are across the street from one another.

Coco's Bar
at Cahuita's main intersection, tel. 506/2755-0437, 10am-2:30am Mon.-Sat., 10am-midnight Sun.
As the sun goes down on the southern Caribbean, the music gets turned up at art-wrapped **Coco's Bar,** where locals and foreigners dance well into the morning on a deck-board dance floor under the glimmer of a disco ball.

Bar & Restaurante Ricky's
at Cahuita's main intersection, tel. 506/2755-0305, 11am-10pm daily
Bar & Restaurante Ricky's competes with happy hours and is a great place to catch Ticos engaging in a much-loved pastime: rounds of dominoes.

El Cangrejo Loco
40 m northwest of Willie's Tours, Cahuita, tel. 506/8822-3844, 4pm-10pm daily
El Cangrejo Loco has live music and an endless happy hour with two-for-one drinks.

© MOON.COM

PUERTO VIEJO
Salsa Brava Beach Restaurant and Bar
Road 256 just east of Avenida 69, Puerto Viejo, tel. 506/8429-2929, 7am-11pm Wed.-Mon.

In Puerto Viejo, kick off your night at the **Salsa Brava Beach Restaurant and Bar,** which has a killer view of the area's best surf break. This small place at the waterfront resembles an informal beach hut with a wrap-around bar and several stools. On the beach, picnic tables and chairs provide additional seating. Expect a chill vibe, smooth reggae beats that play on repeat, and happy hours on the beach.

Hot Rocks
Road 256 at Calle 217, Puerto Viejo, tel. 506/8708-3183, 10am-2am daily

Local favorite **Hot Rocks** is open late. Though it serves all kinds of alcoholic beverages, the semi-out-door bar feels like a beer garden, thanks to its large, open-concept space filled with picnic tables. This place also has funky swing seating (for adults and children) and enter-tains crowds nightly with regularly scheduled events that feature live music, karaoke, free salsa dance lessons, and fire dancing shows. Some early-evening events are family friendly.

SAFETY

Women may find themselves the objects of unsolicited attention from men while in Puerto Viejo's bars and clubs, including invitations to dance, offers of drinks, catcalling, or encroaching on personal space while dancing. The behavior tends to be forward rather than aggressive; most men will back off when asked to do so. It's okay to say *"No, gracias."* If the behavior persists or becomes too aggressive, leave and find another place to hang out. Chances are that the man is a local, so the bar staff won't be helpful. If you ever fear for your safety, call the police. Consider going out with a group, as men are much less likely to approach women in groups.

FOOD

STANDOUTS
Soda Kawe
main street Cahuita, 100 m northwest of the park entrance to the Playa Blanca Sector, tel. 506/2755-0233, 5:30am-7pm daily, $4-8
My preferred eatery, thanks to its yummy Caribbean food and fair prices, is **Soda Kawe.** Hearty breakfast options and fruit *batidos* (smoothies) are great for starting off your day; a plate of coconut rice and beans (with chicken, beef, pork, or vegetables) is my go-to lunch order. If you struggle to find an available picnic table inside the small, bare-bones restaurant, grab a stool and sit at the bar that fronts the property.

Aroma Coffee Bar & Breakfast
downtown Cahuita, just north of the bus station, tel. 506/8808-6445, 8am-6pm Mon.-Sat., $5-15
You cannot beat the food selection and quality at **Aroma Coffee Bar & Breakfast.** The vegetarian and vegan omelets, burgers, wraps, and rolls are each worth a taste. An array of meat dishes appeases visiting carnivores. The relaxing music,

---

Coco's Bar (left); Soda Kawe (right)

CAHUITA TO MANZANILLO FOOD

NAME	LOCATION
★ Soda Kawe	main street Cahuita, 100 m northwest of the park entrance to the Playa Blanca Sector
★ Aroma Coffee Bar & Breakfast	downtown Cahuita, just north of the bus station
★ Cool & Calm Cafe	150 m west of Mr. Maxie's, Manzanillo
★ Take It Easy	Road 256, Playa Cocles
★ Lidia's Place	corner of Avenida 67 and Calle 217, Puerto Viejo de Talamanca
★ Blanca y Selvin's Restaurante	Road 256, 7 km southeast of Puerto Viejo de Talamanca at Punta Uva
★ Bread and Chocolate	Calle 217 between Road 256 and Avenida 69, Puerto Viejo de Talamanca

outdoor patio setting, and stack of board games are much-appreciated extras.

Cool & Calm Café
150 m west of Mr. Maxie's, Manzanillo, tel. 506/8843-7460, 11am-9pm Wed.-Mon., $8-15
In Manzanillo, you can get delicious barbecued food at the seaside **Cool & Calm Café.** Juicy chicken, racks of beef and pork ribs, and fresh fish and seafood caught locally hiss on the restaurant's roadside grill while patrons enjoy frosty bottles of beer and refreshing fruit drinks on a covered outdoor patio. Hailing from Limón, Andy Cook Campbell—the restaurant's cordial owner and chef—lends the place his passion for local Caribbean food, not to mention his lively and carefree vibe.

Take It Easy
tel. 506/8919-0819, 10:30am-5pm Sat.-Sun., under $5
With a bit of luck, you can find the food cart **Take It Easy** parked along Road 256 in front of Playa Cocles. The

cart's palm-thatched roof, old steel grill, and high-flying Pan-American flag are easy to spot if the tantalizing smell of barbecued meat and coconut-flavored rice and beans doesn't lure you in. Most meals are served on the leaf of an almond tree.

Lidia's Place
corner of Avenida 67 and Calle 217, Puerto Viejo de Talamanca, tel. 506/2750-0598, 1pm-9pm Tues.-Sat., 11:30am-8pm Sun., $6-15
When in Puerto Viejo, I regularly dine at the authentic **Lidia's Place.** The simple *soda* (traditional Costa Rican family restaurant) may be unimpressive to the eyes, but it produces the most flavorful home-cooked meals in the region, most prepared by Lidia, the kind cook. Top dishes include chicken drenched in Caribbean sauce, coconut curry shrimp, *pargo rojo* (red snapper), and coconut rice and beans. Lidia's sons (and other relatives) demonstrate warm, genuine service that boosts the place from a delicious Caribbean diner to

CONTACT INFO	FOOD	PRICE
tel. 506/2755-0233	Costa Rican	$4-8
tel. 506/8808-6445	café with vegetarian and vegan options	$5-15
tel. 506/8843-7460	Costa Rican	$8-15
tel. 506/8919-0819	Costa Rican	under $5
tel. 506/2750-0598	Costa Rican	$6-15
tel. 506/2750-0664, www.selvinpuntauva.com	Costa Rican	$8-16
tel. 506/2750-0723, www.breadandchocolatecr.com	café and bakery	$6-9

the best traditional-style restaurant in town.

Blanca y Selvin's Restaurante

Road 256, 7 km southeast of Puerto Viejo de Talamanca at Punta Uva, tel. 506/2750-0664, www.selvinpunta uva.com, noon-8pm Thurs.-Sun., $8-16

Since 1982, **Blanca y Selvin's Restaurante** has been serving up some of the best local Caribbean fare, from bowls of *rondón* to plates of *patacones* (smashed and fried green plantains). For a roadside spot not far from the beach, the laid-back and open-air restaurant is surprisingly clean; service is quick and friendly, and the entire operation feels organized.

Bread and Chocolate

Calle 217 between Road 256 and Avenida 69, Puerto Viejo, tel. 506/2750-0723, www.breadand chocolatecr.com, 6:30am-6:30pm Wed.-Sat., 6:30am-2:30pm Sun., $6-9

The rustic **Bread and Chocolate** is a beloved café tucked away off Puerto Viejo's main street and has a slightly hippie vibe. Choose from waffles, French toast, or biscuits and gravy for breakfast; sandwiches, soups, and salads for lunch; cakes, pies, and tarts for dessert; plus loads of other fresh baked goods. Many items (including breads, butters, sauces, jams, and granolas) are prepared in-house. Other ingredients are sourced locally.

★ CARIBBEAN CUISINE

plates of flavorful Caribbean food

The pristine beaches on Costa Rica's Pacific coast steal much of the country's spotlight, but where the Caribbean shines is in the kitchen. Caribbean cooking relies on freshly grated coconut milk, spices, and homemade sauces. You can taste the difference for yourself by trying any of the following dishes typically served on the Caribbean coast.

- **Coconut rice and beans:** Rice and beans is the Caribbean's take on the rest of the country's *gallo pinto* (a traditional rice and bean blend), although the grain and protein are sometimes served separately on the plate. The major difference between the two?

LODGING

STANDOUTS

El Encanto Inn
on the road to Playa Negra, 150 m east of La Union, Cahuita, tel. 506/2755-0113, www.elencanto cahuita.com, $90 s, $101 d

I like **El Encanto Inn** because it offers decent value and a pleasurable stay. The two-story boutique hotel has 11 rooms amply furnished with beds, wardrobes, desks, end tables, safes, and fans. Two pools (one saltwater) and outdoor lounge areas are set amid the property's attractive landscaping of palms and other tropical plants. Slump in a hammock or a chair on your room's terrace and enjoy the oasis-like feel of the fully enclosed hotel. Kind hosts add to the quality of the experience.

Magellan Boutique Hotel
Plaza Víquez, 50 m southwest of the road to Playa Negra, Cahuita, tel.

The rice here is cooked in coconut milk, so it's sweeter and a bit softer than regular rice. Much like *casado* (a traditional dish of rice and beans, accompanied by a variety of side dishes), coconut rice and beans is regularly enjoyed with meat and vegetables on the side.

- **Rondón:** Essentially fish soup, this slow-cooked stew also has vegetables, coconut milk, and curry powder. The result is a creamy, flavorful bowl of piping-hot goodness.

- **Jerk marinades and *salsa caribeña*:** Caribbean food is rarely bland because it's often doused in delicious dressings. Jamaican-style jerk comes in a variety of flavors, but it's typically a smoky and spicy blend. My personal favorite, *salsa caribeña* (Caribbean sauce), is a slightly sweet brown sauce that looks like watered-down gravy. Both sauces are commonly rubbed on or poured over chicken, beef, and fish.

- **Patís:** The small, turnover-style snacks known as *patís* (also referred to as **patties**) are perfect if you're on the go. They're filled with either meat or fruit and can be baked or fried.

- **Pan bon:** Roadside stalls along Highway 32 sell *pan bon*. The dark, sweet bread is a local delicacy. Ingredients like coconut, cinnamon, and nutmeg are typical, but some varieties feature nuts and dried fruit.

- **Agua de sapo:** Ignore the off-putting translation (toad water): *Agua de sapo* is a delicious drink. The potent concoction of ginger, lime, and *tapa de dulce* (unrefined cane sugar) is part sweet and part sour. It will help clear your palate after a plateful of flavorful Caribbean food.

506/2755-0035, www.magellan boutiquehotel.com, $130 s/d

The six simple but sophisticated guest suites at the **Magellan Boutique Hotel** add a touch of class to a Cahuita stay. An aura of romance wafts throughout the hotel, where guests are treated to king-size beds with orthopedic mattresses, high-quality linens, flat-screen TVs, generously sized rooms, and French doors that open to views of the property's gardens. The rate includes a nourishing breakfast, complimentary beach mats, and access to the hotel's concierge service. Yogis should register for the hotel's yoga retreat package; classes take place in a tranquil open-air studio.

Hostel Pagalu
Avenida 69 between Calle 211 and Calle 213, Puerto Viejo, tel. 506/2750-1930, www.pagalu.com, dorm $13 pp, private $35 s/d

One of the quietest hostels in Puerto Viejo, **Hostel Pagalu** has a wonderfully relaxed vibe. The four dorms sleep four or six people each, and the six private rooms (three have shared baths) have a queen bed. Big lockers and hot water keep guests

CAHUITA TO MANZANILLO LODGING

NAME	LOCATION
★ El Encanto Inn	on the road to Playa Negra, 150 m east of La Union, Cahuita
★ Magellan Boutique Hotel	Plaza Víquez, 50 m southwest of the road to Playa Negra, Cahuita
Alby Lodge	150 south of the park entrance to the Playa Blanca Sector, Cahuita
★ Hostel Pagalu	Avenida 69 between Calle 211 and Calle 213, Puerto Viejo de Talamanca
★ Casa Verde Lodge	Avenida 69 between Calle 217 and Calle 219, Puerto Viejo de Talamanca
★ Umāmi Hotel	at the southern end of Calle 219, Puerto Viejo de Talamanca
★ Playa 506	Road 256, 2.5 km southeast of Puerto Viejo de Talamanca at Playa Cocles
★ Punta Mona	on the beach at Punta Mona, Manzanillo
Pachamama Jungle River Lodge	Road 256, 8 km southeast of Puerto Viejo de Talamanca at Punta Uva
Samasati Retreat & Rainforest Sanctuary	Hone Creek, 8 km west of Puerto Viejo de Talamanca
Shawandha Lodge	Road 256, 6 km southeast of Puerto Viejo de Talamanca at Playa Chiquita

happy. The two-story building gets lots of light and is open-concept and airy. The main-floor common area opposite the shared kitchen is a good place to you can curl up with a book or socialize with others in a low-key setting.

Casa Verde Lodge
Avenida 69 between Calle 217 and Calle 219, Puerto Viejo, tel. 506/2750-0015, www.casaverde lodge.com, $79 s/d
The **Casa Verde Lodge** feels like its own little oasis in downtown Puerto Viejo. The small property packs a lot into its one-story structure, including 17 spacious and well-furnished rooms (each for 1-3 people), terraces with hammocks, and a decent-size pool. Pillow-top mattresses, safes, and mini-refrigerators are welcome in-room extras. Best of all, thick tropical vegetation completely encloses the hotel, creating a quiet, private place to rest where you'll forget you're in the middle of one of the most-visited destinations in the Caribbean.

Umāmi Hotel
at the southern end of Calle 219, Puerto Viejo, tel. 506/2750-3200, www.umamihotel.com, $179 s/d
Luxury in downtown Puerto Viejo is practically nonexistent, but the adults-only **Umāmi Hotel** is changing the scene. Twelve modern rooms

CONTACT INFO	OPTIONS	PRICE
tel. 506/2755-0113, www. elencantocahuita.com	hotel rooms	$90 s, $101 d
tel. 506/2755-0035, www. magellanboutiquehotel. com	hotel suites	$130 s/d
tel. 506/2755-0031, www.albylodge.com	bungalows with private bathrooms	$60 s/d, cash only
tel. 506/2750-1930, www.pagalu.com	dorm rooms, private rooms	dorm $13 pp, private $35 s/d
tel. 506/2750-0015, www. casaverdelodge.com	lodge rooms	$79 s/d
tel. 506/2750-3200, www.umamihotel.com	luxury hotel rooms; adults only	$179 s/d
tel. 506/2750-3158, www.playa506.com	dorm rooms, private rooms	dorm $21 pp, private $50 s, $59 d
www.puntamona.org	basic rooms and casitas at an off-the-grid farm and retreat center	dorm $95, casita $145 s, $205 d, cash only
tel. 506/8531-4845, www. pachamamacaribe.com	villas with bathrooms and kitchens	$105 s/d
tel. 506/8428-3918, www.samasati.com	casitas	$210 s, $235 d
tel. 506/2750-0018, www.shawandha.com	bungalows and poolside tepees	bungalow $180 s/d, tepee $215 s/d

with a comfortable king or queen bed, tile floors, high-end furniture, rainfall showerheads, air-conditioning, and designer finishes like Indigenous-style wall art and sculptures create an aura of elegance in each room and encourage relaxation. The outstanding pool area has roofed cabanas with mattresses and lounge chairs with umbrellas. At night, the place sparkles in soft lighting and is ultraromantic. Breakfast is included in the rate.

Playa 506
Road 256, 2.5 km southeast of Puerto Viejo de Talamanca at Playa Cocles, **tel. 506/2750-3158, www.playa506. com, dorm $21 pp, private $50 s, $59 d**

If you're looking to socialize, head to the beachfront hostel **Playa 506.** It has a fun energy and a laid-back vibe, and is a great place to grab a beer, play some beach volleyball, catch a movie, and meet new friends. The staff are helpful, the sea is steps away, and breakfast is included—what more could you want? Three mixed dorms sleep eight people each and have shared bathrooms. There are three private rooms; two of them share access to outdoor bathrooms.

Punta Mona

on the beach at Punta Mona, Manzanillo, no phone, www.puntamona. org, dorm $95, casita $145 s, $205 d, cash only

Committed to regeneration, **Punta Mona** is an 85-acre, community-driven sustainable farm and educational retreat center accessible only by boat or a two-hour hike from Manzanillo. Visits are opportunities to go off the grid, live a different way of life in the jungle, and learn about permaculture, herbalism, and other holistic practices. Though the dry composting toilets, intermittent Internet service, and rough-hewn wooden rooms (for 1-3 people) and bamboo casitas (for 1-2 people) suggest Punta Mona is overpriced, what you're really paying for is the invaluable experience of establishing a deeper connection with the earth, other travelers, and yourself. Three daily communal (mostly vegan) meals are also included with your stay.

INFORMATION AND SERVICES

Cahuita's medical **clinic, Ebais Cahuita** (tel. 506/2755-0383, 7am-4pm Mon. and Wed.-Fri.), is just west of the town's mini-mall and bus station. There's a **pharmacy,** known as **Farmacia Cahuita** (tel. 506/2755-0505, 9am-5pm Mon.-Sat.), in town as well. Cahuita has a **police station** (north end of town, road to Playa Negra, tel. 506/2755-0217, 24 hours daily). Just north of Highway 36 on the main road into town, the mini-mall and bus station have the town's only bank, **Banco de Costa Rica** (9am-4pm Mon.-Fri.), which has an **ATM** (5am-midnight daily).

In Puerto Viejo de Talamanca, the **Centro de Especialidades Médicas San Gabriel** (Calle 213, 100 m southeast of Road 256, tel. 506/2750-0079, 9am-9pm Mon.-Sat., 9am-6pm Sun.) is a **medical clinic** with an on-site pharmacy. **Banco Nacional** (near the corner of Road 256 and Calle 211, tel. 506/2212-1212, 8:30am-3:45pm Mon.-Fri., ATM 5am-midnight daily) has an ATM. Surprisingly, Puerto Viejo does not have a **police station.** For travelers in Puerto Viejo or Manzanillo, there's a **tourist police office** (Road 256 at Playa Cocles, tel. 506/2750-0452, 10am-10pm daily) in Playa Cocles, which has officers available to assist foreign travelers. In the event of an emergency after hours, the closest official **police station** (Bribri, tel. 506/2751-0003, 24 hours daily) is in the community of **Bribri,** 13 kilometers southwest of Puerto Viejo and 27 kilometers west of Manzanillo. The police station in Cahuita is about the same distance from Manzanillo as the one in Bribri.

Hospital Tony Facio Castro (Paseo Dr. Rubén Umaña Chavarría, 1 km north of the cruise dock, Limón, tel. 506/2758-2222, 24 hours daily) in Limón serves most of the Caribbean region. It is a 45-kilometer, 45-minute drive northwest of Cahuita, a 60-kilometer, one-hour drive northwest of Puerto Viejo, and a 75-kilometer, 90-minute drive northwest of Manzanillo.

TRANSPORTATION AND TOURS

Getting to Cahuita

From **San José,** Cahuita is a 200-kilometer drive east on Highway 32 and southeast on Highway 36, which takes around three hours and 45 minutes. From **Liberia,** Cahuita is 395 kilometers east on Highway 1, Road 142, Highway 4, and Highway 32, and southeast on Highway 36, a drive that takes approximately 7 hours. From **La Fortuna,** the drive is 255 kilometers east on Road 142, Highway 4, and Highway 32, and southeast on Highway 36; it's a 4.5-hour journey. From **Limón,** Cahuita is a 45-kilometer, 45-minute drive southeast on Highway 36. From **Puerto Viejo de Talamanca,** it's just 15 kilometers, a 15-minute drive west on Road 256 and northwest on Highway 36.

The regional **bus station** in Cahuita is at the entrance to town, 500 meters east of Highway 36. You can reach Cahuita by **bus** from **San José** (multiple times 6am-6pm daily, 4 hours, $8.50), **Limón** (multiple times 5:30am-8pm daily, 1-1.5 hours, $2-2.50), **Puerto Viejo de Talamanca** (multiple times 5:30am-8pm daily, 30 minutes, $1.50), and **Manzanillo** (multiple times 5:30am-6:30pm daily, 1 hour, $2-2.50).

Getting to Puerto Viejo de Talamanca

Travelers arrive in Puerto Viejo from all over the country. From **San José,** Puerto Viejo is a 215-kilometer, four-hour drive east on Highway 32, southeast on Highway 36, and east on Road 256. From **Liberia,** it's a 410-kilometer, 7-hour drive east on Highway 1, Road 142, Highway 4, and Highway 32, southeast on Highway 36, and east on Road 256. From **La Fortuna,** the almost five-hour drive is 270 kilometers east on Road 142, Highway 4, and

Highway 32, then southeast on Highway 36 and east on Road 256.

To get to Puerto Viejo from **Limón,** you'll travel southeast on Highway 36, following the Caribbean coast to the small community of Hone Creek (marked by a gas station along the highway). Highway 36 intersects with Road 256, which you'll follow east before reaching Puerto Viejo. This 60-kilometer drive takes one hour. From **Cahuita,** Puerto Viejo is just 15 kilometers southeast on Highway 36 and east on Road 256, a 15-minute drive.

The **regional bus station** in Puerto Viejo is by the water on Avenida 73 at Calle 213. You cannot miss it; the open-air station is one of Costa Rica's most colorful. You can reach Puerto Viejo de Talamanca by **bus** from **San José** (multiple times 6am-6pm daily, 4.5 hours, $10), **Limón** (multiple times 5:30am-8pm daily, 1.5 hours, $3-3.50), **Cahuita** (multiple times 5:30am-8pm daily, 30 minutes, $1.50), and **Manzanillo** (multiple times 5am-6pm daily, 30 minutes, $1.50). Make sure you board a bus to Puerto Viejo de Talamanca, not Puerto Viejo de Sarapiquí. You may see Puerto Viejo de Talamanca referred to as Puerto Viejo de Limón or Puerto Viejo del Caribe at stations, on tickets and schedules, or on signs on the buses themselves.

Getting to Manzanillo

The section of the southern Caribbean spanning Playa Cocles to Manzanillo is considered the eastern outskirts of Puerto Viejo de Talamanca. You'll drive through Puerto Viejo de Talamanca first. If you don't have your own vehicle, most accommodations in the area can pick you up in Puerto Viejo for an extra cost.

From Puerto Viejo, **Playa Cocles** is roughly three kilometers southeast on Road 256, a five-minute drive. **Playa Chiquita** is 6 kilometers (a 12-minute drive) and **Punta Uva** is 8.5 kilometers (a 15-minute drive) southeast of Puerto Viejo. **Manzanillo** is farthest from Puerto Viejo, at 13 kilometers (a 20-minute drive) southeast on Road 256.

Public **buses** travel to Manzanillo daily. You can catch one from **San José** (noon daily, 5-5.5 hours, $11), **Limón** (multiple times 5:30am-6:30pm daily, 1.5-2 hours, $4.50), **Cahuita** (multiple times 5:30am-6:30pm daily, 1 hour, $2-2.50), and **Puerto Viejo de Talamanca** (multiple times 5:30am-6:30pm daily, 30 minutes, $1.50). The bus that travels along Road 256 between Puerto Viejo de Talamanca and Manzanillo provides access to Playa Cocles, Playa Chiquita, and Punta Uva.

Private Transfer and Shared Shuttle Services

The Puerto Viejo-based transportation service **Caribe Shuttle** (corner of Road

256 and Calle 213, tel. 506/2750-0626, www.caribeshuttle.com, 6am-9pm daily) is your best bet for **private transfer services** to the Caribbean region. They provide service to Cahuita and Puerto Viejo de Talamanca from all corners of Costa Rica. One-way prices average around $170 from San José and $225 from La Fortuna for up to 10 people.

Another reliable option is **Exploradores Outdoors** (Road 256, 85 m east of Salsa Brava Beach Restaurant and Bar, tel. 506/2750-2020, www.exploradoresoutdoors.com, 7:30am-9pm Mon.-Fri., 11am-9pm Sat.-Sun.), which offers **private transfer services** to Puerto Viejo de Talamanca from San José and La Fortuna, as well as private transfer services to destinations within the Caribbean region as far south as Manzanillo ($120-413 for up to 9 people).

Caribe Shuttle also provides **shared shuttle services** to Cahuita and Puerto Viejo de Talamanca, as do **Interbus** (tel. 506/4100-0888, www.interbusonline.com) and **Grayline Costa Rica** (tel. 506/2220-2126, www.graylinecostarica.com). Together, the three companies cover routes to Cahuita and Puerto Viejo de Talamanca from Limón, San José, and La Fortuna, among other locales. Depending on the route, one-way services cost $22-67 per person. Caribe Shuttle is usually the least expensive by a few dollars. Most shuttles offer drop-offs at Cahuita and Puerto Viejo de Talamanca hotels.

Organized Tour
Exploradores Outdoors (tel. 506/2222-6262, www.exploradoresoutdoors.com) offers Río Pacuare white-water rafting trips ($99-224 pp) with **post-tour onward transportation.** These tours can be arranged to include a pickup from your hotel in San José or La Fortuna, then a drop-off at your hotel in Cahuita or Puerto Viejo de Talamanca.

Getting Around
Cahuita and Puerto Viejo are both small and easily explored on foot or by bike. Rent a bike from operators in downtown Cahuita or Puerto Viejo; don't pay more than $10 per day. Some hotels provide complimentary bikes for guest use.

There aren't a ton of great options for parking (especially overnight) in Puerto Viejo, unless you select an accommodation with a secure or private lot.

Road 256, the road that runs from Puerto Viejo to Manzanillo, is paved and easy to walk, bike, or drive. If you plan to beach-hop, you'll appreciate having a rental car.

Playa Tamarindo

TAMARINDO

Known for its vibrant surf culture, Tamarindo is Guanacaste's most developed coastal destination—a tight-knit beach community bursting at the seams with accommodations, restaurants, bars, tour offices, and shops. Tamarindo is more commercialized than other remote beach towns, but that means you can get by without a rental car, you have access to dining options of varied cuisines and prices, and numerous recreational options are at your fingertips.

You cannot find two neighboring destinations that are more different from each other than Tamarindo and Playa Grande. Though a mere four kilometers separates the two beach towns, they feel much farther apart, thanks to the estuary that divides them. Tamarindo is superbly energetic. It can feel a bit overwhelming during the high season, when the main drag is crowded and businesses vie for tourists' attention. Playa Grande is calm year-round. But quiet Playa Grande is no ordinary coastal community: It is part of Las Baulas National Marine Park (Parque Nacional Marino Las Baulas), one of the world's top nesting sites of leatherback sea turtles.

Nine kilometers down the coast from Tamarindo, one of this region's best-kept secrets is the span of coastline that includes Playa Avellanas and Playa Negra—few foreigners even know it exists. Visit this far-flung area if you want to base yourself in an isolated beach community with little development, where you can relax with little distraction and surf the day away.

surfers on the Pacific coast

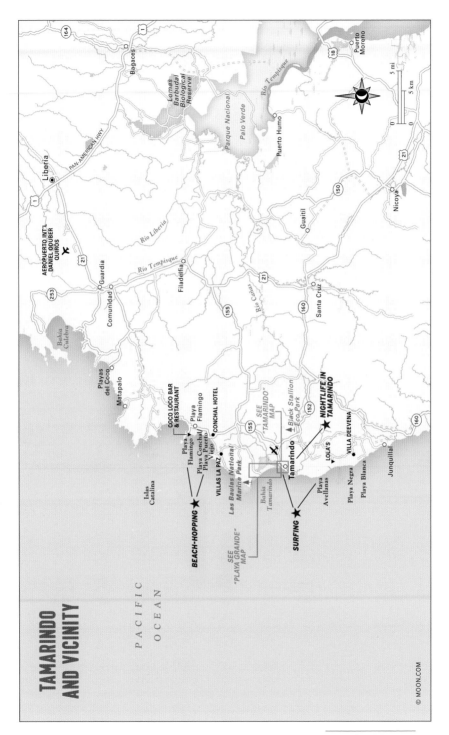

TAMARINDO AND VICINITY

PACIFIC OCEAN

BEACH-HOPPING ★

SURFING ★

NIGHTLIFE IN TAMARINDO ★

COCO LOCO BAR & RESTAURANT

CONCHAL HOTEL

VILLAS LA PAZ

Las Baulas National Marine Park

SEE "PLAYA GRANDE" MAP

SEE "TAMARINDO" MAP

Black Stallion Eco Park

LOLA'S

VILLA DEEVENA

Tamarindo

Playa Flamingo
Playa Conchal/
Playa Puerto Viejo
Playa Flamingo

Bahía Tamarindo

Playa Avellanas

Playa Negra

Playa Blanca

Junquillal

Islas Catalina

Playas del Coco

Matapalo

Bahía Calebra

Comunidad

Guardia

AEROPUERTO INT'L DANIEL ODUBER QUIROS

Liberia

PAN-AMERICAN HWY

Bagaces

Lomas Barbudal Biological Reserve

Parque Nacional Palo Verde

Río Tempisque

Puerto Humo

Puerto Moreno

Filadelfia

Río Liberia

Río Tempisque

Río Cañas

Santa Cruz

Guaitil

Nicoya

164

1

18

21

21

150

160

160

152

155

155

253

21

21

1

5 mi

5 km

© MOON.COM

1

TOP 3

★ **1. SURFING:** The breaks at Witch's Rock, Ollie's Point, and Playa Avellanas are world-class (page 129).

★ **2. BEACH-HOPPING:** The most magnificent stretches of sand in the country sweep along this coastline (page 133).

★ **3. NIGHTLIFE:** Beachside socializing begins before the sun sets and continues into the early morning (page 135).

BEST 5 DAYS IN TAMARINDO

DAY 1

Familiarize yourself with Tamarindo's vibrant spirit and rustic roots. Take a morning stroll along the beachside boulevard for people-watching. Then pop into **Nogui's**—a Tamarindo institution—for lunch. Book an afternoon horseback ride at the **Black Stallion Eco Park,** which ends with a hearty buffet dinner after the sun sets.

DAY 2

If you're an advanced-level surfer, sign up for an unforgettable one-day **surf tour** to legendary **Witch's Rock** and **Ollie's Point.** Spend the day riding gnarly waves and swapping stories with other diehard wave riders. Lunch is not included with the tour, so be sure to pack one for the trip. Back in Tamarindo in the evening, celebrate the day of epic surf with dinner and drinks at **El Vaquero Pub.**

DAY 3

Treat yourself to soft sand and sunshine on a beach-hopping road trip north of Tamarindo. Start at postcard-perfect **Playa Flamingo,** where you can enjoy lunch on the sand at the **Coco Loco Bar & Restaurant.** Next, head to the west end of **Playa Conchal** for an afternoon swim in aquamarine waters. Then head down the bumpy road to **Playa Puerto Viejo** to round out the afternoon with some solitude. Return to Tamarindo for a sunset dinner at the **Pangas Beach Club.**

DAY 4

Whether you're a novice or an expert, carve out a day to catch some waves south of Tamarindo. Beginner-, intermediate-, and advanced-level surf breaks await at **Playa Avellanas** and **Playa Negra.** Surf lessons are available at **Avellanas Surf School.** Once you work up an appetite, enjoy lunch on the beach at **Lola's.** Plan on a romantic dinner at the **Dragonfly Bar & Grill** back in Tamarindo.

DAY 5

Swim, surf, sunbathe, or people-watch at Playa Tamarindo in the morning, followed by an afternoon **sailing tour** up and down the picturesque coast, which includes a sunset dinner and drinks. Night owls can end their time in Tamarindo sampling local **nightlife.**

the beachfront Coco Loco Bar & Restaurant in Playa Flamingo

PLANNING YOUR TIME

Weather

Tamarindo is in the Guanacaste province, which boasts the highest percentage of sunshine across Costa Rica, an average temperature over 80°F, and has very little rainfall, with next to none from January through March. Prepare for scorching sun along the coast and take water, a hat, and sunscreen wherever you go. Rain showers between May and November provide some relief. The wettest months are June, September, and October.

Transportation

A few paved highways make it easy to get to and from Tamarindo. Side roads can be made of asphalt, flattened gravel, or dirt. Most routes in the region do not require a 4x4 vehicle, but it's smart to have one if you plan to explore back roads or venture into mountainous areas. During wet periods, rain can make poorly maintained roads impassable.

Connect with...

Many people follow up active days in La Fortuna and Monteverde by unwinding in Tamarindo. **Tenorio Adventure Company** (Hwy. 1 at Río Corobicí, 5 km northwest of Cañas, tel. 506/2668-8203, www.tenorioadventurecompany. com, 8am-10pm daily) helps connect Tamarindo with either La Fortuna or Monteverde via organized tours that can include transportation between the destinations.

To explore more than one coastal community, consider adding a stay in Montezuma, Santa Teresa, Manuel Antonio, or Costa Ballena. Travel between Tamarindo and the Caribbean coast and Bahía Drake is time-consuming and not recommended.

---

seed pod from a guanacaste tree (top); *guaro* (sugarcane liquor), common in Costa Rican cocktails (bottom)

HIGHLIGHTS

★ SURFING

Surfing is the heart of Tamarindo. Two of the country's top surf spots are found here, off the southwestern coast of **Santa Rosa National Park** (Parque Nacional Santa Rosa). Umpteen surf schools and camps are located in Tamarindo—not to mention instructors offering impromptu lessons.

Witch's Rock, known as Roca Bruja in Spanish, is impossible to miss: It's the giant rock (inhabited by a witch, legend suggests) just off the coast at **Playa Naranjo.** The surf is stellar, thanks to the area's sandbar, and it offers both left and right wave breaks. Advanced surfers from around the globe flock to this world-class spot in the North Pacific Ocean every day of the year. The surf is not safe for beginner surfers. **Ollie's Point** is located up the coast from Witch's Rock, in front of **Playa Potrero Grande.** Experienced surfers love this spot for its razor-cut walls and long rights, not to mention its appearance in the 1994 movie *The Endless Summer II.* Access to the sweet swell is permitted only by boat. Surf trips to Witch's Rock and Ollie's Point depart daily from Tamarindo. **Advance reservations** are required. Because both breaks are within Santa Rosa National Park, you must pay the park entrance fee, even if you never step foot on land. Confirm with your chosen operator whether the fee is included in the cost of their excursions. If not, be prepared to pay it in cash upon arrival.

South of Tamarindo, avid surfers ride the waves around **Playa Avellanas.** Several breaks are nearby, but **La Purruja, El Parqueo, Las Olas, El Palo** (or **Palo Seco**), and **El Estero** are where most beginner-to-intermediate surfers congregate. The pros walk to the north end of Playa Avellanas (across the river mouth), where beautiful barrels await at the **Little Hawaii** break. Additional waves roll further south, near **Playa Negra.** Centrally located in front of Hotel Playa Negra is the area's namesake and most notorious break, a consistent reef break. For less intimidating surf and fewer onlookers, check out **Callejones,** a beach break just down the coast from Playa Negra.

Witch's Rock Surf Camp

Playa Tamarindo, 350 m north of the Tamarindo Diria, tel. 506/2653-1262, www.witchsrocksurfcamp.com

Since 2001, **Witch's Rock Surf Camp** has been Tamarindo's premier full-service surf education provider. They have every aspect of the experience covered, from high-quality instruction to hotel accommodations and a restaurant on the beach where you can fuel up when you're not on the water. Their **weeklong surf programs** ($1,183-3,478 pp) accommodate beginner, intermediate, and advanced surfers. The program packages include accommodations, breakfast, lessons, seminars, board rentals, and more. They even design custom family surf vacations and host women-only surf retreats a few times each year.

Iguana Surf

Playa Tamarindo, 100 m north of the Tamarindo Diria, tel. 506/2653-0091, www.iguanasurf.net, 8am-6pm daily

If you're just interested in taking

Witch's Rock at Playa Naranjo, a top surfing site

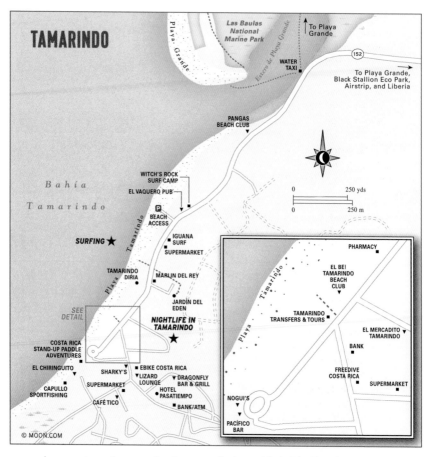

TAMARINDO

Las Baulas National Marine Park

To Playa Grande

WATER TAXI

To Playa Grande, Black Stallion Eco Park, Airstrip, and Liberia

152

PANGAS BEACH CLUB

Bahía Tamarindo

WITCH'S ROCK SURF CAMP

EL VAQUERO PUB

BEACH ACCESS

0   250 yds

0   250 m

SURFING ★

IGUANA SURF

SUPERMARKET

PHARMACY

EL BE! TAMARINDO BEACH CLUB

TAMARINDO DIRIA

MARLIN DEL REY

TAMARINDO TRANSFERS & TOURS

EL MERCADITO TAMARINDO

JARDÍN DEL EDEN

BANK

SEE DETAIL

NIGHTLIFE IN TAMARINDO ★

COSTA RICA STAND-UP PADDLE ADVENTURES

FREEDIVE COSTA RICA

SUPERMARKET

EL CHIRINGUITO

SHARKY'S

EBIKE COSTA RICA

LIZARD LOUNGE

DRAGONFLY BAR & GRILL

CAPULLO SPORTFISHING

SUPERMARKET

HOTEL PASATIEMPO

NOGUI'S

CAFÉ TICO

BANK/ATM

PACÍFICO BAR

© MOON.COM

a class or two, **Iguana Surf** runs three different types of **surf lessons** (9am, noon, and 3pm daily, 1.5 hours): group ($45 pp, 4 students per instructor), semiprivate ($65 pp, 2-3 students per instructor), and private ($80 pp, 1 student per instructor). Each lesson includes a board and rash guard rental for the duration of the class. If you wish to keep renting the board until the end of the day (or for additional days), as a lesson graduate you'll pay half the standard rental rate.

If you just need a board, Iguana Surf keeps a variety in stock, including shortboards, longboards, and funboard hybrids ($10 for 2 hours; $120 for 1 week). The optional board insurance is $5 per day. They also have stand-up paddleboards ($25 for 2 hours; $220 for 1 week) and boogie boards ($5 for 2 hours; $60 for 1 week).

Frijoles Locos
500 m north of the beach at Playa Grande, tel. 506/2652-9235, www. playagrandesurfshop.com, 9am-6pm daily

In the center of Playa Grande, **Frijoles Locos** is a reputable surf school, surf shop, tour concierge, and spa. They run three different types of **surf lessons** (on the hour 9am-4pm daily, 1.5 hours): group ($40 pp, 4 students per instructor, min. age 12), semiprivate ($55 pp, 2-3 students per instructor), and private ($120 pp, 1 student per instructor). The semiprivate and private lessons are ideal for couples, small families, and children under the age of 12. Operating since 2008, this outfitter knows not only how to maneuver the area's swells but also how to avoid its difficult current to keep surfers safe.

Playa Grande Surf Camp

3 km south of Playa Grande center, in Palm Beach Estates, tel. 506/2653-1074, www.playagrandesurfcamp.com

Playa Grande Surf Camp offers weeklong **surf packages** ($879 pp) that target beginner and intermediate surfers, as well as weeklong **surf tours** ($1,079 pp) for experienced wave riders in search of breaks up and down the coast. Both programs include accommodations, breakfast or lunch, and board rentals. Additionally, surf packages include surf lessons, and surf tours include travel to beaches. Perfectly suited for relaxed Playa Grande, the surf camp is a small but well-organized operation that prioritizes student experience through tailored instruction.

Avellanas Surf School

Lola's, at Playa Avellanas, tel. 506/7105-8809, www.avellanas-surf-school.com, 8am-6pm daily

A fantastic small-scale operation, the **Avellanas Surf School** is driven by passion for the sport and is particularly patient with young or novice surfers. They run four different types of **surf lessons** (times depend on the tide, 1.5 hours): group ($55 pp, 3 students per instructor), semiprivate ($65 pp, 2 students per

instructor), private ($75 pp, 1 student per instructor), and lessons specifically designed for children ($65 pp, 1-2 students per instructor, min. age 6). The school also has **water sport equipment rentals,** including surfboards ($10 for 1 hour) and boogie boards ($5 for 1 hour).

★ BEACH-HOPPING

Parallel to much of Calle Central, **Playa Tamarindo** is almost always speckled with sunbathers, pedestrians, and surfers, but this bustle is part of the beach's appeal. If you want space to yourself, you can find it along the kilometer of beach that extends southwest past the end of Calle Central, toward the small village of Playa Langosta.

For easy beach-hopping from Tamarindo, head about 20 kilometers north. There you'll find the beachside towns of **Playa Flamingo** and **Brasilito.** This is where to come to stretch out on soft, light-colored sand. Some of the country's most magnificent beaches sweep the coastline here, and the gentle waves and clear waters create ideal conditions for swimming. Brasilito's stunning Playa Conchal alone is worth the road trip.

Playa Flamingo

Stunning **Playa Flamingo,** located in the town of the same name, is the area's biggest draw. Filled with silky, postcard-worthy, nearly white sand, this deep beach has a wide-open view of Bahía Brasilito, which sparkles in emerald, teal, and steel-blue hues. Over one kilometer long, the beach provides more than enough room for stretching out away from others, and its proximity to a variety of restaurants means that food and drinks are never far away. This beach is a great day-trip destination that is worth the drive from Tamarindo. To access the beach, follow Road 180 west through the town of Playa Flamingo.

Playa Conchal

Without a doubt, Brasilito's primary draw is **Playa Conchal.** Comprising millions of tiny shell fragments and dusty white sand, this place is unique among Costa Rica's beaches. The stunning landscape sweeps the coastline just south of town, separated from **Playa Brasilito** by Punto Conchal, a red rock formation.

Shell fragments (and the occasional complete shell) fill the east end of the beach. Polished like sea glass, the shells are soft enough to walk on barefoot, and you'll love digging your feet into them for a natural foot massage. Long walks here can be a challenge, as you have to work harder than usual to pull your feet out of the sand each time you step. The view from this part of the beach

west end of Playa Conchal (top); Playa Puerto Viejo (bottom)

is particularly pretty, with craggy headlands framing the coast to the north and south. Swimming is decent here around the shore of **Bahía Brasilito,** but beware of a rocky seabed immediately south of Punto Conchal. Nearest to Brasilito and a few high-end resorts, this eastern section of Playa Conchal is the most frequented.

The west end of the beach, separated from Punto Conchal by one kilometer, is wildly different. It has fine sand (arguably the lightest in the country), hardly any shells, and fewer visitors than the opposite end of the beach. A swim here, among aquamarine waters that glide into Playa Conchal in rows, is paradisiacal. Choose this section of Playa Conchal if you want to isolate yourself from other beachgoers.

Vegetation backs the entirety of the beach, but it is sparse in areas and offers no opportunities for shade in others. Come prepared to stretch out on a largely exposed beach.

As striking as the beach's shells may be, removing them from the beach is strictly prohibited. Also forbidden is driving anywhere on the beach between Brasilito and Playa Conchal.

To reach the east end of Playa Conchal from town, you can walk along Playa Brasilito and make an easy 100-meter climb up and over Punto Conchal. To reach the west end of Playa Conchal, you can drive or take a taxi to Playa Conchal's alternate access point at Playa Puerto Viejo, then follow the one-kilometer forest trail that connects the two beaches.

Playa Puerto Viejo

Playa Puerto Viejo is essentially an extension of the west end of Playa Conchal, with a sandy, one-kilometer forest trail connecting the two beaches. It's perfect for swimming and sunbathing and has gentle waves that creep up the soft, sandy shore. Because the beach can only be accessed from the south via an unnamed, bumpy dirt road from Matapalo, Playa Puerto Viejo receives a fraction of the visitors that Playa Conchal does.

★ NIGHTLIFE

There's a lot to do in Tamarindo after dark. Most of the action takes place on the beach, where you can kick back with a cocktail and listen to the waves roll in or enjoy more lively entertainment. Stroll along the waterfront and you'll find happy hours and live music at **El Chiringuito** (Playa Tamarindo, near Calle Cruz, tel. 506/2438-9569, 7am-10pm daily), the **Pacífico Bar** (south end of Calle Central, tel. 506/2653-4406, 8pm-2:30am Mon.-Sat.), and **El Be! Tamarindo Beach Club** (Playa Tamarindo, near Calle del Parque, tel. 506/8804-0042, 10am-10pm Tues.-Fri. and Sun., 10am-2:30am Sat.). All three establishments are within walking distance of one another, making for easy barhopping along the shore.

Lizard Lounge
south end of Calle Central, tel. 506/8345-1604, 4pm-2:30am daily
At the upscale **Lizard Lounge,** DJs spin reggae, reggaeton, and hip-hop jams well into the morning.

Sharky's
Avenida Central, 150 m south of Calle Central, tel. 506/2653-4705, www.sharkysbars.com, 11:30am-12:30am daily
Tamarindo's best sports bar, **Sharky's** is also a favorite hangout joint. Theme nights like Margarita Monday

and Sangria Saturday feature discounted cocktails. The evening will fly by while you're watching televised games, singing karaoke, and playing beer pong.

El Vaquero Pub

Witch's Rock Surf Camp, Playa Tamarindo, tel. 506/2462-6432, 7am-midnight daily
Head to **El Vaquero Pub** for artisan beer brewed locally. The pale and dark ales are crafted by the town's own Volcano Brewing Company.

El Mercadito Tamarindo

Calle del Parque, tel. 506/8727-5227, 11am-11pm daily
El Mercadito Tamarindo resembles a food court more than a bar, but it's a neat place to be on nights with live music (see their Facebook page for specific events).

HORSEBACK RIDING

BLACK STALLION ECO PARK

7.5 km east of Tamarindo, off Road 152/155, tel. 506/8869-9765, www.blackstallionhills.com, 8:30am-10pm Mon.-Sat.

Visits to Tamarindo are all about having fun in the sun. But what I love most about this place is that it pays homage to the region's *sabanero* roots. Just up the hill from town is the fantastic **Black Stallion Eco Park,** a ranch where you can explore cowboy culture and take adventure tours all in one spot. Most authentic are the ranch's barbecue fiestas, hosted in a rustic, all-wood saloon.

The guided adventures offered here include **zip-lining, ATV tours,** and a **ropes course** called the Monkey Walk. The best option is the **Sunset Horseback Ride and Gourmet BBQ Combo** (3pm Mon.-Sat., ride 2-2.5 hours, $89 adults, $55 children 4-11, min. age 4), a horseback ride through the park's private 1,500-acre property. The ride ends with a panoramic view of the Tamarindo highlands as the sun goes down, followed by the park's legendary buffet dinner, a feast of ribs, sausages, chicken, rice, and potatoes hearty enough to feed a hundred cowboys. Drinks, both alcoholic and nonalcoholic, are included.

SAILING

MARLIN DEL REY

Plaza Esmeralda, across from Tamarindo Diria, tel. 506/2653-1212, www.marlindelrey.com, 8am-7pm daily
Sailing along the Pacific coast is one of my favorite activities. **Marlin del Rey** provides an unforgettable sailing experience. Choose between the Morning Sailing Tour (8am daily, 4 hours, $75 adults, $65 children 6-11) and **Afternoon Sailing Tour** (1:30pm daily, 4 hours, $95 adults, $65 children 6-11). Both are opportunities to relax on a catamaran, search for dolphins and other marine life, and snorkel near the Bahía de los Piratas.

A delicious homemade meal and drinks (both alcoholic and nonalcoholic) are included with either tour.

On the afternoon tour, you'll also be treated to a gorgeous sunset (weather permitting).

SNORKELING AND DIVING

FREEDIVE COSTA RICA

Plaza Conchal, Avenida Central, tel. 506/8353-1290, www.freedive costarica.com, 7:30am-6:30pm daily

Free diving (also known as apnea diving) is starting to catch on in Costa Rica. Essentially, you're diving without the "scuba," inviting you into the underwater world in the least restrictive way possible. If you have ever tried free diving, you know there is no other experience quite like it. With **Freedive Costa Rica,** you can join in by taking a free-diving discovery course ($150 pp, min. age 10) or a two-day, PADI-certified free-diving course ($350 pp, min. age 15). Avid anglers can combine the free-diving discovery course with one in spearfishing ($290 pp, min. age 18). A valid fishing license is required to spearfish; the license fee is not included in the cost of the discovery course. You can buy one online through the **Instituto Costarricense de Pesca y Acuicultura** (Costa Rican Institute of Fisheries and Aquaculture, www.incopesca. go.cr); licenses start at $17 per person.

STAND-UP PADDLING

COSTA RICA STAND-UP PADDLE ADVENTURES

50 m south of Nogui's, tel. 506/8780-1774, www.costaricasupadventures. com, 10am-6pm Mon.-Sat., 11am-4pm Sun.

Adding to the plethora of water sports in Tamarindo is **Costa Rica Stand-Up Paddle Adventures.** You'll often see their boards lined up along the sand or out on flat water as beginners participate in **stand-up paddleboarding lessons** (2 hours, $85 pp). The company's most interesting offering is lessons in **stand-up paddle surfing** (2-2.5 hours, $95 pp), the ingenious mashup of stand-up paddling and surfing; it's a lot harder than it looks. Lesson times depend on wind conditions, which can usually be predicted up to one week in advance. Advance reservations are required; the tour operator can confirm lesson start times a day or two before the lesson date.

stand-up paddling

TAMARINDO AND VICINITY FOOD

NAME	LOCATION
★ Nogui's	south end of Calle Central, Tamarindo
★ Pangas Beach Club	Calle Central, 750 m north of Tamarindo Diria, Tamarindo
★ Dragonfly Bar & Grill	Calle Corona behind Hotel Pasatiempo, Tamarindo
★ Café Tico	Calle Tigris, Tamarindo
★ El Huerto	Road 933, Playa Grande center
★ Lola's	Playa Avellanas
★ Coco Loco Bar & Restaurant	on the beach at Playa Flamingo
Angelina's Restaurant	Centro Comercial La Plaza, Playa Flamingo
Ander's Restaurant	Road 180, Brasilito
Fish & Cheeses	Calle Cardinal, Playa Langosta

FISHING

CAPULLO SPORTFISHING

tel. 506/8569-3516, www.capullo. com, 7am-5pm Sun.-Fri.

Capullo Sportfishing operates directly from Tamarindo. They'll save you from having to travel far, since their charter boats depart from Playa Tamarindo. Their operation is small, with just two boats to choose from, but they offer both inshore and offshore fishing trips. The smaller boat can take three people; excursions start at $475 for a half day. The larger boat can hold 6-7 people; excursions start at $900 for a half day.

PAPAGAYO SPORTFISHING

tel. 506/8991-7289, www.papagayo sportfishing.com

Papagayo Sportfishing is based out of Playas del Coco up the coast, but they can pick you up in Tamarindo at extra cost.

CONTACT INFO	FOOD	PRICE
tel. 506/2653-0029, www.noguistamarindo.com	Costa Rican	$8-25
tel. 506/2653-0024, www.pangasbeachclubcr.com	fine dining	$19-40
tel. 506/2653-1506, www.dragonflybarandgrill.com	fine dining	$14-21
tel. 506/8861-7732, www.cafeticotamarindocr.com	café	$4-8
tel. 506/2653-1259, www.elhuertodeplayagrande.com	international	$12-24
tel. 506/2652-9097, www.lolascostarica.info	international	$10-18
tel. 506/2654-6242, www.cocolococostarica.com	seafood	$7-21
tel. 506/2654-4839, www.angelinasplayaflamingo.com	upscale Italian	$15-48
tel. 506/2654-6034	upscale seafood	$11-21
tel. 506/4700-6947, www.fishandcheeses.com	Italian	$10-28

FOOD

STANDOUTS
Nogui's
south end of Calle Central, Tamarindo, tel. 506/2653-0029, www.noguistamarindo.com, 6am-10pm Thurs.-Tues., $8-25

Your stay isn't complete without a meal, dessert, or drink at **Nogui's,** a Tamarindo institution. The restaurant is, as locals say, *"más Tico que el gallo pinto"* ("more Costa Rican than a spotted rooster"). It's most sought after for its seafood selections, especially the locally caught mahimahi and tuna. Locals also flock to this spot for less-traditional treats like milkshakes and cream pies. The bright yellow, two-story, open-air establishment is hard to miss. Inside, it has café-style tables on the 1st floor and casual seating that creates a lounge setting on the 2nd floor.

Pangas Beach Club
Calle Central, 750 m north of Tamarindo Diria, Tamarindo, tel. 506/2653-0024, www.pangasbeach clubcr.com, noon-9pm Mon.-Fri., noon-7pm Sat.-Sun., $19-40

At **Pangas Beach Club,** you can dine on prime beef cooked tableside, all while enjoying a great seaside view. Their smoked salmon lasagna is another favorite.

Nogui's (top); Lola's (middle); Villas La Paz (bottom)

Dragonfly Bar & Grill

Calle Corona behind Hotel Pasatiempo, Tamarindo, tel. 506/2653-1506, www.dragonflybar andgrill.com, 5:30pm-10pm daily, $14-21

Dragonfly Bar & Grill serves elegant entrées like filet mignon and sesame-seared yellowfin tuna. Its intimate setting is ideal for a romantic dinner.

Café Tico

Calle Tigris, Tamarindo, tel. 506/8861-7732, www. cafeticotamarindocr.com, 7am-1pm Mon.-Sat., $4-8

Finding Costa Rican coffee in Tamarindo is never a problem; cafés are all around. **Café Tico,** my favorite, has lattes, espresso, cappuccinos, iced coffee, and decaffeinated brews, as well as yummy baked goods and full breakfast and lunch menus.

El Huerto

Road 933, Playa Grande center, tel. 506/2653-1259, www.elhuertode playagrande.com, 2pm-9:30pm Tues.-Sun., $12-24

When you're hungry, head to **El Huerto.** Mixing casual dining with a sophisticated ambience, this restaurant features hanging lanterns, tropical plants, and beautifully crafted tables made from giant tree trunks. Its menu covers all the bases—salads, seafood, meat, pizza, and decadent desserts—but locals swear the linguine is the best around.

Lola's

Playa Avellenas, tel. 506/2652-9097, www.lolascostarica.info, 9am-5pm daily, $10-18

Established in 1998, the laid-back **Lola's** has long served cold drinks and good eats to anyone who stumbled upon Playa Avellanas. It's now a modern, open-air structure that reminds me of a giant pergola. Lola's supplies beachgoers with shaded seating under umbrellas, hammocks for lounging, and bathrooms. Food options include burgers, salads, pizza, and tacos. Be sure to get a snap with the resident pig, Lolita, who saunters freely about the beach.

Coco Loco Bar & Restaurant
on the beach at Playa Flamingo, tel. 506/2654-6242, www.cocoloco costarica.com, 11am-9pm daily, $7-21
On scorching-hot days, the beachfront **Coco Loco Bar & Restaurant** is a lifesaver. Cool down with a Coco Loco cocktail—a *guaro*, rum, and tequila blend added to coconut water and cream—or fill up on the Loco Coco entrée, a mix of rice, fish, shrimp, octopus, and mussels; both are served in an actual coconut. This relaxed spot has wooden tables on Playa Flamingo's silky sand, each one equipped with a large umbrella so you can enjoy your meal under cooling shade.

LODGING

STANDOUTS
Hotel Pasatiempo
Avenida Central, 400 m south of the beach at Playa Tamarindo, tel. 506/2653-0096, www.hotelpasa tiempo.com, $114 s/d
Tamarindo's best-value standard accommodation, **Hotel Pasatiempo** is tucked away enough from the main drag to feel private, yet it's within walking distance of nearly everything, including the beach. The 22 rooms are clean, and the beds are comfy, but the property's secluded location among the trees is the reason to visit. Don't be surprised if you see howler monkeys snooping around while you relax by the pool or in the on-site restaurant **Monkey La-La** (7am-10am and 11:30am-9:30pm daily).

Tamarindo Diria
Playa Tamarindo, tel. 506/2653-0032, www.tamarindodiria.com, Family Poolview and Tropicana Village $255 s/d, Sunset Oceanview $333 s/d
Taking up much of Playa Flamingo's town center, the sprawling **Tamarindo Diria** is a 242-room resort complex providing everything you might want: 10 restaurants and bars, five pools, attentive and warm customer service, a central location in the heart of Tamarindo, and a big breakfast buffet that won't leave you hungry. Essentially three hotels in one, Tamarindo Diria consists of the Sunset Oceanview building (on the west side of Calle Central) with beachfront rooms and the Family Poolview and Tropicana Village buildings with additional rooms tucked back from Playa Tamarindo (on the east side of Calle Central). All rooms impress guests with beds as soft as clouds, flat-screen televisions, air-conditioning, and spotless bathrooms. Tropicana Village is an adults-only section that provides a more intimate stay; the remainder of the complex is family friendly.

Jardín del Eden
100 m east of Playa Tamarindo, tel. 506/4070-0303, www.jardindeleden. com, $306 s/d
Sister to Tamarindo Diria, **Jardín del Eden** is a lovely adults-only paradise

TAMARINDO AND VICINITY LODGING

NAME	LOCATION
★ Hotel Pasatiempo	Avenida Central, 400 m south of the beach at Playa Tamarindo
★ Tamarindo Diria	Playa Tamarindo
★ Jardín del Eden	100 m east of Playa Tamarindo
★ RipJack Inn	100 m south of MINAE office, Playa Grande
★ Villa Deevena	300 m east of Café Playa Negra, Pargos
★ Conchal Hotel	Road 180, 400 m south of Playa Brasilito
★ Villas La Paz	750 m south of Playa Puerto Viejo, west of Playa Conchal

with pretty gardens, a tranquil pool, and plenty of thatched-roof cabanas equipped with queen-size daybeds perfect for lounging. Each of the hotel's 46 rooms has a king-size bed, soft lighting, tropical decor, and a romantic feel. Although the property isn't on the beach, a direct path from the hotel leads to Playa Tamarindo via a private waterfront garden shared with Tamarindo Diria.

RipJack Inn
100 m south of the MINAE office, Playa Grande, tel. 506/2653-1636, www.ripjackinn.com, $115 s/d
The **RipJack Inn** boasts the funkiest vibe in town. This boutique hotel's 21 eclectic rooms have touches like vintage-style wardrobes, colorful artwork, and crisp white bed linens. Some rooms are grouped together in standalone buildings, perfect for families or groups desiring their own space. A teakwood yoga shala, where the hotel runs yoga classes and retreats, adds to this place's uniqueness. The RipJack is named after the kind owners' beloved past

dogs—Ripley and Jack—so it comes as no surprise that pets are welcome at the hotel (with prior approval).

Villa Deevena
300 m east of Café Playa Negra, Pargos, tel. 506/2653-2328, www. villadeevena.com, $135 s/d
The small, six-room **Villa Deevena** is a great choice close to Playa Negra. The property's rooms frame the property's saltwater lap pool, creating an enclosed, intimate space where you can swim or lie on a lounge chair while enjoying a drink. Extras like rainforest showerheads, fragrant gardens, and patios with Adirondack chairs add comfort and a touch of elegance to the place. The on-site restaurant offers fine dining in a casual setting.

Conchal Hotel
Road 180, 400 m south of Playa Brasilito, tel. 506/2654-9125, www. conchalcr.com, $115 s/d
The bright, colorful **Conchal Hotel** is the best in Brasilito, with 16 clean and cozy guest rooms centered on

CONTACT INFO	OPTIONS	PRICE
tel. 506/2653-0096, www.hotelpasatiempo.com	hotel rooms	$114 s/d
tel. 506/2653-0032, www.tamarindodiria.com	hotel rooms in three buildings	$255-333 s/d
tel. 506/4070-0303, www.jardindeleden.com	hotel rooms	$306 s/d
tel. 506/2653-1636, www.ripjackinn.com	boutique hotel rooms	$115 s/d
tel. 506/2653-2328, www.villadeevena.com	hotel rooms	$135 s/d
tel. 506/2654-9125, www.conchalcr.com	hotel rooms	$115 s/d
tel. 506/8307-9423, www.conchalcostarica.com	small and large villas	$80-240

the small property's flora-framed pool. A tropical buffet breakfast (included in the rate) is served on the 2nd floor at the hotel's open-air Papaya Restaurant. The restaurant has the healthiest food in the area and offers ample vegetarian and vegan options. Service at the hotel and the restaurant is above average.

Villas La Paz

750 m south of Playa Puerto Viejo, just west of Playa Conchal, tel. 506/8307-9423, www.conchal costarica.com, $80-240
Southwest of Brasilito, on the west side of Playa Conchal, each of the lodgings at tropical **Villas La Paz** is unique in design, decor, and size (they can sleep 2-12 people). The villas mimic mini houses; large villas resemble full-size homes and small villas feel like apartments. The complex is a short walk south of Playa Puerto Viejo and the west end of Playa Conchal, and 4.5 kilometers north of the hamlet of Matapalo, the closest place to grab the groceries you need to prepare your own meals in your villa's fully equipped kitchen. I often spot monkeys, iguanas, and a variety of birds around the peaceful grounds, which have plenty of open-air gathering spaces and a communal pool. The Costa Rican family that owns the place goes above and beyond to make your stay memorable.

INFORMATION AND SERVICES

The hospital that serves most of the region's communities is **Hospital Enrique Baltodano Briceño** (Calle 3 between Avenida Central and Avenida 2, Liberia, tel. 506/2690-2300, 24 hours daily) in Liberia, a 75-kilometer, 75-minute drive northeast of Tamarindo. **Ebais Villareal** (4 km east of Tamarindo center, tel. 506/2653-0736, 7am-4pm Mon.-Fri.), the closest **clinic** to Tamarindo, is 15 minutes east of Tamarindo in the small village of Villareal.

Villareal also has a **post office** (3 km east of Tamarindo center, tel. 506/2653-0676, 8:30am-5pm Mon.-Fri.) and a **police station** (3 km east of Tamarindo center, tel. 506/2244-6173, 24 hours daily).

Downtown Tamarindo has a handful of **pharmacies,** including **Farmacia Pacífico** (Calle Central across from the Diria Grand Boulevard, tel. 506/2653-0711, 9am-8pm daily), as well as **supermarkets, banks,** and **ATMs,** along Calle Central and Avenida Central. The biggest bank in town, which has an ATM, is **Banco Nacional** (Avenida Central, 350 m south of Calle Central, tel. 506/2653-1724, 8:30am-3:45pm Mon.-Fri.).

The closest **gas station** is seven kilometers northeast of Tamarindo, on Road 155, and two kilometers north of the village of Villareal.

TRANSPORTATION AND TOURS

Getting There

Air

The fastest way to get to Tamarindo is by catching a domestic flight to **Aeropuerto Tamarindo** (TNO). **SANSA Airlines** (tel. 506/2290-4100, www.flysansa.com) flies to Tamarindo daily from San José (45 minutes).

Car

The drive to Tamarindo from other parts of Guanacaste is easy, thanks to favorable road conditions and significant signage. To get to Tamarindo from **Liberia,** it's a 75-kilometer, 75-minute drive southwest on Highway 21, Road 155, and Avenida de las Palmas, a side road that leads into town from the village of Villareal.

From **San José,** it's a 290-kilometer, 4.5-hour drive to Tamarindo, heading west on Highways 1, 18, and 21, Roads 160, 152, and Avenida de las Palmas.

From Tamarindo, the 20-kilometer, half-hour drive to **Playa Grande** loops around national park land on Avenida de las Palmas and Roads 155, 180, and 933. **Playa Flamingo** is a 25-kilometer, 30-minute drive from Tamarindo. To get there, head north on Roads 155 and 180.

It can be tricky to reach **Playa Avellanas** from Tamarindo, so it's best to have a GPS. Take Avenida de las Palmas east to Villareal. Follow Road 152 south for three kilometers, then take the unnamed road west off Road 152 and follow the signs to Hacienda Pinilla. After two kilometers, the road forks at a bridge; stay left and follow the signs to Playa Avellanas. The route passes through the small community of Pinilla along the way. A 4x4 vehicle is recommended since many roads in the area are dirt.

Boat

Small boats commute between Tamarindo and **Playa Grande** multiple times daily. They do not operate according to set schedules or accept advance reservations. You can hire one of these boats at either of two docks in Playa Grande (The Grateful Hotel or the southernmost end of Playa Grande). The boat will take you to the dock in Tamarindo (northern end of town, near the Pangas Beach Club). Expect to pay $2-6 per person for a brief ride that lasts 5-15 minutes, depending on where you depart from. Some boat captains speak English and others do not. To hire a captain, ask: *"¿Por favor, me puede llevar a Tamarindo?"* ("Please, can you take me to Tamarindo?") To confirm the cost of the service, also ask: *"¿Cuánto cobra por el viaje?"* ("How much do you charge for the trip?")

Bus

You can reach Tamarindo by **bus** from **Liberia** (multiple times 3:15am-6:10pm daily, 2.5 hours, $2.50) or **San José** (7am, 11:30am, and 4pm daily, 5.5 hours, $9). The bus can drop you off at the bus stop in Tamarindo (Calle Central, 150 m north of Tamarindo Diria).

Private and Shared Transfer Services

Many **private transfer services** travel to and from Tamarindo daily. My top two recommendations are **Ecotrans Costa Rica** (tel. 506/2654-5151, www.ecotranscostarica.com) and **Tamarindo Transfers & Tours** (Centro Comercial Galerías del Mar, Tamarindo, tel. 506/2653-4444, www.tamarindoshuttle.com, 8am-8pm daily). With Ecotrans Costa Rica, prices range $80-140 for pickups in Guanacaste and $190-320 for pickups elsewhere in the country. With Tamarindo Transfers & Tours, prices range $75-120 for pickups in Guanacaste and $220-380 for pickups elsewhere in the country.

Both Ecotrans Costa Rica and Tamarindo Transfers & Tours also provide **shared shuttle services** to Tamarindo, as do **Interbus** (tel. 506/4100-0888, www.interbusonline.com) and **Grayline Costa Rica** (tel. 506/2220-2126, www.graylinecostarica.com). Together, the four companies cover routes to Tamarindo from Liberia, San José, La Fortuna, Monteverde, Montezuma, Santa Teresa, and Manuel Antonio, among other locales. One-way services cost $20-96 per person.

Most shuttles offer drop-offs at Tamarindo hotels.

Organized Tour

A few adventure and nature tours by **Tenorio Adventure Company** (Hwy. 1 at Río Corobicí, 5 km northwest of Cañas, tel. 506/2668-8203, www.tenorioadventurecompany.com, 8am-10pm daily) include **post-tour onward transportation** to Tamarindo. White-water rafting tours, safari float tours, and hiking tours to **Río Celeste** at Tenorio Volcano National Park ($149-154 pp) can be arranged to include a pickup from your hotel in La Fortuna, Monteverde, or a variety of Guanacaste beach towns, then a drop-off at your hotel in Tamarindo.

Getting Around

Tamarindo's roads are flat, paved, and lined with **parking** spaces. Although Tamarindo has a few **taxis**, the most common way to explore town is on foot. If the heat has you beat, seek out **eBike Costa Rica** (Centro Comercial Plaza Tamarindo, tel. 506/8458-7963, www.ebikecostarica.com, 10am-6pm daily, rentals $15 for 2 hours; $200 for 1 week). Rent one of their funky electric bikes, easy riders, or street surfers to help you get around.

The outfitter and gear shop **Frijoles Locos** (500 m north of the beach at Playa Grande, tel. 506/2652-9235, www.playagrandesurfshop.com, 9am-6pm daily) can help you get around Playa Grande. Their **Fetch Me, Frijoles service** (9am-5:30pm daily with advance reservation) covers transportation between Playa Grande, the area's southern end (known as the Palm Beach Estates), and the estuary dock at The Grateful Hotel. The service costs $5 per person, but the fee is returned to you as a credit that you can use in their shop. Frijoles Locos also has beach cruiser **bike rentals** (from $5 for 4 hours) for local use.

view of the Nicoya Peninsula

SANTA TERESA AND MONTEZUMA

The sun is setting over western Costa Rica. Surfers line up in the Pacific Ocean, eager to ride the day's last waves. Sunbathers relax on sand that glows in colorful hues under an iridescent sky. Yogis stretch out in peaceful shalas and welcome nightfall with a gentle namaste. This is the Nicoya Peninsula, a corner of the country where water, land, and spirit come together.

An assortment of travelers gathers in the beach towns of Santa Teresa and Montezuma. First-time and lifelong surfers, soul searchers, health nuts, socialites, artists, and bohemians are drawn to the region for different reasons, but they share a common interest in its tranquil, slow-paced way of life. Regardless of which coastal destination you choose, it will rid you of stress the moment you roll into town.

The region's calm and positive vibe materializes in many forms. Resorts here are typically small-scale boutique hotels. Health food restaurants and shops are the norm, not anomalies. Organized tours are less popular than surf lessons, yoga classes, retreats, and other opportunities to better yourself or your skills. If you don't have a checklist of things to do or see while in Costa Rica, the Nicoya Peninsula is the place for you.

bridge from the mainland to the Nicoya Peninsula

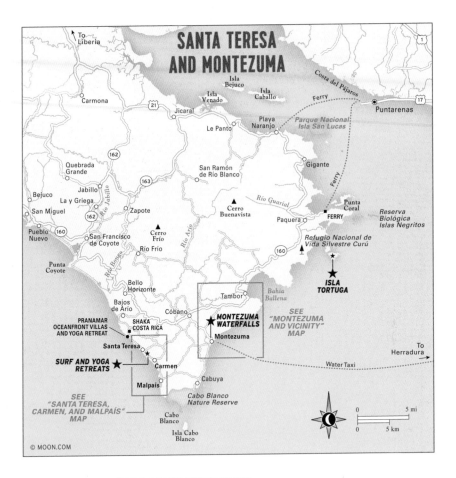

SANTA TERESA AND MONTEZUMA

To Liberia

Carmona

Costa del Pájaros

Puntarenas

Isla Bejuco

Isla Venado

Isla Caballo

Jicaral

Le Panto

Playa Naranjo

Ferry

Parque Nacional Isla San Lucas

Ferry

Quebrada Grande

San Ramón de Río Blanco

Gigante

Bejuco

Jabillo

La y Griega

San Miguel

Zapote

Cerro Buenavista

Río Guarial

Punta Coral

Paquera

FERRY

Reserva Biológica Islas Negritos

Pueblo Nuevo

San Francisco de Coyote

Cerro Frío

Río Frío

Refugio Nacional de Vida Silvestre Curú

Punta Coyote

Bello Horizonte

Bajos de Ario

Cóbano

Tambor

Bahía Ballena

ISLA TORTUGA

SEE "MONTEZUMA AND VICINITY" MAP

PRANAMAR OCEANFRONT VILLAS AND YOGA RETREAT

SHAKA COSTA RICA

MONTEZUMA WATERFALLS

Santa Teresa

Montezuma

SURF AND YOGA RETREATS

Carmen

To Herradura

Water Taxi

Malpaís

Cabuya

Cabo Blanco Nature Reserve

SEE "SANTA TERESA, CARMEN, AND MALPAÍS" MAP

Cabo Blanco

0   5 mi

0   5 km

Isla Cabo Blanco

© MOON.COM

Bali Beach Deli, on the main drag in Santa Teresa

TOP 3

⭐ **1. SURF AND YOGA RETREATS:** Get your zen on in Santa Teresa (page 155).

⭐ **2. MONTEZUMA WATERFALLS:** There's nowhere else you would rather be than soaking in these beloved swimming holes (page 166).

⭐ **3. DAY TRIP TO ISLA TORTUGA:** It's the deserted island paradise of your dreams (page 169).

BEST 5 DAYS IN SANTA TERESA AND MONTEZUMA

DAY 1

Ease into your visit to peaceful Santa Teresa by practicing **yoga,** either on your own or during a morning yoga class at **Casa Zen.** Fuel up on superfoods for lunch at the **Bali Beach Deli** before spending the afternoon **surfing.** After dark, head to the **Drift Bar** for dinner and cocktails.

DAY 2

Rise with the sun to enjoy the morning **surf.** Take the afternoon off to explore Santa Teresa's main drag on foot or with the help of a rented ATV, starting with lunch at the popular **Banana Beach Restaurant.** Catch a sunset yoga class at the **Horizon Hotel and Yoga Center,** then enjoy an intimate dinner at **Koji's.**

DAY 3

Pack a lunch for a day of beach-hopping. Start the day with a jaunt along the tranquil **Playa Los Suecos** to soak in its lovely tide pools and hear the bats at **Punta Murciélago.** In the afternoon, lounge at the beach of your choice: **Playa Santa Teresa** or **Playa Carmen.**

DAY 4

Escape to the remote, uninhabited **Isla Tortuga** and pretend to be a castaway for a day. Take a **snorkeling** or **diving** tour, swim in crystalline waters, or simply laze on silky beaches. (Many tours include lunch.)

DAY 5

Pack a lunch and set out on a morning hike to the **Montezuma Waterfalls.** Give yourself a few hours to swim at both the upper and lower falls. In the afternoon, trade the falls for the pale sands at the nearby **Playa Las Manchas.** Eat dinner at the oceanfront **Playa de los Artistas** in Montezuma.

snorkeling off Isla Tortuga

PLANNING YOUR TIME

Independent surfing and yoga practice are possible from sunup to sundown. If you need more structure, though, you'll need to plan ahead and be patient: Surf lessons can depend on the tide, and yoga classes run according to set schedules. Closures of restaurants, bars, and shops in Santa Teresa and Montezuma are common late in the low season, especially between September and November. Most accommodations and tour operators remain open throughout the year.

Best Bases

An approximate 30-minute drive separates Santa Teresa and Montezuma, so choose one beach town as your home base knowing you can make day trips to the other as you like. Choose Santa Teresa if you prefer health-conscious restaurants and high-end accommodations, or want to practice surf or yoga in a peaceful community that some call Costa Rica's surf and yogic soul. Smaller, less-polished Montezuma has food, lodging, and services that slant toward the economical.

Weather

Between December and July, the region is hot—temperatures average over 80°F—famously sunny, and dry. Rainfall is most significant between September and October, which is also when road conditions in the region are at their worst.

Connect with...

Slow days spent taking it easy in the dreamy Santa Teresa and Montezuma region complement jam-packed days that seem to fly by in La Fortuna and Monteverde. They also provide a slower pace than busier beach destinations like Tamarindo and Manuel Antonio. Travel from either Santa Teresa or Montezuma to Manuel Antonio or the Costa Ballena is unique in that the journey includes a ferry crossing. It's not easy to reach Santa Teresa and Montezuma from the Caribbean or Bahía Drake.

---

view of the Nicoya Peninsula (left); an ATV, a common way to explore the Nicoya Peninsula (right)

SANTA TERESA

This long, flat stretch of coastline comprises several beaches separated by rocky outcroppings, coves, and headlands. Spread out along the coast are three laid-back beachfront communities: Santa Teresa, Carmen, and Malpaís (sometimes styled as Mal País). Thanks to the monster waves that develop offshore here, surfing is one of the area's main attractions. Yoga is another principal draw. Travelers from around the world come to this remote part of the country for surf and yoga retreats. This is a place where it's easy to feel calm and relaxed.

Santa Teresa adjoins Carmen to the north, but there is little distinction between them. Together, they serve as the area's commercial hub, with the majority of the area's hotels, restaurants, offices, services, and shops. The two communities also front the area's best surf breaks, so either makes a good home base if you wish to catch some waves. Most places where you can practice yoga are centered on Santa Teresa.

Smaller and less-visited Malpaís, a dispersed settlement dotted with development, is five kilometers south of Carmen. Stay in Malpaís only if you wish to isolate yourself from the area's low-key action.

HIGHLIGHTS

★ SURF AND YOGA RETREATS

The calmness that wafts throughout Santa Teresa makes it an ideal and peaceful place to surf and practice yoga. It isn't too developed, and so lacks distracting sights and sounds, and it's remote enough to avoid big crowds. Both residents and visitors share an interest in the same recreational activities, lending an inclusive vibe. Retreats here don't just teach surf skills and provide yoga classes; they also welcome you into a community that some call Costa Rica's surf and yogic soul.

Lucero Surf Retreats
east of the main road parallel to Playa Santa Teresa, 2 km northwest of the intersection at Carmen, tel. 506/8427-6587, www.

costarica-surfvacations.com, $1,575 pp

Come ready to learn how to surf, have fun, and meet new friends with **Lucero Surf Retreats.** Conducted in the heart of Santa Teresa, these social retreats consist of five lessons, complete with in-depth surf theory and photo souvenirs, and unlimited surfboard rentals throughout the week. The retreat also includes accommodations, a healthy breakfast and lunch each day, and a farewell dinner at the end of the retreat. A team of friendly, detail-oriented, and encouraging instructors works hard to make sure you enjoy the entire experience.

Shaka Costa Rica
main road parallel to Playa Santa Teresa, 6.5 km northwest of the intersection at Carmen, tel.

506/2640-1118, www.shakacostarica. com, $1,625-1,925 pp, min. age 15

For a remote retreat, head 20 minutes northwest of Santa Teresa to **Shaka Costa Rica.** The six- or eight-day retreats take place in a tranquil setting and include daily surf lessons, surfboard use, accommodations, a snack, brunch, and dinner each day, plus complimentary yoga classes and snorkeling gear. In collaboration with the **Ocean Healing Group** (www.oceanhealinggroup.org), a handful of Shaka's surf camps are designed for youths who use wheelchairs.

Pranamar Oceanfront Villas and Yoga Retreat

main road parallel to Playa Santa Teresa, 6 km northwest of the intersection at Carmen, tel. 506/2640-0852, www.pranamar villas.com, prices vary

Choose **Pranamar** for a yoga getaway with high-quality accommodations set amid a beautiful tropical setting just steps from the beach. Diverse options are led by a revolving list of guest instructors and vary in duration and inclusions, but typically last 1-2 weeks. In addition to yoga classes, retreats can include room and board, meditation, dharma talks, and beach walks.

Funky Monkey Lodge

east of the main road parallel to Playa Santa Teresa, 2 km northwest of the intersection at Carmen, tel. 506/2640-0272, www.funkymonkey lodge.com, $450-1,300 pp

Love both yoga and surfing? The **Funky Monkey Lodge** combines the two pleasures during its five-, six-, and eight-day surf and yoga camps. Along with accommodations, you'll get surf lessons, yoga classes, and breakfast and dinner daily. You can swap some of the camp's complimentary yoga classes for aerial silk classes or sign up for a combined yoga and aerial silk package if you'd rather not surf. These are some of the most affordable surf and yoga retreats in Santa Teresa. The base package price includes shared accommodations; pricing increases with room upgrades.

Pura Vida Adventures

at Trópico Latino, tel. 506/2640-0062, www.puravidaadventures. com, $3,195-3,895 pp

Pura Vida Adventures hosts empowering women-only surf and yoga retreats. The best thing about these retreats is the feeling of community that comes from joining your own band of "surf sisters." Beyond common inclusions, like accommodations, daily surf lessons and yoga classes, and complimentary surfboard use, these retreats also provide video analysis of your surf progress, a rash guard you can keep, and a therapeutic massage. Three healthy, gourmet meals are offered daily and can be cooked to accommodate vegetarian, vegan, lactose intolerant, and gluten-free dietary preferences.

Yoga Classes

Casa Zen (south of the main road parallel to Playa Santa Teresa, 1.5 km northwest of the intersection at Carmen, tel. 506/2640-0523, www. zencostarica.com) and the **Horizon Hotel and Yoga Center** (east of the main road parallel to Playa Santa Teresa, 500 m northwest of the intersection at Carmen, tel. 506/2640-0524, www.horizon-yogahotel.com) have drop-in **yoga classes** (Casa Zen: 9:30am daily, 90 minutes, $10 pp; Horizon Hotel: schedule and class duration vary, $15 pp).

BEACHES

PLAYA LOS SUECOS

The primary reason to venture south from Carmen and Santa Teresa toward Malpaís is to experience the cove at **Playa Los Suecos.** Bounded on three sides by lush vegetation and tall rock formations, the place is private, quiet, and the epitome of paradise. The beach has nearly white sand with finely crushed shells; the water is aquamarine, almost teal in places; and the shore deepens gradually. At high tide, the spot is great for **snorkeling;** marine life from the nearby Reserva Natural Absoluta Cabo Blanco comes to visit. Low tide exposes rocky areas and creates lovely little pools perfect for soaking in as if they were your own personal bath.

Low tide is also when **Punta Murciélago** (Bat Point) becomes the main attraction. You can't miss the charcoal-colored escarpment at the north end of the beach. Less obvious are the hundreds of **bats** that occupy the giant rock's crevice. To see the creatures, or at least to hear their communal squeaks, you'll need to wade through water and climb over large rocks. These rocks are uneven and slippery, and they also hide mollusks and tiny crabs. Watch out for waves that crash into the spot and can throw you off-balance. Strap-on shoes are a must. Only attempt the walk at low tide: If you get caught on the point as the tide rises and swallows your path, it's a rough, dangerous swim back to the shore. As you approach the bats, be sure to remain quiet. Don't disturb the colony by going too far into the rock's opening.

To find Playa Los Suecos, take the road to Malpaís as far south as it leads—roughly four kilometers from the intersection at Carmen, an approximate 15-minute drive. Just after the gate that leads to the Reserva Natural Absoluta Cabo Blanco (a staff-only entrance), a clearing in the forest has room for a handful of

Punta Murciélago at Playa Los Suecos (top); Playa Santa Teresa (bottom)

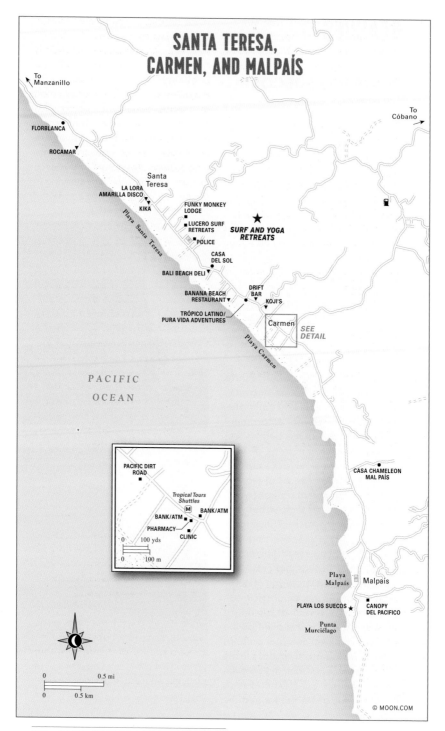

SANTA TERESA, CARMEN, AND MALPAÍS

To Manzanillo

To Cóbano

FLORBLANCA

ROCAMAR

Santa Teresa

LA LORA
AMARILLA DISCO

KIKA

FUNKY MONKEY
LODGE

LUCERO SURF
RETREATS

★ SURF AND YOGA
RETREATS

POLICE

CASA
DEL SOL

BALI BEACH DELI

BANANA BEACH
RESTAURANT

DRIFT
BAR

KOJI'S

TRÓPICO LATINO/
PURA VIDA ADVENTURES

Playa Santa Teresa

Carmen

SEE
DETAIL

Playa Carmen

PACIFIC
OCEAN

CASA CHAMELEON
MAL PAÍS

Detail inset:

PACIFIC DIRT
ROAD

Tropical Tours
Shuttles

Ⓜ

BANK/ATM

BANK/ATM

PHARMACY

CLINIC

0   100 yds
0   100 m

Playa
Malpaís   Malpaís

PLAYA LOS SUECOS ★   CANOPY
DEL PACIFICO

Punta
Murciélago

0   0.5 mi
0   0.5 km

© MOON.COM

vehicles to park. A short trail, sometimes with a small stream running through it, leads from the lot to the beach. As with any secluded beach, don't go alone.

PLAYA CARMEN

At the end of the main road that leads into town, **Playa Carmen** is close to several restaurants, shops, and services. It's the central beach in the area and a popular choice with visitors, but it's large enough that there's always enough space to stretch out. The striking, light-colored sand pleases sunbathers, and the consistent beach break (with a long right and short left) speaks to surfers. Lifeguards are stationed at this beach.

PLAYA SANTA TERESA

The area's best-known beach, **Playa Santa Teresa** is beautiful: It has 2.5 kilometers of shimmery, cream-colored sand with hardly any debris and a verdant green backdrop. It's also an advanced surf site. There's plenty to impress the pros, from predictable beach breaks to first-rate point breaks. If you're a nonsurfer, you can watch the action from anywhere along the beach, especially at the waterfront restaurant and bar **Rocamar** (main road parallel to Playa Santa Teresa, 4 km northwest of the intersection at Carmen, tel. 506/2640-0250, noon-10pm Mon.-Sat., noon-7pm Sun. Nov.-July), which has a direct view of the area's best surf spot: **Suck Rock.** Lifeguards are stationed at this beach.

PLAYA MALPAÍS

The jagged coastline at Malpaís has rocky outcroppings and sandy stretches. Near the beached fishing boats at the *pescadería* (fish market) is **Playa Malpaís.** Locals hang out at this beach, which has beautiful turquoise water you can swim in. It also has sand strewn with stones and a shore roughened by several rock formations. While a much more pristine and secluded swimming spot awaits 400 meters down the coast at Playa Los Suecos, this beach is a decent option if you're based in Malpaís and would prefer not to isolate yourself from most other beachgoers.

ZIP-LINING

CANOPY DEL PACÍFICO

700 m east of the fish market at Playa Malpaís, tel. 506/2640-0360, www.canopymalpais.com, office 8am-5pm daily, tours 9am, 11am, and 3pm daily, 1.5-2 hours, $55 pp, min. age 3

The panoramic views of the ocean and the Reserva Natural Absoluta Cabo Blanco are the best reason to take the eight-cable tour with Canopy del Pacífico. If you're the gutsy type, you'll also love the forward-facing superman cable and the option to give zip-lining upside down a go. The tour's surf line lets you try out the newest zip-lining trend: riding a zip-line cable while standing on a dual-cable-controlled surfboard. Fun and attentive tour guides make this zip-line tour full of zany adventures a blast to complete.

SANTA TERESA FOOD

NAME	LOCATION
★ Bali Beach Deli	main road parallel to Playa Santa Teresa, 1.5 km northwest of the intersection at Carmen
★ Banana Beach Restaurant	south of the main road parallel to Playa Santa Teresa, 1 km northwest of the intersection at Carmen
★ Koji's	50 m east of the main road parallel to Playa Santa Teresa, 550 m northwest of the intersection at Carmen
★ Drift Bar	main road parallel to Playa Santa Teresa, 650 m northwest of the intersection at Carmen

NIGHTLIFE

Rocamar
main road parallel to Playa Santa Teresa, 4 km northwest of the intersection at Carmen, tel. 506/2640-0250

Santa Teresa's old-school beach bar **Rocamar** hosts events that bring together locals, expats, and travelers to catch an epic sunset, listen to live music, and enjoy a bonfire on the sand. Variety acts demonstrate hula hooping, aerobatics, and poi (fire dancing). Don't expect a booze fest, although drinks are poured. On a Sunday, there's nowhere else you should be other than soaking up the last of the day's rays at family-friendly **Sunday Funday beach parties** (3pm-7pm Sun. Nov.-July, weather permitting).

Kika
main road parallel to Playa Santa Teresa, 2.5 km northwest of the intersection at Carmen, tel. 506/2640-0408, 6pm-10pm daily

Thursdays are thumping at the chill bar **Kika,** when the house band puts on a live music show (10pm-midnight).

La Lora Amarilla Disco
main road parallel to Playa Santa Teresa, 2.5 km northwest of the intersection at Carmen, tel. 506/2640-0132, 6pm-2am Wed.-Mon.

La Lora Amarilla Disco, Santa Teresa's classic dance spot, features DJs and karaoke. Thursday nights are reggae nights.

Drift Bar
main road parallel to Playa Santa Teresa, 650 m northwest of the intersection at Carmen, tel. 506/8496-6056, www.driftbar cr.com, 11am-11pm Mon.-Thurs., 11am-midnight Fri.-Sat., 3pm-11pm Sun.

For fruity and boozy cocktails any night of the week, head to the contemporary **Drift Bar.** Most cocktails are prepared using natural, cold-pressed juices; mojitos, margaritas, mules, and other specialty drinks, plus wine and beer, are also served.

CONTACT INFO	FOOD	PRICE
tel. 506/2640-0797	vegetarian and vegan lunch	$6-9
tel. 506/2640-1117, www.bananabeachcr.com	international	$10-23
tel. 506/8414-8122, www.kojisrestaurant.com	Japanese	$10-22
tel. 506/8496-6056, www.driftbarcr.com	vegetarian	$7-16

Prefer to drink with your travel mates at your hotel? Drift Bar's signature cocktails can be ordered to go in 200-milliliter and one-liter bottles.

FOOD

STANDOUTS
Bali Beach Deli
main road parallel to Playa Santa Teresa, 1.5 km northwest of the intersection at Carmen, tel. 506/2640-0797, 7:30am-3:30pm Mon.-Sat., $6-9

The health-conscious **Bali Beach Deli** knows how to stack a sandwich, blend a smoothie, and artfully present bowls full of superfoods. Though the café caters primarily to vegetarians, there are a few vegan meals and a few meat dishes. This fun and colorful diner has seats out front—perfect for people-watching on the main drag—and knickknacks to smile at inside, like old-school lunchboxes and Lego toys. It's wonderfully quirky.

Banana Beach Restaurant
south of the main road parallel to Playa Santa Teresa, 1 km northwest of the intersection at Carmen, tel. 506/2640-1117, www.bananabeachcr.com, 7am-1am daily, $10-23

Everything goes at **Banana Beach Restaurant,** everyone's favorite hangout. Kick around a soccer ball, play volleyball, twist in aerial silks, or simply lounge in a hammock while waiting for your food: succulent burgers and nontraditional mains like oxtail pasta and pork spareribs.

Koji's
50 m east of the main road parallel to Playa Santa Teresa, 550 m northwest of the intersection at Carmen, tel. 506/8414-8122, www.kojis restaurant.com, hours vary, $10-22

Quite possibly the tastiest Japanese food you can get in Costa Rica is served at **Koji's,** an intimate restaurant that invites you to dine casually in a lovely garden setting.

SANTA TERESA LODGING

NAME	LOCATION
★ Florblanca	main road parallel to Playa Santa Teresa, 4.5 km northwest of the intersection at Carmen
★ Casa Chameleon Mal País	450 m east of the main road parallel to Playa Santa Teresa, 2 km south of the intersection at Carmen
★ Casa del Sol	main road parallel to Playa Santa Teresa, 1.5 km northwest of the intersection at Carmen
Trópico Latino	main road parallel to Playa Santa Teresa, 750 m northwest of the intersection at Carmen

Drift Bar

main road parallel to Playa Santa Teresa, 650 m northwest of the intersection at Carmen, tel. 506/8496-6056, www.driftbar cr.com, 11am-11pm Mon.-Thurs., 11am-midnight Fri.-Sat., 3pm-11pm Sun., $7-16

A mod cocktail bar by night, **Drift Bar** is a 100 percent vegetarian restaurant by day. Grab a table or booth on the covered patio and peruse an inclusive menu full of flavorful entrées (some vegan, some gluten-free) from around the world, including Indian samosas, Chinese *gyozas* (dumplings), Thai coconut curry, French croquettes, Spanish gazpacho, Italian cannelloni, and more. Most restaurants in Costa Rica don't offer such a wide array of culturally significant dishes, so come with an interest in trying something new or enjoying your favorite international meal.

LODGING

STANDOUTS
Florblanca

main road parallel to Playa Santa Teresa, 4.5 km northwest of the intersection at Carmen, tel. 506/2640-0232, www.florblanca. com, $600 s/d, min. age 6

One of my favorite luxury accommodations in the entire country, **Florblanca** is where urban sophistication and rural naturalness meet, forming idyllic spaces where comfort comes first. Any one of the 10 villas equipped with bedrooms, bathrooms, and open-air living spaces will woo you with plush bedding, soaking tubs, cozy seating options, and tons of natural light. Each villa is also rich in exotic wood, bamboo, stone, and tile textures. The rest of the property will impress you with its two-tier pool, Pilates studio, and renowned health-conscious restaurant **Nectar** (7am-9:30pm daily).

CONTACT INFO	OPTIONS	PRICE
tel. 506/2640-0232, www.florblanca.com	luxury villas	$600 s/d
tel. 506/2103-1212, www.casachameleonhotels.com	resort villas, adults-only	$525 s/d
tel. 506/2101-4877	dorm rooms and private rooms	dorm $50 pp, private $165 s/d
tel. 506/2640-0062, www.hoteltropicolatino.com	hotel rooms and bungalows	room $150 s/d, bungalow $265 s/d

Casa Chameleon Mal País

450 m east of the main road parallel to Playa Santa Teresa, 2 km south of the intersection at Carmen, tel. 506/2103-1212, www.casachameleonhotels.com, $525 s/d

If you're aiming for indulgence, your target should be the adults-only **Casa Chameleon Mal País.** Blissful is the best way to describe stays at this cosmopolitan resort with 10 intimate and romantic villas, each with a king-size canopy bed, a palatial bathroom with modern facilities, and a personal plunge pool with an ocean view. Expect truly top-notch, personalized service from all staff, who go out of their way to make you feel welcome and help you enjoy your stay. Breakfast and your choice of lunch or dinner are included in the room rate.

Casa del Sol

main road parallel to Playa Santa Teresa, 1.5 km northwest of the intersection at Carmen, tel. 506/2101-4877, dorm $50 pp, private $165 s/d

Steps from Playa Santa Teresa, Playa Carmen, and the area's best restaurants and bars is **Casa del Sol.** This quiet hotel and hostel has a two-story, hammock-wrapped bunkhouse with shared bathrooms and mixed-dormitory rooms (for 1-6 people). The four standard rooms (for 1-3 people), each with air-conditioning, a double bed and a twin rollaway bed, an enormous bathroom, and a semi-private front porch facing Santa Teresa's main drag provide an upgraded stay at a below-average price for accommodations in the area.

INFORMATION AND SERVICES

Often discussed interchangeably, Santa Teresa, Carmen, and Malpaís share the various services provided within their six-kilometer span of coastline.

Nicoya's **Hospital La Anexión** (Road 150, 300 m north of the justice courts, Nicoya, tel. 506/2685-8400, 24 hours daily) serves most of the Nicoya Peninsula. It's about a 140-kilometer, three-hour drive northwest of Santa Teresa and Malpaís.

Santa Teresa has a **tourist police office** (northeast side of the *fútbol* field, tel. 506/2640-0856, 24 hours daily) with officers available to assist foreign tourists.

At the main intersection in Carmen, you'll find two **banks** with **ATMs,** one of which is **Banco de Costa Rica** (tel. 506/2640-1019, 9am-4pm Mon.-Fri., ATM 5am-midnight daily). Across the street is a pharmacy, **Farmacia Amiga** (tel. 506/2640-0830, 8am-8pm Mon.-Sat., 8am-4pm Sun.), and a clinic, **Clínica y Emergencias de la Peninsula** (tel. 506/2640-0976, 8am-5pm Mon.-Fri.).

Head to Cóbano, a town about 10 kilometers north of Santa Teresa, to find the area's official **police station** (on the coastal road, 350 m north of Road 624, Cóbano, tel. 506/2642-0770, 24 hours daily), as well as the closest **post office** (Road 624, 50 m east of the coastal road, Cóbano, tel. 506/2783-3500, 8:30am-5pm Mon.-Fri.).

The area's only **gas station** is two kilometers northeast of Carmen.

TRANSPORTATION AND TOURS

Getting There

Car

Carmen is a 145-kilometer, 4.5-hour journey west from downtown **San José** that consists of a 100-kilometer, two-hour drive to Puntarenas on Highways 1 and 17, a one-hour ferry crossing to Paquera, and a 45-kilometer, 75-minute drive to Carmen on Road 160 and an unnamed principal access road. If you'd prefer to skip the ferry crossing, Carmen, Santa Teresa, and Malpaís can also be reached from downtown San José via a tiring 315-kilometer, 5.5- to 6-hour drive around the gulf via Highways 1, 18, and 21, Road 160, and the unnamed principal access road.

Carmen is a 215-kilometer, 4.5-hour drive southeast from downtown **Liberia** via Highway 21, Road 160, and an unnamed principal access road.

From **Montezuma,** a pressed-gravel road known locally as "the road to Delicias" cuts east-west across the peninsula and connects with Carmen, passing the farming community of Delicias along the way. This 15-kilometer drive takes 40 minutes.

Bus

Public **buses** travel daily to Carmen and Santa Teresa from **San José** (2pm daily, 6 hours, $13 includes ferry ticket). There's also a 6am bus from San José each day that will get you to Carmen and Santa Teresa, but it requires transferring buses in Cóbano.

To get to Carmen or Santa Teresa from **Montezuma,** take the bus to Cóbano (multiple times 6:20am-8pm daily, 30 minutes, $1) and catch one of many buses from there to Carmen or Santa Teresa. To identify a bus bound for Carmen and Santa Teresa, look for signage in the front window.

If you're transferring buses in Cóbano, board your new bus and ask the driver, *"¿Por favor, puede parar en Carmen?"* ("Please, can you stop in Carmen?") or *"¿Por favor, puede parar en Santa Teresa?"* ("Please, can you stop in Santa Teresa?"). Buses can stop at the main intersection in Carmen or 2.5 kilometers up the coast (in front of the small commercial center signed as Plaza Kahuna) where they end their run in Santa Teresa.

Private Transfer Service

Private transfer services can be hired through **Tropical Tours Shuttles** (main road parallel to Playa Santa Teresa, 50 m northwest of the intersection at Carmen, tel. 506/2640-1900, www.tropicaltour-shuttles.com, 8am-9pm daily). Prices average around $240-310 from San José and $270 from Liberia.

Shared Shuttle Service

Both **Tropical Tours Shuttles** and the Montezuma-based **Zuma Tours** (tel. 506/2642-0024, www.zumatours.net) provide shared shuttle services to the Santa Teresa and Malpaís area from San José, Liberia, La Fortuna, Monteverde, and Tamarindo. Zuma Tours can also shuttle you to Santa Teresa and Malpaís from Manuel Antonio and other Pacific coast locales. Services departing from San José and Manuel Antonio consist of ground transportation and either a ferry ride or water taxi ride. Services departing from Liberia, La Fortuna, Monteverde, and Tamarindo are ground transfer services only. One-way services cost $50-155 per person. Most shuttles offer drop-offs at Santa Teresa, Carmen, and Malpaís hotels.

If you plan to travel with your own surfboard to Santa Teresa or Malpaís, you'll love that Tropical Tours Shuttles accepts surfboards on their shuttles at no extra cost. Zuma Tours charges a fee of $10 per board. Shortboards are typically accepted without issue; longboards are best preapproved by Zuma Tours.

Water Taxi

To get from the central Pacific coast to Santa Teresa or Malpaís, take one of the water taxis that commute daily between Playa Herradura and Montezuma. **Zuma Tours** (tel. 506/2642-0024, www.zuma-tours.net) operates a **taxi boat service** ($55 adults, $45 children age 5-10) that takes approximately 75-90 minutes for the water crossing, with an additional hour for ground transportation to Santa Teresa, Carmen, or Malpaís. You're permitted to bring up to 50 pounds of luggage per person on the taxi boat. There's an extra fee to travel with a surfboard ($5-20).

Getting Around

The unnamed principal access road leads to Santa Teresa, Carmen, and Malpaís from the northeast at Cóbano. It enters the area just shy of the ocean at Carmen. It intersects with the main drag, an unnamed, north-south coastal road. The intersection, called *el cruce* (the crossing), is a common point of reference. Turn right at the intersection (head north) and you'll travel through the area's concentrated center, which blends with Santa Teresa. Make a left turn (head south) and you'll drive along a forlorn-feeling road through the spread-out community of Malpaís.

The coastal road is a wide-open, sometimes dusty, walkable stretch. From Carmen to Malpaís, the road is a rather desolate three-kilometer span with only a handful of hotels and restaurants along it. Stick to the area north of Carmen if you wish to walk around aimlessly, and only stray south of Carmen if you have a predetermined endpoint in mind.

If you need a taxi, Cóbano-based **taxi driver Gilberto Rodríguez** (tel. 506/8826-9055), who services the Santa Teresa, Carmen, and Malpaís areas, is well known and provides reliable service.

If you really want to blend in with the crowd, rent an **ATV** to get around. ATVs are the most common method of transportation within the beach community, and tons of places in Santa Teresa and Carmen have them. The outfitter **Pacific Dirt Road** (main road parallel to Playa Santa Teresa, 225 m northwest of the intersection at Carmen, tel. 506/8875-8452, www.quadtourscostarica.com, 8am-5pm daily) includes helmets, safe driving instruction, and hotel delivery with their ATV rentals ($50-100 per day).

MONTEZUMA

Montezuma is a coastal village heavy in hippiedom, popular for its soft sand and swimmable, bright blue water. Bohemian locals, expats, and visitors converge here to form a carefree community rich in the arts. You'll likely come across fire dancers, jugglers, aerial silk and trapeze artists, musicians, kirtan (a type of religious performance art) performers, and other surprising talents. Economy lodging and informal dining options are the standard in the heart of Montezuma. Tucked away in the hills on the outskirts of the village are newer options.

About 20 kilometers north of Montezuma, an assortment of midrange and high-end hotels and homes form the small community of Tambor. The town is spread out across flat, easy-to-navigate land on both sides of the Río Panica, which drains into the bay. Largely geared toward international retirees (who both live and vacation here), Tambor is often overlooked. Here you'll find a quiet, largely undeveloped place with a noticeably mature vibe. Farther north is the uninhabited, paradisiacal Isla Tortuga, a few kilometers offshore.

Nature trails cut through the Reserva Natural Absoluta Cabo Blanco, satisfying active visitors who seek nature exploration to supplement their beach time.

HIGHLIGHTS

- -

★ MONTEZUMA WATERFALLS

lower waterfall entrance: Road 624, 50 m north of the road to Delicias, 24 hours daily, free; upper waterfall entrance: at Suntrails, on the road to Delicias, 1.5 km northwest of Road 624, 8:30am-5pm daily, $4 pp

The triad of cascades that form the **Montezuma Waterfalls** (Cataratas Montezuma) are not only a fine display of Mother Nature's remarkable craftsmanship but are also home to Montezuma's most beloved swimming holes. Each waterfall has its own freshwater pool set amid a natural landscape with nothing made by humans in sight. There's truly nowhere else you need to be in Montezuma than in one of the pools, soaking up your surroundings and patting yourself on the back for selecting Costa Rica as your travel destination. Technically, the three waterfalls are one giant cascade. Each is part of the **Río Montezuma,** which tumbles over three rockfaces one after the other. The top two waterfalls are known as the **upper falls.** Slightly downriver and closer to the village of Montezuma is the **lower fall.**

There are a few ways to access the falls and their respective swimming holes. The cheapest way is to follow the free **entrance trail** (1 km one-way, 20 minutes, moderate). It begins just beyond the bridge at the south end of town, roughly a 15-minute walk from Montezuma center. There's a parking lot at the trailhead. The trail leads to the lower waterfall,

the most visited of the bunch. It has the largest swimming hole and is the tallest—some people say 24 meters, others say 30 meters. If you're on a budget or you're only interested in seeing the most impressive cascade, stop here, swim if you wish, and then head back the way you came.

If you want to swing or jump into pools, or swim where fewer people are, opt to visit the upper falls. (If you're itching for adrenaline, you can give the rope swing at the uppermost fall a go.) One way to reach these two cascades is to take the **unnamed trail** (1 km one-way, 45 minutes, difficult) on the north side of the lower waterfall. This trail is free to access. The rough route will take you on a steep uphill trek through the forest and alongside rocks; ropes are provided to aid in the journey. Don't attempt to tackle this challenging terrain in flip-flops. To exit from the upper falls, carefully retrace your steps to the lower waterfall and return to Montezuma.

A third and much easier way to access the falls is through the property of **Suntrails** (on the road to

Montezuma Waterfalls

Delicias, 1.5 km northwest of Road 624, 8:30am-5pm daily, $4 pp), the providers of Montezuma's zip-line canopy tour. To enter, you need to pay a fee. Suntrails provides an unnamed trail that trades uphill hikes for hanging bridge crossings and descents to the waterfalls, saving more challenging ascents for your exit. The first section (1.5 km one-way, 20 minutes, easy-moderate) begins just beyond the Suntrails office and leads to the upper falls. The second section (500 m one-way, 10 minutes, easy-moderate) travels onward to the lower waterfall. The well-maintained Suntrails paths are the safest to trek and the better choice if you're traveling with children. The Suntrails office, which has a parking lot, is an approximate five-minute drive up the hill from downtown Montezuma.

If you plan to visit the area, please be cautious. Rocks can be slippery, flash floods are a possibility, and cliff jumps can be deadly.

★ DAY TRIP TO ISLA TORTUGA

Travel time: 1 hour from Montezuma to tour departure point

If you envision paradise as an island with lush vegetation and snow-white sand surrounded by gentle, turquoise-tinged waters, you're dreaming of **Isla Tortuga**. The uninhabited island lies a mere three kilometers off the coast of the Nicoya Peninsula, just east of the Refugio Nacional de Vida Silvestre Curú, yet it remains largely undeveloped. The smell of barbecued food, the warm touch of sunshine, and the sight of palm trees swaying in the breeze here are enough to make you giddy with glee.

The island, whose official name is Isla Tolinga (though you'll just hear it referred to as Isla Tortuga), is one of the Nicoya Peninsula's most popular destinations, and its stunning beauty attracts hordes of travelers. All-inclusive day trips include boat transportation to and from the island, meals, and optional activities like snorkeling, banana boat rides, and kayaking. Overnight stays are not permitted. Most excursions are full-day adventures that depart in the early morning, dock at Playa Tolinga—Isla Tortuga's main beach—and return in the late afternoon.

Turismo Curú

inside Refugio Nacional de Vida Silvestre Curú, tel. 506/2641-0014, www.turismocuru.com, 7am-9pm daily

Here's the secret to having a slice of dreamy Isla Tortuga all to yourself: sign up for the **Tortuga Island Tour** (9am daily, 3.5 hours, $30 pp plus $15 pp wildlife refuge entrance fee) run by **Turismo Curú**. Following an hour-long snorkeling excursion at the **Islas Mortero,** a group of islets encountered on the way to Isla Tortuga, the no-frills, half-day tour visits **Playa Tropical,** a secluded beach on Isla Tolinga that's separated from the crowds at Playa Tolinga by a rocky headland. At this heavenly bare beach, you'll have a few hours to sunbathe in solitude, wade in shallow water away from other swimmers, and bask in the blissfulness of the island with little distraction. Longer day trips can be arranged (subject to boat availability). Turismo Curú is based out of the Refugio Nacional de Vida Silvestre Curú, a 35-kilometer drive from Montezuma. Though you'll need your own vehicle to reach their establishment on the beach inside the refuge, round-trip transportation to Isla Tortuga (10-15 minutes by small boat) is included in the tour cost.

Calypso Cruises

Avenida 3, 100 m east of Calle 7, Puntarenas, tel. 506/2256-2727, www.calypsocruises.com

Calypso Cruises has been operating classy excursions to the island since 1975. Their standout **Tour to Tortuga Island** (8:30am daily, 9 hours, $150 adults, $90 children 4-12) is far more than a boat trip—it's a comprehensive experience. First comes breakfast, served at a private dock in Puntarenas. After a 90-minute scenic cruise across the Golfo de Nicoya, you'll spend at least five hours on Isla Tortuga, where you can enjoy a complimentary snorkeling excursion and banana boat ride, along with plenty of free time at the beach. Included with the tour are unlimited nonalcoholic drinks (alcoholic drinks are available for purchase), a four-course gourmet lunch served under shade on the sand, and free downloadable photographs of the day's events. Calypso doesn't skimp on extras, like hiring local musicians to play marimba music and providing free beach chairs, hammocks, a volleyball net, a slack line, and private bathrooms. They even take different routes to and from the island to showcase unique views during each trip. Expect superior service from the outfitter, from their friendly staff to the use of a high-quality yacht, the *Manta Raya*, that delivers tour participants to the island in style. Calypso can provide ground transportation to their dock in Puntarenas from destinations including San José, Jacó, Manuel Antonio, and Monteverde.

Zuma Tours

Road 624, across from the *fútbol* field, tel. 506/2642-0024, www.zumatours.net, 7am-8pm daily

Montezuma-based **Zuma Tours** attracts a young crowd. Their **Tortuga Island Snorkeling Tour** (9am daily, 7 hours, from Montezuma: $65 adults, $45 children 4-10; 8am daily, 8 hours, from Santa Teresa or Malpaís: $79 adults, $60 children 4-10) includes boat transportation, snorkel gear, lunch, nonalcoholic drinks, and two cans of beer.

Getting There

The island is typically accessed by boat. Excursions run year-round with departures from (and returns to) Tambor, Montezuma, Santa Teresa, Malpaís, San José, Manuel Antonio, and Monteverde.

HIKING

CABO BLANCO NATURE RESERVE

Road 624, 9 km south of Montezuma, tel. 506/2642-0093, www.sinac.go.cr, 8am-4pm Wed.-Sun., $12 adults, $5 children 2-12

Declared the country's first protected land area in 1963, the **Cabo Blanco Nature Reserve** (Reserva Natural Absoluta Cabo Blanco) has led the way for nature conservation in Costa Rica. Comprising roughly 3,400 acres of land and 4,200 acres of water, the reserve encompasses the entire southern tip of the Nicoya Peninsula and a wide perimeter of ocean.

Come to the reserve to walk its

forested trails. After you've hiked up a sweat, spend some time relaxing on the beach near Cabo Blanco, the cape for which the reserve is named; this is the southernmost part of the peninsula. Two kilometers due south of the cape and visible from the beach is the rocky **Isla Capitán,** sometimes called **Isla Cabo Blanco.** Anteaters, armadillos, deer, monkeys, pacas, and the odd jungle cat inhabit the forest. Frigatebirds, brown boobies, pelicans, and other seabirds congregate at the cape, making it the region's best bird-watching locale. A seemingly endless list of marine life fills the reserve's protected waters and the expansive ocean beyond.

Cabo Blanco Nature Reserve

The reserve has two official entrances, but only the eastern entrance, closer to Montezuma, is open to the public. A **biological station** equipped with bathrooms and picnic tables marks the public entrance.

The **Arboretum Trail** (1-km loop, 20-30 minutes, easy) is a quick loop that offers a peek at the reserve's rare tree collection, which flourishes within a contradictory mix of tropical dry forest and moist forest ecosystems.

The **Danés Trail** (2-km loop, 45 minutes, moderate) and the challenging **Sueco Trail** (4 km one-way, 2 hours, difficult) are the park's most trekked trails. The Danés Trail will lead you through secondary forest. The Sueco Trail, an offshoot of the Danés Trail, will have you trudging uphill and downhill through thick brush and humid air, and possibly muddy patches too, with the goal of reaching **Playa Cabo Blanco,** the reserve's principal beach. Although stones largely cover the light-sand coastline, visits to the spot are hardly disappointing. Simply being at this remote beach surrounded by dramatic hills, and viewing a limitless and thought-provoking sky and ocean, is rewarding enough.

You can explore the reserve's three trails on your own, but tour operators around the peninsula will gladly sell you the services of a guide. Based in Santa Teresa, **Tropical Tours Shuttles** (main road parallel to Playa Santa Teresa, 50 m northwest of the intersection at Carmen, Santa Teresa, tel. 506/2640-1900, www.tropicaltourshuttles.com, 8am-9pm daily) runs a popular **Cabo Blanco Nature Reserve Tour** (7am daily, 5 hours, $75 pp) that includes round-trip transportation from Montezuma, Santa Teresa, Carmen, or Malpaís, a naturalist tour guide, snacks, and the reserve's entrance fee.

Getting There

The reserve, in the southern corner of the Nicoya Peninsula, is best accessed by car from Montezuma. Follow Road 624 south out of Montezuma for 8.5 kilometers until it ends at the reserve's entrance. Worth momentarily pulling over for as the road enters Cabuya, a hamlet

MONTEZUMA FOOD

NAME	LOCATION
★ Playa de los Artistas	Road 624, 250 m north of the road to Delicias
Puggo's	750 m north of the road to Delicias, 3 km west of Road 624

you'll pass through approximately 2.5 kilometers before arriving at the reserve's entrance, is the giant, hollow *higuerón* tree (strangler fig, or ficus) you can stand inside. Look for it on the right side of Road 624 behind the "Bienvenidos a Cabuya" sign.

BEACHES

PLAYA COLORADA

Northeast of Montezuma are bare beaches that invite you to walk for miles—and aren't accessible by car. A quick, 200-meter coastal trail that begins at the Ylang Ylang Beach Resort at Playa Montezuma, a 15-minute walk from the center of town, leads to the pretty cove known as **Playa Colorada.** Here, you can spot rocks in coral, turquoise, amber, and purple hues, and wade in a freshwater swimming hole just west of the beach fed by the gentle Río Piedra Colorada.

PLAYA COCALITO

Farther up the coast from Montezuma is the deserted **Playa Cocalito,** immediately south of Tambor. At the east end of this beach, you can watch the eight-meter **El Chorro Waterfall,** also known as **Cocalito Falls,** pour off a rockface into the ocean. It's a seven-kilometer, two-hour walk from the center of Montezuma to the base of the waterfall at Playa Cocalito. The top of the waterfall, an escarpment that stuns with a bird's-eye view of the cascade, the Pacific Ocean, and Montezuma's coastline, can be reached via a combined road and forest trail (1 km one-way, 30 minutes, easy) that departs from the property of Tango Mar. The escarpment doesn't have guardrails, so keep a safe distance from the cliff's edge when you go and don't loosen your grip on any young ones in tow. When visiting the bottom of the waterfall via the beach, most sections of the walk offer no shade, so don't go without a hat, sunscreen, and water. There is no way to reach the top of the waterfall from its base (or vice versa).

PLAYA LAS MANCHAS

My vote for the best beach in the area goes to **Playa Las Manchas,** 1.5 kilometers south of downtown Montezuma on Road 624. Many expats in the area also favor it, so you may not get the beach all to yourself, although it remains off the tourist radar. This local hangout spot, less than a half-hour walk south of Montezuma, has white sand, turquoise

CONTACT INFO	FOOD	PRICE
tel. 506/2642-0920	seafood	$8-19, cash only
tel. 506/8913-7091	international	$8-16

water, tons of tide pools, and enough fish to warrant breaking out your snorkel gear. It also has a strong rip current at times, so remain mindful when you swim.

PLAYA QUIZALES

The most beautiful beach in the Tambor area is **Playa Quizales**, a long stretch of smooth light brown sand. Jagged escarpments bookend this beach, making it nearly impossible to reach on foot from the east or the west. The best way to access this sequestered hidden gem is to spend a night at Tango Mar, the hotel that fronts the beach. The hotel allows public access to the beach through its property, but non-guests aren't allowed to use its facilities. Beach visitors must park in Tango Mar's visitors parking lot.

YOGA

ANAMAYA BODY, MIND, AND SPIRIT RESORT

on the road to Delicias, 900 m west of Road 624, tel. 506/2642-1289, www. anamayaresort.com, $995-1,995 pp

Montezuma's best yoga resort, **Anamaya Body, Mind, and Spirit Resort** (on the road to Delicias, 900 m west of Road 624, tel. 506/2642-1289, www.anamayaresort.com), is arguably also one of the top yoga resorts in the country. Sway in a hammock, swim in a tranquil infinity pool, reward yourself with spa services, dine on gourmet organic cuisine, and surround yourself with nature; then breathe in fresh air and exhale any remaining stress. The resort encourages you to do it all and more, including practicing yoga in an open-air shala with a panoramic view of the Pacific Ocean. One-week **yoga retreats** ($995-1,995 pp) run back-to-back throughout the year. The 200-hour **yoga teacher training program** ($3,438-5,155 pp) typically starts at the beginning of each month. Both include accommodations and all meals.

MONTEZUMA YOGA

Road 624, 250 m north of the road to Delicias, tel. 506/8704-1632, www.montezumayoga.com, 8:30am-7:30pm daily

To take in the laid-back local vibe, join one of **Montezuma Yoga**'s many **classes** (8:30am and 6pm daily, 90 minutes, $15 pp). Mainly vinyasa flow yoga and vin yoga are practiced. Drop-ins are permitted. Mats and props are provided free of charge.

MONTEZUMA AND TAMBOR LODGING

NAME	LOCATION
★ Sunshine Sanctuary	on the road to Delicias, 750 m west of Road 624
Ylang Ylang Beach Resort	Playa Montezuma, 1 km northeast of downtown Montezuma
★ Tango Mar	1.5 km south of the coast road, 7 km south of Aeropuerto Tambor, Tambor

NIGHTLIFE

CHICO'S BAR
on the main road that runs parallel to Playa Montezuma, tel. 506/2642-0578, 11am-2am daily
Beachfront **Chico's Bar** is the main gathering place in town, if for no good reason than that there are few places to go. During the day, it's a decent place to grab a drink. After dark, it gets loud, attracts a mix of locals and tourists, and has DJs and dancing.

ORGÁNICO
on the main road that runs parallel to Playa Montezuma, tel. 506/2642-1322, 8:30am-9:30pm Wed.-Mon.
The small but trendy **Orgánico** has live music and open mic nights.

FOOD

STANDOUTS
Playa de los Artistas
Road 624, 250 m north of the road to Delicias, tel. 506/2642-0920, 4:30pm-9:30pm Mon.-Fri., noon-9:30pm Sat., $8-19, cash only
For high-quality food, Montezuma's standout restaurant is the beachfront **Playa de los Artistas.** The chef creates a new, handwritten short menu daily inspired by the freshest ingredients available, so part of the fun of dining here is the element of surprise. Regardless of what is served (usually fish dishes), meals regularly receive rave reviews for their exquisite preparation, presentation, and taste. Grab a table on the beach before dark so you can fully appreciate the ocean view.

CONTACT INFO	OPTIONS	PRICE
tel. 506/7014-8394	lodge rooms	$135 s/d
tel. 506/2642-0636, www.ylangylangbeachresort.com	tent cabins, hotel rooms, bungalows	tent cabin $198 s/d, room $220 s/d, bungalow $295
tel. 506/2683-0001, www.tangomar.com	resort rooms, Polynesian-style tiki suites	room $278 s/d, suite $361 s/d

LODGING

STANDOUTS
Sunshine Sanctuary
on the road to Delicias, 750 m west of Road 624, tel. 506/7014-8394, $135 s/d

Perched atop the hill that descends into town, **Sunshine Sanctuary** offers astounding ocean and forest views. Rooms have comfortable king or queen beds, shiny tile floors, air-conditioning, flat-screen televisions, and a wall of glass with sliding doors. I've seen aracaris in the trees, heard monkeys howl, and even spotted a whale breaching offshore from the room's private balcony. As a guest, you'll have free access to the hotel's hanging bridge and a private trail that connects to the Montezuma Waterfalls.

Tango Mar
1.5 km south of the coastal road, 7 km south of Aeropuerto Tambor, tel. 506/2683-0001, www.tangomar.com, room $278 s/d, suite $361 s/d

My favorite place to stay in Tambor is the beachfront **Tango Mar.** Contained within a guarded complex that houses private residences, a golf course, and horse stables is the hotel's row of Polynesian-style tiki suites, each one steps away from the beautiful Playa Quizales. Additional rooms are up a steep hill. All accommodations are fresh, clean, classy, tropical-themed, and outfitted with one or two king or queen beds, wood furniture, and a television. As a guest of Tango Mar, you'll get exclusive trail access to the top of the nearby El Chorro Waterfall, keyed entry to a phenomenal viewpoint that overlooks the Pacific coastline, and the convenience of having one of Tambor's best restaurants, **El Cristobal** (7am-10am and 6:30pm-10pm daily), at your hotel.

INFORMATION AND SERVICES

There are few services in Montezuma proper. You'll need to go to nearby **Cóbano,** five kilometers northwest on Road 624, for most services.

Nicoya's **Hospital La Anexión** (Road 150, 300 m north of the justice courts, Nicoya, tel. 506/2685-8400, 24 hours daily) serves most of the Nicoya Peninsula. It's a 2.5- to 3-hour drive northwest of Montezuma.

In Cóbano, you'll find the **clinic Ebais Cóbano** (Road 624, 250 m west of the coastal road, Cóbano, tel. 506/2642-0208, 24 hours daily) and **Farmacia Montecristo** (Road 624, 75 m west of the coastal road, Cóbano, tel. 506/2642-1119, 7am-7pm Mon.-Fri., 7am-6pm Sat.).

The closest **bank** is the **Banco Nacional** (corner of the coastal road and Road 624, Cóbano, tel. 506/2212-2000, 8:30am-3:45pm Mon.-Fri.) in Cóbano. Most businesses, with the exception of some small shops, accept credit cards.

Cóbano also has a **post office** (Road 624, 50 m east of the coastal road, Cóbano, tel. 506/2783-3500, 8:30am-5pm Mon.-Fri.) and a **police station** (on the coastal road, 350 m north of Road 624, Cóbano, tel. 506/2642-0770, 24 hours daily).

Fuel up at Cóbano's **gas station** (on the coastal road, 1 km northeast of Road 624); Montezuma doesn't have a *bomba* (gas station) of its own. There's a **gas station** in Paquera (on Road 621), north of Tambor.

TRANSPORTATION AND TOURS

Most routes at the southern end of the Nicoya Peninsula lead to Cóbano. From there, a quick five-kilometer (10-minute) journey down the hillside on **Road 624** ends in Montezuma. Tambor is 20 kilometers north of Montezuma on Road 160, a 30-minute drive.

Getting There

Car

Montezuma is a 140-kilometer, four-hour journey west from downtown **San José** that consists of a 100-kilometer, two-hour drive to Puntarenas on Highways 1 and 17, a one-hour ferry crossing to Paquera, and a 40-kilometer, one-hour drive to Montezuma on Roads 160 and 624. This combination of ground and water transportation is a prime opportunity to take in the views of the gulf. Montezuma can also be reached from downtown San José via a tiring 310-kilometer, 5.5-hour drive around the gulf via Highways 1, 18, and 21, and Road 160.

From downtown **Liberia,** it's a 210-kilometer, four-hour drive southeast on Highway 21, Road 160, and Road 624 to **Montezuma.**

From **Santa Teresa** and **Malpaís,** a pressed-gravel road known locally as "the road to Delicias" cuts east-west across the peninsula and connects with Montezuma, passing the farming community of Delicias along the way. This 15-kilometer drive takes 40 minutes.

Air

The local domestic airport, **Aeropuerto Tambor** (TMU), is four kilometers north of Tambor. **SANSA Airlines** (tel. 506/2290-4100, www.flysansa.com) flies to Tambor daily from San José and Liberia.

Bus

Public **buses** travel daily to Montezuma from **San José** (6am and 2pm daily, 5.5 hours, $13 includes ferry ticket). This route includes a timed transfer in Cóbano, where you'll get off the bus you boarded in San José and immediately board a bus bound for Montezuma.

To get to Montezuma from **Santa**

Teresa and **Malpaís,** take the bus from Carmen (between Santa Teresa and Malpaís) to Cóbano (multiple times 3am–8pm daily, 45 minutes, $1.50–2) and catch one of many buses from there to Montezuma (multiple times 5:30am–7:30pm daily, 30 minutes, $1). When you board in Carmen, ask the bus driver, *"¿Por favor, puede parar en Cóbano?"* ("Please, can you stop in Cóbano?"). Buses stop in front of Banco Nacional, on the corner of Roads 624 and 160 in Cóbano. To identify a bus bound for Montezuma, look for signage in the front window. In Montezuma, buses end their run on Road 624 by the waterfront, one block south of the village center.

Private Transfer Service

Private transfer services can be hired through **Montezuma Expeditions** (10 m southeast of Road 624 on the main road in Montezuma, tel. 506/2441-3394, www.montezumaexpeditions.com, 8am–8pm daily). Prices average $275 from San José and $315 from Liberia. Vehicles vary in size; most accommodate up to eight people plus luggage.

Shared Shuttle Service

Local operators **Zuma Tours** (Road 624, across from the *fútbol* field, tel. 506/2642-0024, www.zumatours.net, 7am–8pm daily) and **Montezuma Expeditions** (10 m southeast of Road 624 on the main road in Montezuma, tel. 506/2441-3394, www.montezumaexpeditions.com, 8am–8pm daily) both run shared shuttle services to Montezuma from San José, Liberia, Tamarindo, and Sámara. Additionally, Zuma Tours can shuttle you to Montezuma from Santa Teresa, Malpaís, Tambor, La Fortuna, Monteverde, Jacó, Manuel Antonio, Dominical, Uvita, and Sierpe. Routes from Jacó, Manuel Antonio, Dominical, Uvita, and Sierpe consist of ground transportation and either a ferry or water taxi ride. Except for departures from San José, all other routes are ground transfer services only; San José departures can be booked with or without the ferry or water taxi ride. One-way services cost $45–140 per person. Most shuttles fit eight people with luggage and offer drop-offs at Montezuma hotels.

Water Taxi

To get to Montezuma from the central Pacific coast, take one of the water taxis that commute daily between Playa Herradura and Montezuma. **Zuma Tours** (tel. 506/2642-0024, www.zumatours.net) operates a **taxi boat service** ($45 adults, $35 children age 5–10) that takes approximately 75–90 minutes. A luggage weight limit (50 lbs pp) is enforced, and there's an extra fee ($5–20) to travel with a surfboard.

Getting Around

Montezuma's tiny core comprises two unnamed roads. One runs parallel to Playa Montezuma, and the other runs perpendicular to the beach for no more than 100 meters until it connects with Road 624, the village's principal access road. Walking around town is easy and only takes a few minutes. The **Ylang Ylang Beach Resort** (Playa Montezuma, 1 km northeast of downtown Montezuma, tel. 506/2642-0636, www.ylangylangbeachresort.com) has **bikes for rent** ($18 for 1 day) if you wish to speed up the process.

Accommodations and other businesses dot the hills that surround the village; several are on roads with a steep incline or decline. If you are driving, a 4x4 vehicle is not required but is recommended. Taxis, although scarce in Montezuma, can help you get up or down the area's hills if you prefer not to hike. Cóbano-based **taxi driver Gilberto Rodríguez** (tel. 506/8826-9055), who services the Montezuma area, is well known and provides reliable service.

Playa Manuel Antonio, inside Manuel Antonio National Park

MANUEL ANTONIO AND COSTA BALLENA

Midway along Costa Rica's central Pacific coast is one of the country's most visited attractions. Manuel Antonio National Park impresses with soft and beautiful beaches, several hiking trails, and diverse ecosystems that support abundant wildlife. The park's sprawling, mountainous namesake community has its own draws: beach access, cliffside properties, varied cuisines, and an energetic vibe.

South of Manuel Antonio, the highway angles toward the coast and passes through dense plantations of lofty African palms, leading to the Costa Ballena. Leisurely drives through this region are particularly scenic, thanks to rainforest-covered mountains in the northern sections and up-close ocean views in the southern parts. Detours off the highway lead to empty beaches, forest-wrapped waterfalls, mountainside homesteads, and hotels with panoramic views.

Half of the experience of this region is the journey: Drive alongside steep, verdant hills, pass through rows of swaying tropical palms, spot the sparkle of the glassy ocean, and marvel at a rainbow-colored sky come sunset.

a pair of scarlet macaws in an *almendro* (almond) tree

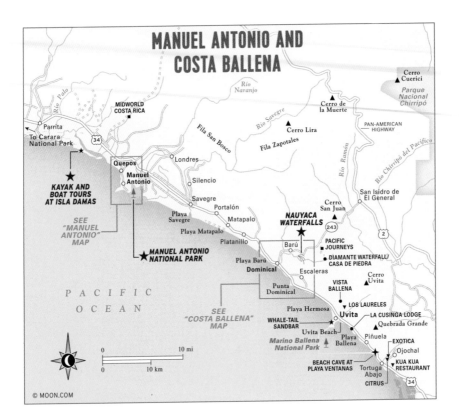

MANUEL ANTONIO AND COSTA BALLENA

Cerro Cuerici

Parque Nacional Chirripó

Río Naranjo

Río Savegre

Cerro de la Muerte

PAN-AMERICAN HIGHWAY

MIDWORLD COSTA RICA

Cerro Lira

Fila San Bosco

Fila Zapotales

Río Palo

Parrita

To Carara National Park

Quepos

Londres

Manuel Antonio

Silencio

Savegre

San Isidro de El General

KAYAK AND BOAT TOURS AT ISLA DAMAS

Cerro San Juan

SEE "MANUEL ANTONIO" MAP

Playa Savegre

Portalón

NAUYACA WATERFALLS

Matapalo

PACIFIC JOURNEYS

MANUEL ANTONIO NATIONAL PARK

Playa Matapalo

Platanillo

Barú

DIAMANTE WATERFALL CASA DE PIEDRA

PACIFIC OCEAN

Playa Barú

Dominical

Escaleras

Cerro Uvita

Punta Dominical

VISTA BALLENA

SEE "COSTA BALLENA" MAP

Playa Hermosa

LOS LAURELES

Uvita

LA CUSINGA LODGE

WHALE-TAIL SANDBAR

Uvita Beach

Quebrada Grande

Marino Ballena National Park

Playa Ballena

Piñuela

EXOTICA

Ojochal

10 mi

KUA KUA RESTAURANT

10 km

BEACH CAVE AT PLAYA VENTANAS

Tortuga Abajo

CITRUS

© MOON.COM

capuchin monkey

3

TOP 3

★ **1. MANUEL ANTONIO NATIONAL PARK:** Spot wildlife such as monkeys and sloths—or follow their examples by playing or lounging on the beach (page 187).

★ **2. ISLA DAMAS:** Kayak or float among its tranquil mangroves (page 190).

★ **3. NAUYACA WATERFALLS:** Hike or ride a 4x4 to the stunning falls, where you can swim in their idyllic pools (page 209).

BEST 5 DAYS IN MANUEL ANTONIO AND COSTA BALLENA

DAY 1

Start the day at **Manuel Antonio National Park.** Give yourself at least a few hours to spot wildlife while wandering its nature trails and to enjoy a swim along its beaches. Exit the park to head up the mountainside for lunch at **El Patio de Café Milagro,** then retreat to **Playa Espadilla Norte** or **Playa Biesanz** for more beach time. In the evening, enjoy a plateful of barbecued food at **El Lagarto.**

DAY 2

Spend the day on the water. Depending on the tides, schedule either the morning or afternoon **kayak tour** of the mangroves at **Isla Damas.** Devote the other half of the day to a **sailing, snorkeling,** and **dolphin-watching tour** from the marina in **Quepos.** Each tour includes a meal.

DAY 3

Devote a full day to participating in a guided excursion. Bird-watchers should head up the coast to the **Carara National Park.** If you want adventure, choose either a **white-water rafting tour** or **canyoneering** on the 10-in-1 Adventure Tour. All three experiences depart from Manuel Antonio in the morning, return in the mid-afternoon, and can be arranged to include lunch. In the evening, suit up for fine dining at **La Luna.**

DAY 4

In the morning, take a scenic **hike** or **horseback ride** to the stunning **Nauyaca Waterfalls** and swim in the pool at the bottom of the two-tiered cascade. Some waterfall tours include lunch; you can also grab food at **Café Mono Congo** in nearby **Dominical.** Spend a low-key afternoon wandering Dominical. If you're still there in the evening, enjoy dinner at the **Fuego Brew Company.**

DAY 5

From Bahía (near Uvita), set out on an early-morning **boat tour** in the protected waters of **Marino Ballena National Park** to try your luck at spotting whales. If it's low tide when the tour returns to shore, stroll along the **whale-tail-shaped sandbar.** Pop into **Los Laureles Restaurant** in Uvita for lunch before moving down the coast to **Playa Ventanas** for a restful afternoon at the beach. End your stay by indulging in a gourmet dinner in Ojochal, known for its cuisine. Choose from **Exotica, Citrus,** or the **Kua Kua Restaurant** (make reservations in advance).

trail at Carara National Park

PLANNING YOUR TIME

Some activities, attractions, and tours can only be experienced at high or low tide, so familiarize yourself with the **local tide schedule.** If tide-dependent activities interest you, create a flexible itinerary that allows for activities with start times beyond your control.

Reservations

This region is in high demand. Especially if you intend to stay in Manuel Antonio, **book accommodations 3-6 months in advance** if you will be in the country between the end of **December** and **April**—even earlier if your visit coincides with Christmas, New Year's, or Easter. Transportation and activity arrangements can be made a few weeks prior to your trip, as can accommodation arrangements if you plan to travel between May and mid-December.

Best Bases

This region's attractions dot the central Pacific coast. No matter where you park yourself, you will need to travel to capture the best experiences. Fortunately, it only takes a little over an hour to drive the full coastline from Manuel Antonio (in the northwest) to Ojochal (in the southeast), so jaunts between towns and attractions are relatively short.

Not all destinations provide the same beach-town experience. Stay in entertaining **Manuel Antonio** to enjoy myriad dining and activity options and the closest access to Costa Rica's most visited national park. If you'd rather have a less developed home base that receives **fewer visitors,** choose **Dominical, Uvita,** or **Ojochal. Food lovers** should consider staying—or at least eating—in **Ojochal,** which offers rich culinary experiences that shouldn't be missed.

Weather

This emerald-green region receives a consistent dose of rain and sun. **Showers** ranging from drizzles to downpours are not uncommon throughout the year, but most of the annual precipitation falls between June and November. September through November is the wettest time to visit.

Destinations near the water, including Manuel Antonio, Dominical, and Bahía (part of Uvita), receive **average temperatures of 80°F,** rivaling some of the country's hottest areas. Temperatures drop as elevation rises inland, so it is cooler around the hillside destinations of Uvita and Ojochal. Prior to travel, prepare for two climates—pack plenty of **sunscreen** and a **waterproof rain jacket** or **poncho.**

Connect with...

Manuel Antonio and the Costa Ballena are easily reached from any of the regions covered in this guide except for the Caribbean. These destinations, centrally located on the Pacific coast, connect well with time spent in **Bahía Drake.** To experience two contrasting beach destinations, consider connecting Manuel Antonio with either **Santa Teresa** and **Montezuma** or **Tamarindo.** Travel from either Manuel Antonio or the Costa Ballena to Santa Teresa or Montezuma includes a ferry crossing.

MANUEL ANTONIO

In Manuel Antonio you'll find beautiful coastlines of soft sand, abundant wildlife, and a vivacious community. Manuel Antonio and the neighboring town of Quepos to the north offer an endless number of day tours, mainly water-based activities and nature expeditions that showcase the area's wildlife and marine life.

Quepos is a bustling town jam-packed with shops, restaurants, and other businesses that cater primarily to locals. Just southwest of town, the Marina Pez Vela has some of the most tourist-friendly services, restaurants, and tour operator offices in Quepos.

From the southeast corner of Quepos, Road 618 is an easy but curvy 15-minute drive up and down the mountainside, ending at beach level. Lacking clear borders and an obvious center, Manuel Antonio sprawls across the entire stretch of Road 618 and down small side streets. Most accommodations, restaurants, and shops sit along this stretch. A handful of others cluster near Playa Espadilla Norte, Manuel Antonio's principal beach.

Separating Playa Espadilla Norte in the south from Quepos in the north is Punta Quepos, a small, hilly, forest-covered peninsula that extends into the ocean. A few of Manuel Antonio's upscale resorts dot the peninsula.

HIGHLIGHTS

- -

★ WILDLIFE AT MANUEL ANTONIO NATIONAL PARK

500 m northeast of Road 618 at Playa Espadilla Norte, tel. 506/2777-5185, www.sinac.go.cr, 7am-4pm Wed.-Mon., last entry 3pm, $16 adults, free for seniors and children under 12

One of Costa Rica's most beloved and busiest attractions, **Manuel Antonio National Park** (Parque Nacional Manuel Antonio) is also one of its smallest national parks, occupying less than 5,000 acres of land and an additional 60,000 acres of ocean. The park's nearly 500,000 visitors each year come for beautiful crescent beaches where **monkeys** are known to fraternize with people on the sand. Despite its relatively small size, the park is jam-packed with trails, beaches, and lookout points. Well-designed and -maintained trails lead through forested areas, and sightings of **sloths** (both two-toed and three-toed varieties) are nearly guaranteed. If your ideal day in Costa Rica combines beach relaxation, light nature exploration, and wildlife encounters, you can tick all three off your travel list with just a few hours in this park.

Purchase park tickets online (www.sinac.go.cr). Tickets are assigned for set days and time slots, and they tend to sell out weeks in advance, especially during the high season. An iron gate marks the **entrance** to the park. Just beyond the gate is the park's **ranger station.** Your ticket is good for one entry; come-and-go access is not permitted.

Manuel Antonio Expeditions

tel. 506/8365-1057, www.juan brenes.blogspot.com, 8:30am and 1pm daily, 3 hours, $51 adults, $35 children under 12

An overwhelming number of tour guides congregate near the park entrance, but the best guides are secured in advance. I've always had a blast touring the park with—and learning a lot from—**Manuel Antonio Expeditions,** also known as **Águila Tours.** Guides on their wildlife-spotting expedition come ready with spotting scopes, trained eyes, and years of experience that help them catch what others miss. The guided tour experience includes the park entrance fee and round-trip transportation from Manuel Antonio and Quepos hotels. If you have a rental car and buy your own park ticket, one of the company's guides can be hired for $25 per person. If you're drawn to the park for its beaches, you won't need a tour guide; simply buy your ticket and go.

Hiking

The park's most popular trails are **El Manglar Trail** (785 m one-way, 15 minutes, easy), a raised boardwalk bordered by mangrove ecosystems; and the narrow forest path **El Perezoso Trail** (650 m one-way, 15 minutes, easy), which provides access to Playa Manuel Antonio. El Manglar's wheelchair-accessible boardwalk allows a peek at the area's woody mangroves. It also includes informational placards in Braille. El Perezoso is aptly named (*perezoso* means "lazy"), as its namesake **sloths** sleep in the trees that line the trail, while **frogs, lizards,** and **iguanas** scurry below. From Playa Manuel Antonio, **Playa Espadilla Sur Trail** (650 m one-way, 15 minutes, easy) leads west to Playa Espadilla Sur, then runs north along the beach and connects with El Manglar.

To really get to know the park and uncover its less obvious beauty, explore one of its other trails. The **Punta Catedral Trail** (1.4-km loop, 1 hour, moderate-difficult) begins just south of Playa Manuel Antonio. This dense forest hike offers decent **bird-watching** and ocean and island views.

squirrel monkey (left); iguana (right)

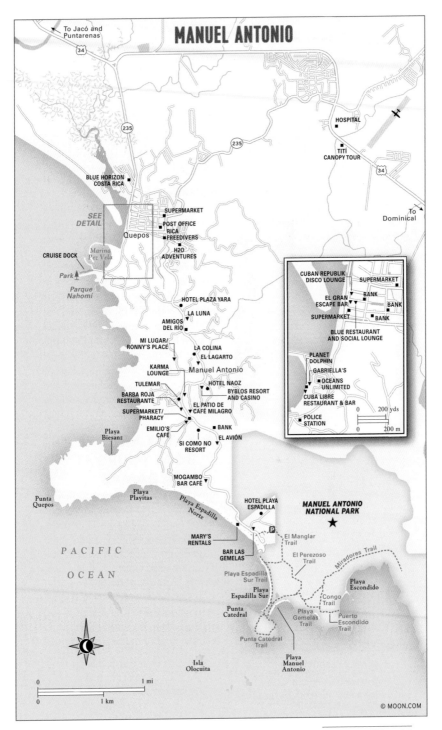

MANUEL ANTONIO

To Jacó and Puntarenas

34

235

235

34

To Dominical

HOSPITAL

TITÍ CANOPY TOUR

BLUE HORIZON COSTA RICA

SEE DETAIL

Quepos

SUPERMARKET

POST OFFICE
RICA FREEDIVERS

H2O ADVENTURES

CRUISE DOCK

Marina Pez Vela

Park

Parque Nahomi

HOTEL PLAZA YARA

LA LUNA

AMIGOS DEL RÍO

MI LUGAR/ RONNY'S PLACE

LA COLINA
EL LAGARTO

KARMA LOUNGE

Manuel Antonio

TULEMAR

HOTEL NAOZ

BARBA ROJA RESTAURANTE

BYBLOS RESORT AND CASINO

SUPERMARKET/ PHARACY

EL PATIO DE CAFÉ MILAGRO

EMILIO'S CAFÉ

BANK

EL AVIÓN

SI COMO NO RESORT

Playa Biesanz

MOGAMBO BAR CAFÉ

Punta Quepos

Playa Playitas

Playa Espadilla Norte

HOTEL PLAYA ESPADILLA

MANUEL ANTONIO NATIONAL PARK ★

P

El Manglar Trail

MARY'S RENTALS

BAR LAS GEMELAS

El Perezoso Trail

Miradores Trail

PACIFIC

Playa Espadilla Sur Trail

Playa Espadilla Sur

Playa Escondido

OCEAN

Congo Trail

Punta Catedral

Playa Gemelas Trail

Puerto Escondido Trail

Punta Catedral Trail

Playa Manuel Antonio

Isla Olocuita

0   1 mi

0   1 km

Inset (Quepos detail)

CUBAN REPUBLIK DISCO LOUNGE

SUPERMARKET

EL GRAN ESCAPE BAR

BANK

BANK

SUPERMARKET

BANK

BLUE RESTAURANT AND SOCIAL LOUNGE

PLANET DOLPHIN

GABRIELLA'S

OCEANS UNLIMITED

CUBA LIBRE RESTAURANT & BAR

POLICE STATION

0   200 yds

0   200 m

© MOON.COM

Playa Gemelas Trail (550 m one-way, 10 minutes, easy-moderate), **Puerto Escondido Trail** (450 m one-way, 10 minutes, easy-moderate), **Congo Trail** (300 m one-way, 10 minutes, easy-moderate), and **Miradores Trail** (1.3 km one-way, 1 hour, moderate-difficult) connect with one another and are best completed as a set. They lead through the least visited areas of the park where you're most likely to run into one of the park's 107 animal varieties. Keep an eye open for endangered **squirrel monkeys,** referred to by locals as mono tití monkeys; Manuel Antonio is one of only a few places in the country where you can spot them. Lookout points that frame lush, textured headlands juxtaposed with soft stretches of sandy coast are abundant, but be prepared to climb lengthy staircases to reach them.

Getting There

The park is within walking distance of Playa Espadilla Norte and most beachfront hotels. Many high-end Manuel Antonio hotels include a complimentary shuttle to the park entrance.

To drive to the park from Quepos or the mountainous section of Manuel Antonio, take Road 618 south to beach level and turn left at the Marlin Restaurant. Follow the short side road until it ends just before the park's entrance. Parking lots are scattered all around; expect to pay roughly $10 for the day.

★ KAYAK AND BOAT TOURS AT ISLA DAMAS

A mere seven kilometers northwest of Quepos is **Isla Damas,** a tranquil mangrove ecosystem. This area, technically an estuary, lends itself to quiet, slow, up-close exploration of nature—and it is truly replete with wildlife. You're bound to run into a capuchin monkey (or an entire troop) at this spot, which is full of birds, iguanas, lizards, caimans, and my favorite local inhabitants: tiger crabs.

tiger crab at Isla Damas (top); scarlet macaws in Carara National Park (bottom)

Manuel Antonio Expeditions

tel. 506/8365-1057, www.juanbrenes.blogspot.com, 4 hours, $65 pp

You can learn about the important role tiger crabs and other creatures play in the ecosystem's life cycle during a narrated boat or kayak tour of the mangroves. Mangrove experts **Manuel Antonio Expeditions,** also known as **Águila Tours,** run fantastic guided boat and kayak tours through the swampy Isla Damas and its web of intertwined tree roots. Regardless of whether you're cruising through the ecosystem in a pontoon boat (with protection from the sun or rain) or floating through it in a kayak, you'll have an enjoyable and informative experience. Knowledgeable guides share tons of fascinating facts about mangroves and how their survival is vital to the protection of our oceans. The activity is a must if you're interested in ecology or unique ecosystems. The boat tour is a favorite among less active travelers and families with young children. Tour times are tide dependent, and round-trip transportation from Manuel Antonio and Quepos hotels is included.

DAY TRIP TO CARARA NATIONAL PARK

Travel time: 1.5 hours from Manuel Antonio

Hwy. 34, 90 km north of Manuel Antonio, tel. 506/2637-1083, www.sinac.go.cr, 7am-4pm daily Dec.-Apr., 8am-4pm daily May-Nov., last entry 3pm, $10 adults, $5 children 6-12

Carara National Park (Parque Nacional Carara) is one of the best **bird-watching** locales in the country. Located between dry forest and humid climates, the protected land area not only provides refuge to more than 400 bird species (roughly half of all of Costa Rica's bird species), but it also offers an opportunity to see birds that aren't usually spotted in the same place.

The 13,000-acre park is also one of the most accessible national parks in the country, making it a top destination for visitors of all ages and mobility levels. It's easy to get to, one of its trails is accessible by wheelchair, and numerous informational placards make even unguided visits educational ones. Recorded audio narrations and Braille supplement the park's signage. A **visitors center** marks the park's main entrance.

Bird-Watching

There's an array of birds along the park's **Laguna Meándrica Trail,** including **trogons, bellbirds, woodcreepers, hawks, owls,** and a list of others. If you're lucky, you'll be dazzled by the smooth moves of a male **red-capped manakin**—nicknamed the Michael Jackson bird—as it moonwalks along tree branches as part of a mating ritual. Sightings of colorful **scarlet macaws** are most sought after. Hundreds inhabit the area, and several can often be seen flying overhead around the park; sightings are usually at dawn and dusk but are possible throughout the day. All bird sightings vary significantly depending on the time of day and the time of year.

Both **Costa Rica Birding Journeys** (tel. 506/8417-9015, www.costaricabirdingjourneys.org) and **Vic-Tours** (tel. 506/8723-3008, www.victourscostarica.com) are experts at pinpointing when you're most likely to see precise species. Both outfitters coordinate custom park tours that can help you spot the elusive birds you're eager to see. Prices typically begin around $45 per person.

Hiking

Three of the park's trails are accessible beyond the visitors center. A fourth trail is located two kilometers up the road; stop at the visitors center first to pay the entrance fee. The trails here are easy to explore on your own; no reservations are needed.

The first trail beyond the visitors center is the **Universal Access Trail** (1.2-km loop, 30 minutes-1 hour, easy). This paved, flat, and wheelchair-friendly trail provides ample resting stations, water fountains, and a bathroom halfway along the route. Leisurely walkers should give themselves an hour to complete the walk; however, speedier hikers can cover the trail in much less time. There is plenty to see as you meander through the forest, including leaf-cutter ants, iguanas, giant ceiba and espavé trees, and the endemic cafecillo shrub.

The **Quebrada Bonita Trail** (1.5-km loop, 30-45 minutes, easy-moderate) juts off from the Universal Access Trail. **Las Aráceas Trail** (1.2-km loop, 30 minutes, easy-moderate) connects to the Quebrada Bonita. Each of these trails is its own loop and travels over flat land through an area of the forest where small bridges cross gentle streams. If you choose to explore Las Aráceas, backtrack through the Quebrada Bonita and the Universal Access Trail when you wish to leave. (Note that the marked exit signs lead to a point where the park meets the highway. If you follow them, you'll need to walk alongside the high-traffic road to get back to the visitors center and your vehicle.)

Birders in particular love strolling the **Laguna Meándrica Trail** (2 km one-way, 45 minutes, easy-moderate), which originates north of the visitors center. The out-and-back path darts into the protected land area and ends just beyond the large Laguna Meándrica. Part of the trail crosses open areas where there is little cover from the sun. Visit during the early morning when the sun is not directly overhead. You can explore the park's other trails, which are mainly shaded, at midday.

Getting There

From Manuel Antonio, it's a 90-kilometer, 1.5-hour drive along Highway 34 to reach the national park. The park is to the immediate east of the town of Tárcoles. It's a four-kilometer, five-minute drive from Tárcoles to the main entrance of the park.

The well-marked turnoff to the entrance is along Highway 34. There's a large parking lot at the main entrance; a second, smaller lot is at the trailhead for the Laguna Meándrica Trail.

BEACHES

INSIDE MANUEL ANTONIO NATIONAL PARK

Upon buying their ticket ($16 adults, free for seniors and children under 12) and entering the park, many visitors head straight for **Playa Manuel Antonio** to stretch out on its idyllic stretch of supple white sand. Long visits are made easy by nearby bathrooms, showers, picnic tables, and a water station. You'll revel in calm waves, a shallow shoreline, and turquoise waters. Get there by taking El Manglar Trail and keeping straight toward El Perezoso Trail when the trail forks.

If Playa Manuel Antonio is too crowded for you to relax at comfortably, retreat to one of the park's other, equally stunning beaches, including the tiny cove at **Playa Gemelas** to the east of Playa Manuel Antonio, or the long **Playa Espadilla Sur** to the west. Nearly enclosed by forest, Playa Gemelas is two small beaches split by a rocky outcrop; it's one of the quietest, most private beaches in the park. Playa Gemelas Trail leads right to it. Playa Espadilla Sur is a wide, long beach frequented by park visitors who find Playa Manuel Antonio too busy. From the south end of Playa Manuel Antonio, Playa Espadilla Sur Trail provides access to this beach.

PLAYA ESPADILLA NORTE

Manuel Antonio's most visited beach is **Playa Espadilla Norte.** Not to be confused with Playa Espadilla Sur, which is inside Manuel Antonio National Park, Playa Espadilla Norte is the principal beach that spans much of Manuel Antonio up to the boundary of the park. The beach has soft, light brown sand; a shallow shore perfect for strolling along in your flip-flops; and small, crashing waves that are fun to play in. There's a strong undertow, so keep a close eye on young swimmers.

Most visitors congregate at the south end of the beach, where there are restaurants, souvenir shops, and the occasional food cart. Park yourself farther north to avoid crowds or to watch local surfers maneuver the break that fronts the nearby **Playa Playitas,** which is accessible by crossing over the rocks that separate it from Playa Espadilla Norte. You can rent umbrellas from vendors on the beach; however, lush vegetation backs the sand and provides plenty of shade for free. **Mary's Rentals** (Playa Espadilla Norte, tel. 506/8827-5305, 7am-5:30pm daily) rewards customers with free access to parking, lockers, a tented dressing room, and an outdoor shower. In addition to umbrellas (rented together with two chairs and one table for $16 pp), they have surfboards, bodyboards, stand-up paddleboards, kayaks, snorkeling gear, and towels to loan ($4-20 per hour; $12-60 per day).

PLAYA BIESANZ

Manuel Antonio's best-kept secret is out. Tucked away on the north side of Punta Quepos is the white-sand cove known as **Playa Biesanz.** When empty, the small spot is your own private oasis, but it doesn't take much

Playa Espadilla Norte

for the small beach to feel full. The busiest times are from the end of December to the beginning of April and weekends year-round.

This is a great spot for snorkeling right off the beach, as schools of tropical fish frolic in the bay's warm waters. Vendors rent equipment on the beach ($10 per day). The beach is accessed via a short but steep forested trail near the Shana by the Beach hotel.

SAILING

Take to the ocean on a sailboat or catamaran to capture a stunning view of Manuel Antonio. From the water, you'll see luxury resorts adorning lush hills and sandy stretches speckled with beachgoers spanning the coast. Most boat tours sail as far south as the national park, where you can catch a glimpse of **Punta Catedral,** a wide, tall, tree-filled landform edged by a sharp, rocky escarpment that slices into the ocean. The pristine scene is particularly beautiful from the water, where waves crash into rough rock faces, and seabirds soar between the point's treetops and nearby islets.

Planet Dolphin

at Marina Pez Vela, Quepos, tel. 506/2777-1647, www.planetdolphin. com, office 7am-9pm daily, tours 9am and 2pm daily, 3.5-4 hours, $79 adults, $50 children 6-11
The **sailing, snorkeling, and dolphin-watching tour** run by **Planet Dolphin** is one of the most enjoyable experiences I have had in Manuel Antonio. More a relaxing jaunt on the water than a booze cruise (although an open bar is included), the tour provides a leisurely sail along the coast, an opportunity to snorkel and swim at Playa Biesanz, and plenty of chances to see dolphins swimming alongside the boat. If you're lucky, you can spot sea turtles, rays, and whales in the waters too. Although the surrounding scenery is the tour highlight, a close second is the buffet of fish brochettes, pasta salad, and other delights prepared by the crew and served aboard the boat. Planet Dolphin's tour fleet includes two boats that hold 110 passengers and 150 passengers each. A third boat, carrying up to 12 passengers, can be rented for **private charters** ($680-1,620).

SCUBA DIVING AND FREE DIVING

Twelve small islands just off the coast at Manuel Antonio, each one a short boat ride from Quepos, provide nearly 20 dive sites that range in depth from 10 to 20 meters. Dives in these areas showcase volcanic rock formations and marine life that resides around Parque Nacional Manuel Antonio, including large and small species of fish, dolphins, eels, and crustaceans. Less commonly spotted are whitetip reef sharks, sea turtles, and rays. Offshore deep dives, for experienced divers, bottom out at 40 meters where pelagic species are more frequently seen. Water temperatures average between the low 70s and the mid-80s (Fahrenheit).

Visibility varies by season; December through April offers the best visibility (10-20 meters).

Ocean's Unlimited
Marina Pez Vela, Quepos, tel. 506/2519-9544, www.scubadiving costarica.com, 7am-6pm Mon.-Sat., 7am-4pm Sun.

The best dive operator in the area, **Ocean's Unlimited** specializes in **local day dives** (7:30am and 12:30pm daily, 4.5 hours, $109 pp for 2 tanks) but also runs occasional **night dives** (by demand, Dec.-Apr., 2.5 hours, $75 pp for 2 tanks) and **deep dives** (7:30am daily, 6 hours, $109 pp for 2 tanks) for advanced divers. Equipment rental is included with each option. They also offer a plethora of scuba certification courses including the Discover Scuba Diving course, the minimum accreditation you need to dive in Costa Rica.

Rica Freediving
Marina Pez Vela, Quepos, tel. 506/8725-4908, www.ricafreedivers. com

Rica Freediving teaches free diving (aka breath-hold diving) to beginners with a basic free-diving course ($95 pp, min. age 12) and educates avid divers through a PADI-certified free-diving course ($295 pp, min. age 15).

WHITE-WATER RAFTING

The Manuel Antonio area offers two prime rivers for white-water rafting. The Class II and III **Río Savegre** (90-minute drive from downtown Quepos) stuns with clear waters and a jungle-laden backdrop. The Class III and IV **Río Naranjo** (30-minute drive from downtown Quepos) has more thrilling rapid runs, especially if you opt to tour the steep section known as **El Chorro** (Jan.-Apr. only), which features river drops and infamously narrow lines.

H2O Adventures
Road 618, 300 m southeast of the central church, Quepos, tel. 506/2777-4092, www.h2ocr.com, 7am-8pm daily

Amigos del Río
Road 618, 4.5 km north of the national park, tel. 506/2777-0082, www.amigosdelrio.net, 7am-9pm daily

H2O Adventures and **Amigos del Río (ADR)** run trips down the rivers. Choose the outfitter that offers the time that works best with your itinerary. Tour options include:

Savegre River Rafting Tour: 8am daily with H2O Adventures; 7am and 11:30am daily with ADR; 6 hours, $99-105 pp, min. age 6

Naranjo River Rafting Tour: 8am and 11:30am daily with H2O Adventures, min. age 8; 7am and 11:30am daily with ADR, min. age 12; May-Dec., 4-4.5 hours, $77-79 pp

Naranjo River El Chorro Section Rafting Tour: 8am and 12:30pm daily with H2O Adventures, min. age 15; 7am and 11:30am daily with ADR, min. age 12; Jan.-Apr., 4-4.5 hours, $87-99 pp

ZIP-LINING

MIDWORLD COSTA RICA

15.5 km north of Quepos, San Rafael, tel. 506/2777-7181, www.midworld adventures.com, 6:30am-8pm daily

At the theme park **Midworld Costa Rica,** you can participate in a nine-cable **canopy tour** (7:30am, 10am, and 1pm daily, 2.5 hours, $80 pp, min. age 4) or opt for the forward-facing, one-kilometer **superman cable** (7:30am, 10am, and 1pm daily, 1.5 hours, $70 pp, min. age 8). Each experience is sold separately, but the two activities can be combined for $125 per person. Midworld Costa Rica runs their tours on double-cabled lines, an especially safe setup. The theme park is approximately 45 minutes by car from Manuel Antonio.

TITÍ CANOPY TOUR

La Foresta Nature Resort, Hwy. 34, tel. 506/2777-3130, www.titicanopy tour.com, 6:30am-10pm daily

To minimize your drive time from Manuel Antonio, choose the **canopy tour** (7:30am, 11am, and 2:30pm daily, 2.5 hours, $75-80 adults, $65 children 5-11, min. age 5) operated by **Tití Canopy Tour.** The 12-cable experience takes place 10 minutes outside of Quepos and offers an optional **Tarzan swing** at no extra cost. For a unique zip-lining experience and an opportunity to spot wildlife after dark, sign up for the **night canopy tour** (6pm daily, 2.5 hours, $90 pp, min. age 5).

CANYONEERING

AMIGOS DEL RÍO

Road 618, 4.5 km north of the national park, tel. 506/2777-0082, www.amigosdelrio.net, 7am-9pm daily

One of the wildest adventures you can have around Manuel Antonio is **Amigos del Río**'s adrenaline-pumping **10-in-1 Adventure Tour** (7am, 8:30am, and 11am daily, 7 hours, $130 pp, min. age 8). The experience is a mash-up of waterfall and canyon rappels, zip lines, a Tarzan swing, a via ferrata walk (a route with ladders and cables) along a canyon's edge, a caving ladder, and a free fall into a river pool, plus a crazy 4x4 ride over rough terrain to get to the mountain clearing where the adventure begins. The entire ordeal is a thrilling hodgepodge of stunts and challenges.

NIGHTLIFE

Both Quepos and Manuel Antonio have lively nightlife, with a vibrant gay bar scene that is typically welcoming to all. The bar scene in Quepos is clustered together and a bit louder. In contrast, nightlife venues in Manuel Antonio are spread out around the community. Low-key live music nights are held throughout the week at an endless list of comfortable, unpretentious venues. Featured acts and performance times change regularly, so it's best to ask around for the current schedule.

El Patio de Café Milagro
Road 618, 3 km northwest of the entrance to the national park, tel. 506/2777-2272, www.elpatiode cafemilagro.com, 7am-9pm daily
El Patio de Café Milagro is my favorite place to enjoy live music in Manuel Antonio, hosting musicians every night of the week.

Emilio's Café
off Road 618, 50 m south of El Patio de Café Milagro, Manuel Antonio, tel. 506/2777-6807, 7am-9pm Wed.-Mon.
Emilio's Café offers music to accompany soothing views of the water from its position above the treetops.

Barba Roja Restaurante
Road 618, 3 km northwest of the entrance to the national park, tel. 506/2777-0331, www.barbaroja restaurante.com, noon-10pm daily
You'll find occasional live music and sunset views at Barba Roja Restaurante.

Colina's Steak House and Pizza
at La Colina, 4 km northwest of the entrance to the national park, tel.

506/6101-6007, www.restaurant manuelantonio.com, 2pm-10pm daily
Tucked away on the mountainside, the rustic poolside Colina's Steak House and Pizza also offers live music.

Byblos Resort and Casino
Road 618, 3 km northwest of the entrance to the national park, tel. 506/2777-0411, www.bybloshotel costarica.com, 11am-10pm daily
At Byblos Resort and Casino, you'll find several restaurants and bars that encourage you to drink, dance, gamble, and play pool.

Bar Las Gemelas
Road 618, across from Playa Espadilla Norte, Manuel Antonio, tel. 506/2777-5238, 9am-1am daily
At the beachfront hole-in-the-wall Bar Las Gemelas, you can pass the evening while listening to waves roll in.

Karma Lounge
Road 618, 3.5 km northwest of the entrance to the national park, tel. 506/2777-7230, 8pm-2:30am Tues.-Sun.
Karma Lounge, a hip LGBTQ bar, has DJs, dancing, and an outdoor patio.

MoGamBo Bar Café
Road 618, 2 km northwest of the entrance to the national park, tel. 506/7090-0883, 4pm-midnight Sun.-Mon. and Wed., 4pm-1am Thurs.-Sat.
Another LGBT hotspot, MoGamBo Bar Café offers karaoke, cocktail parties, and a great ocean view.

Cuba Libre Restaurant & Bar
Marina Pez Vela, Quepos, tel. 506/2519-9091, https://cubalibre.

cantondequepos.com, 11am-10pm daily

Sip your choice of wine, whiskey, or beer at the upscale, open-air **Cuba Libre Restaurant & Bar.** You can also opt for one of nearly 45 inventive cocktails and shots, enjoyed while overlooking the Pacific Ocean.

Blue Restaurant and Social Lounge

Centro Comercial La Garzam, 2nd floor, Avenida 1, Quepos, tel. 506/8433-6240, 11am-1am Mon.-Sat., 11am-midnight Sun.

The underwater-themed **Blue Restaurant and Social Lounge** is swanky but without attitude. It's a great place to hang out with friends alongside locals doing the same.

Cuban Republik Disco Lounge

Avenida 3, near Calle 4, Quepos, tel. 506/2777-7438, 8pm-4am Tues.-Sun., $4 cover charge Fri.-Sat.

The **Cuban Republik Disco Lounge** is a hazy, neon-lit club that pumps out dance hits well into the morning. Visit after 11pm when the place begins to build its regular late-night crowd.

FOOD

STANDOUTS
El Lagarto

Road 618, 4 km northwest of the entrance to the national park, tel. 506/2777-6932, www.ellagartobbq.com, 3pm-11pm daily, $10-46

El Lagarto is the go-to spot for food prepared *a la parrilla* (on the grill), with barbecued chicken, vegetables, fish, lobster, shrimp, and octopus, plus loads of beef cuts. To produce meals of the highest caliber, El Lagarto sources ingredients from around the country, bringing in

traditional Costa Rican meal of *gallo pinto, plátanos maduros*, cheese, *picadillo,* and a tortilla

MANUEL ANTONIO FOOD

NAME	LOCATION
★ El Lagarto	Road 618, 4 km northwest of the entrance to the national park, Manuel Antonio
★ El Patio de Café Milagro	Road 618, 3 km northwest of the entrance to the national park, Manuel Antonio
★ La Luna	Gaia Hotel and Reserve, off Road 618, Manuel Antonio
★ El Avión	Road 618, 2.5 km northwest of the entrance to the national park, Manuel Antonio
Lugar/Ronny's Place	off Road 618, 750 m south of Amigos del Río, Manuel Antonio
El Gran Escape	corner of Avenida 1 and Calle 4, Quepos
Gabriella's	Marina Pez Vela, Quepos

high-grade beef from plains around the northern inland region, seafood caught off the coast of the Nicoya Peninsula, and vegetables grown in the Central Valley. The restaurant's open design allows you to watch chefs prepare your meal on wood-burning grills.

El Avión

El Patio de Café Milagro
Road 618, 3 km northwest of the entrance to the national park, tel. 506/2777-2272, www.elpatiode cafemilagro.com, 7am-9pm daily, $10-26
Not only does **El Patio de Café Milagro** provide a warm and cozy ambience, but 18 of its menu items cater to vegetarians, and 10 are suitable for vegans. Several accommodate gluten-free diets too. My favorite thing to order for dinner is La Feria, which features quinoa and grilled vegetables purchased fresh from the market. Go for lunch and you can try the mango and chayote salad, with nuts and greens tossed with a passion fruit vinaigrette.

La Luna
Gaia Hotel and Reserve, off Road 618, tel. 506/2777-9797, www.gaiahr. com, 6am-10pm daily, $10-35
The fine-dining restaurant **La Luna** boasts a special menu for vegan and vegetarian customers separate from

CONTACT INFO	FOOD	PRICE
tel. 506/2777-6932, www.ellagartobbq.com	a la parilla (on the grill)	$10-46
tel. 506/2777-2272, www.elpatiodecafemilagro.com	vegetarian and vegan	$10-26
tel. 506/2777-9797, www.gaiahr.com	fine-dining	$10-35
tel. 506/2777-3378, www.elavion.net	international	$7-20
tel. 506/2777-5120, www.ronnysplace.com	Costa Rican	$8-22
tel. 506/2777-7850, www.elgranescapequepos.com	casual international	$7-23
tel. 506/2519-9300, www.gabriellassteakhouse.com	steak and seafood	$19-53

the restaurant's main menu. Ask for it if it isn't automatically given to you by waitstaff. Must-try appetizers include mango tartare with avocado, and grilled vegetables with chia and mustard dressing. The sweet potato cannelloni is my favorite entrée. There's vegan coconut ice cream for dessert.

El Avión
Road 618, 2.5 km northwest of the entrance to the national park, tel. 506/2777-3378, www.elavion.net, noon-11pm daily, $7-20
Regarded by many as Manuel Antonio's must-see restaurant, **El Avión** is built in and around a C-123 Fairchild cargo plane set among the mountains. The two-story dining establishment offers panoramic ocean and forest views that are spectacular at sunset. The menu lists salad, sandwich, seafood, beef, pasta, rice, and plant-based selections, but the novelty of the restaurant's setting is what's most appealing. A small pub occupies the plane's fuselage. Grab a cocktail and take a photo in the cockpit!

LODGING

Manuel Antonio has both mountain hotels and accommodations near the beach. Most of Manuel Antonio's best hotels are away from the water, perched cliffside on quiet, private, and luxurious properties. They require you to drive or take a bus, taxi, or hotel shuttle to the beach, but the travel time is 10 minutes or less.

There's little reason to base yourself in Quepos. Most of its accommodation options are economical hostels and hotels. If you're on a budget, choose an inexpensive accommodation in Manuel Antonio

MANUEL ANTONIO LODGING

NAME	LOCATION
★ Hotel Playa Espadilla	off Road 618, 400 m northwest of the entrance to the national park, Manuel Antonio
★ Si Como No Resort	Road 618, 2.5 km northwest of the entrance to the national park, Manuel Antonio
★ Hotel Naoz	off Road 618, 4 km northwest of the entrance to the national park, Manuel Antonio
Tulemar	Road 618, 3.5 km northwest of the entrances to the national park, Manuel Antonio
La Colina	Road 618, 4 km northwest of the entrance to the national park, Manuel Antonio
Hotel Plaza Yara	Road 618, 5 km northwest of the entrance to the national park, Manuel Antonio

so you don't miss out on the community's unique energy.

STANDOUTS
Hotel Playa Espadilla
off Road 618, 400 m northwest of the entrance to the national park, tel. 506/2777-0903, www.espadilla.com, $203 s/d

Each time I stay at **Hotel Playa Espadilla,** I awake to the calls of howler monkeys in the nearby national park. Location is key at this hotel, which has 16 rooms in two buildings connected by a set of staircases. The spacious rooms are decorated in warm colors and feature cathedral ceilings with dark wood beams; 2nd-floor rooms have balconies. On-site you'll find a restaurant with a bar, pools, and a tennis court. Down the road, sister property Hotel Espadilla Gardens ($187 s/d) is similarly priced, but don't mistake the two; Hotel Playa Espadilla provides the superior stay.

Si Como No Resort
Road 618, 2.5 km northwest of the entrance to the national park, tel. 506/2777-0777, www.sicomono.com, $330 s/d

My favorite upscale resort here is the family-friendly and rainforest-inspired **Si Como No Resort.** The luxury here is understated. You'll notice it in the resort's multitiered design, beautifully landscaped property, colorful stained glass decor, substantial buffet breakfast, and friendly service. Each of the 58 spacious, comfortable rooms is perched on the Manuel Antonio mountainside and offers a private balcony where you can enjoy jungle or ocean views. There are no televisions around to distract you, and the resort's pools, bars, restaurants, and spa will spoil you. Best of all, the eco-conscious resort, which sparked the development of sustainable hotels in Costa Rica when it opened in 1992, adheres to a long list of sustainable practices and is active

CONTACT INFO	OPTIONS	PRICE
tel. 506/2777-0903, www.espadilla.com	hotel rooms	$203 s/d
tel. 506/2777-0777, www.sicomono.com	resort rooms	$330 s/d
tel. 506/2777-6269, www.hotelnaoz.com	hotel rooms	$170 s/d
tel. 506/4001-5878, www.tulemar.com	octagonal bungalows	$298 s/d
tel. 506/6101-6007, www.lacolina.com	hotel rooms	$85 s/d
tel. 506/2777-4846, www.hotelplazayara.com	suites with kitchenettes	$160 s/d

in protecting Manuel Antonio's land and wildlife. One such effort is the resort-managed, off-site **Greentique Wildlife Refuge** (Refugio de Vida Silvestre Greentique, 100 m west of Si Como No Resort, tel. 506/2777-0850, 8am-4pm daily), which houses a butterfly atrium, among other nature exhibits, that resort guests can visit for free.

Hotel Naoz
off Road 618, 4 km northwest of the entrance to the national park, tel. 506/2777-6269, www.hotelnaoz. com, $170 s/d
The stylishly luxurious and surprisingly affordable **Hotel Naoz** is easy to love. All 17 spacious, spotless rooms (which sleep 1-4 people) in the three-story

boutique hotel treat guests to soft beds, air-conditioning and air purification systems, flatscreen televisions, and posh bathrooms. A courtyard encircled by beautiful tropical gardens provides an intimate space to soak in a heated pool, lay out on a lounge chair under an umbrella, or sip a drink from the poolside bar. Breakfast is complimentary.

view from the Si Como No Resort

INFORMATION AND SERVICES

On the outskirts of Quepos is **Hospital Max Terán Valls** (Hwy. 34, 650 m northwest of the Quepos airport, tel. 506/2774-9500, 24 hours daily), the hospital that serves much of the central Pacific coast.

In town, Marina Pez Vela has a **police station** (Quepos, tel. 506/2777-7140, 24 hours daily) and a **clinic,** called **Hospital Metropolitano** (tel. 506/2519-9733, 9am-6pm Mon.-Fri., 9am-noon Sat.), with a **pharmacy.**

The downtown core has several **banks** and **supermarkets.** The **post office** (tel. 506/2643-2175, Quepos, 8:30am-5pm Mon.-Fri.) is on the north side of the *fútbol* field.

In Manuel Antonio, there are **supermarkets, pharmacies,** and **banks.** You'll find them along Road 618. You can have your clothes washed at **Lavandería Lucimaria** (Road 618 beside Amigos del Río, Manuel Antonio, tel. 506/8492-2233, 8am-9pm daily). However, many hotels in the vicinity offer laundry services to guests.

There is a **gas station** (1 km north of the airport) just east of Quepos where Highway 34, Road 235, and Road 616 meet. There's also a gas station to the north of town, on Highway 34, 2.5 kilometers before the turnoff to Quepos at Road 235.

TRANSPORTATION AND TOURS

Getting There

Air

The **Aeropuerto Quepos** (XQP) is five kilometers (a 10-minute drive) northeast of downtown Quepos. **SANSA Airlines** (tel. 506/2290-4100, www.flysansa.com) offers direct flights to Quepos from San José daily. The flight time from San José is approximately 30 minutes.

Taxis operated by the **Manuel Antonio Taxi Service** (tel. 506/2777-3080, 24 hours daily) can be called to the airport to take you wherever you need to go. Expect to pay $20-25 for a ride to most hotels around Manuel Antonio. Alternatively, **Blue Horizon Costa Rica** (Road 235, 1 km north of Marina Pez Vela, tel. 506/2277-9292, www.bluehorizoncostarica.com) can transport you between the airport and your Manuel Antonio hotel in one of their air-conditioned minibuses ($30 for up to 5 people).

Car

To get to Quepos and Manuel Antonio from **San José,** it's a 170-kilometer drive west on Highway 27, then south on Highway 34 and Road 235; the trip takes nearly three hours. From **Liberia,** it's a 255-kilometer drive south on Highway 1, Highway 23, Highway 27, Highway 34, and Road 235 that takes a little less than four hours. From **La Fortuna,** it's a 245-kilometer drive south on Road 702, Highway 1, Highway 23, Highway 27, Highway

34, and Road 235 that takes almost five hours. From **Monteverde**, it's a 190-kilometer, 3.5-hour drive southeast on Road 606, Highway 1, Highway 23, Highway 27, Highway 34, and Road 235.

Bus

The **regional bus station** is in the heart of Quepos on Avenida Central between Calle Central and Calle 2. Public **buses** travel to Quepos daily. You can catch one from **San José** (multiple times 6am-7:30pm daily, 3.5 hours, $8-8.5), **Dominical** (multiple times 6:30am-7:30pm daily, 1.5-2 hours, $3), and **Uvita** (5:30am, 11:30am, 1pm, and 4pm daily, 2 hours, $3-3.50).

Private Transfer Service

Desafio Adventure Company (tel. 506/2479-0020, www.desafiocostarica.com) offers private transfer services to Quepos and Manuel Antonio with free Wi-Fi on board their vehicles. Prices average around $213 from San José, $192 from La Fortuna, and $180 from Monteverde.

Shared Shuttle Service

Interbus (tel. 506/4100-0888, www.interbusonline.com) offers daily shared shuttle services to Quepos and Manuel Antonio from San José, La Fortuna, Monteverde, Montezuma, Santa Teresa, and Malpaís. **Grayline Costa Rica** (tel. 506/2220-2126, www.graylinecostarica.com) travels to Quepos and Manuel Antonio from San José, Dominical, Uvita, La Fortuna, Monteverde, Tamarindo, Brasilito, and Playa Flamingo. One-way services cost $42-91 per person. Most shuttles offer drop-offs at Quepos and Manuel Antonio hotels.

Organized Tour

A few adventure tours by **Desafio Adventure Company** (tel. 506/2479-0020, www.desafiocostarica.com) include **post-tour onward transportation** to Quepos. White-water rafting tours ($129 pp) can be arranged to include a pickup from your hotel in La Fortuna, then a drop-off at your hotel in Manuel Antonio.

Getting Around

The paved Road 618 that connect Quepos and Manuel Antonio has inclines, declines, curves, and barely any sidewalks. The safest way to travel this stretch is in a vehicle. Walking, biking, or relying on scooters or golf carts is not recommended.

Car and Taxi

Driving around Quepos and Manuel Antonio does not require a 4x4 vehicle. Quepos has a few one-way streets; traffic flows west on **Avenida 5** at the north end of town and traffic flows east on **Avenida 2** at the south end of town. **Road 618,** known as Avenida 2 in Quepos, is a two-way street. It goes through Manuel Antonio and ends at a roundabout in front of the beach.

Bus

Public **buses** (multiple times 5:45am-10pm daily, 25 minutes, $1) travel from Quepos to Playa Espadilla Norte and the national park (and vice versa), passing through Manuel Antonio along the way.

COSTA BALLENA

South of Quepos and Manuel Antonio, the highway meets the water at the lackadaisical and popular surf town of Dominical, continues down the coast to the village of Uvita—home to Marino Ballena National Park—and then bypasses Ojochal, a small collection of upscale establishments. Together, this trio of destinations forms the Costa Ballena, spanning roughly 35 kilometers of coastline. Though hopping between destinations along the Costa Ballena is easy, most visitors base themselves in one area, typically Dominical or Uvita, and make day trips to area attractions.

Dominical is a small, noncommercial surf town and the most popular of the three destinations along the Costa Ballena. From the moment you turn off the highway onto the main dirt road, you'll feel like you've entered a local community, not a tourist trap—except for the row of vendors who display souvenirs on tables near the waterfront. Backpackers and young travelers station themselves here to soak up the sun, socialize, and laze around like sloths.

Located 16 kilometers southeast of Dominical is the blossoming village of Uvita. Uvita is home to a small, tight-knit, and vibrant community composed of locals and expats that gives off a warm and welcoming vibe. It is marked by plazas, restaurants, and hotels around Highway 34. The protected beaches and waters contained within Parque Nacional Marino Ballena draw in most visitors. Bordering Uvita to the south is a neighborhood known as **Bahía** (sometimes called **Bahía Ballena**). You'll find most of Uvita's tour outfitters here, as well as the area's most inexpensive digs and diners. The national park, which sits on the

view of the Costa Ballena at Uvita

COSTA BALLENA

To San Isidro
de El General

To Quepos

Barú

Platanillo

NAUYACA
WATERFALLS

Playa
Barú

Dominical

Playa
Dominical

SEE DETAIL

Fila Cariblanco

Punta
Dominical

PACIFIC
OCEAN

0   2 mi
0   2 km

© MOON.COM

Río Barú

CAFÉ
MONO CONGO

FUEGO BREW
COMPANY

SESAME ST

MAIN ST

PINEAPPLE
TOURS

CAFE
ENSUEÑO

Playa
Dominical

MAIN ST

south side of Bahía, is roughly two kilometers southwest of Uvita.

The southernmost destination on the Costa Ballena is the quiet community of Ojochal. A tight-knit mix of locals and expats inhabits the town, which is spread out in the mountains just north of Highway 34. Many first-time visitors are surprised by Ojochal's greatest contribution to the central Pacific coast: top-notch international cuisine. A cluster of small and casual but polished and revered restaurants puts this remote destination, known as the culinary capital of Costa Rica, on the map.

Nauyaca Waterfalls

HIGHLIGHTS

★ NAUYACA WATERFALLS

Road 243, 10 km north of Domini-cal, tel. 506/2787-0541, www. nauyacawaterfallscostarica.com, 7am-5pm Mon.-Sat., 8am-4pm Sun., last entry 2pm

North of Dominical, the two-tier, 65-meter **Nauyaca Waterfalls** (Cataratas Nauyaca) are some of Costa Rica's most stunning cascades. Tucked among dense rainforest and scenic rolling hills, the two remote waterfalls are especially beautiful to behold as the upper cascade flows freely into the lower. The taller **upper waterfall** is flanked on both sides by craggy canyon walls. Giant boulders at its base add to the dramatic scene. Water flows from here to the **lower waterfall,** where it tumbles into a nat-ural pool that's great for swimming. At this cascade's base, you'll find a quiet, peaceful space, fresh water, bright green flora, and few distractions.

The falls are on the private property of Don Lulo, who grants **hiking access** (trail access fee $10), runs **4x4 trans-portation** to the falls (7am, 8am, 9am, 10am, 11am, and noon Mon.-Sat., $32 pp), and offers guided **waterfall tours** (8am Mon.-Sat., 5.5 hours, $85 pp) and **horseback tours** (8am Mon.-Sat., 5.5 hours, $85 pp, min. age 3).

The guided tours include a light breakfast, lunch, the trail access fee, and transportation to the falls. There's also plenty of time for swim-ming once you reach the falls. Your guide will show you how and where to safely climb and jump off the rocks into the cascade's refreshing pool.

If you choose to hike, be prepared for a long walk. If you don't have a 4x4 vehicle, you'll be hiking six kilo-meters out to the falls from the office where the trail access fee is paid and another six back. If you do have a 4x4, the falls are just four kilometers each way from the parking lot, which is two kilometers down the road from the office. Parking costs $3. The chal-lenging trail is steep and rolling. Be sure to bring sturdy footwear; the dusty route gets muddy and slippery when it rains.

For those who don't want the full tour experience but also don't want to walk a long way, there is another choice. Referred to on Don Lulo's website as the Economic 4x4 Tour, this option is a transportation service rather than a tour. At the appointed time, you'll hop in the back of a 4x4 vehicle that will drive you to the falls. Note: Vehicle seats are limited, and preference is given to guided tour participants.

For your safety, **waterfall jump-ing** is only permitted when a tour guide is present at the falls (typically 10am-11am Mon.-Sat.). If you're a self-guided visitor and you wish to jump off the rocks that edge the falls, schedule your visit accordingly. There are no guided tours offered on Sundays; only self-guided tours are available.

To get to Don Lulo's property from Dominical, take Road 243 northeast for about 10 kilometers. You'll find a small office, well signed for the waterfalls, on the east side of the highway.

MARINO BALLENA NATIONAL PARK

1.5 km southwest of Hwy. 34, Bahía, tel. 506/8946-7134, www.sinac.go.cr, 8am-4pm Wed.-Mon., $6 pp 11 years and older

The beach-filled **Marino Ballena National Park** (Parque Nacional Marino Ballena) is home to countless marine animals and plants, including dolphins, sea turtles, octopuses, crabs, sharks, sponges, and mollusks. Coral reef and mangrove ecosystems are protected by the park, which spans 15 kilometers of coastline from Uvita south to Punta Piñuela on the outskirts of Ojochal. At this mating site for **humpback whales** (*ballena* means "whale"), it is not uncommon to see pods of the giant mammals breaching offshore, especially from December to March, when whales migrate from the north, or from July to October, when whales migrate from the south.

Four **ranger stations** scattered along Highway 34 provide access to the park's coastal areas. Most visitors come through the **Bahía entrance ranger station,** in the southwest corner of Bahía at the end of the main street that leads through the community from Highway 34. The Bahía entrance is the closest to the park's most visited beach, Playa Uvita, and the whale-tail sandbar.

Bahía Aventuras

beside the school, Bahía, tel. 506/2743-8362, www.bahia aventuras.com, 6:30am-8:30pm daily

Local outfitter **Bahía Aventuras** leads water-based adventures in the park from the Uvita area. They dominate tourism in the region with their friendly guides, knowledge of the Costa Ballena, and stellar service. The **snorkeling tour** (Dec.-Apr., 2.5 hours, $75 adults, $35 children 3-9, min. age 3) provides an opportunity to spot several species of fish, including colorful parrotfish, funny-looking pufferfish, and even big fish varieties like marlin. During the **kayaking tour** (3-4 hours, $78 adults, $38 children 6-10, min. age 6), you may see bottlenose dolphins, spinner dolphins, and spotted dolphins playing in the waves. Most sought after is the **whale- and dolphin-watching boat tour** (8:30am and 1pm daily, 3.5-4 hours, $70-85 adults, $40-45 children 3-10, min. age 3), offering an opportunity to spot a breaching humpback whale or, less likely, an orca. All three experiences include the park entrance fee. The times for the snorkeling and kayaking tours are tide dependent.

CAVES
Beach Cave at Playa Ventanas

The coolest thing to see in Ojochal is the **natural beach cave** at the pretty, light gray **Playa Ventanas.** If you visit at low tide, you'll find a narrow passageway that cuts through the craggy rock face, separating the

Marino Ballena National Park

ocean from the beach. The cave's two entrances (or "windows") are large enough to walk through, but stay mindful of the tide. Water levels rise quickly and eventually engulf the tunnel with raging waves. The sight is neat to see from the outside, especially when the cave acts like a blowhole and spits out a powerful mist. Do not get caught in the middle at high tide.

Additional caves are accessible to kayakers. The seasonal **Ventanas Cave Ocean Kayak Tour** run by Dominical's **Pineapple Tours** (beside the police station, Dominical, tel. 506/8873-3283, www.pineapple kayaktours.com, 9am-5pm daily, tour times tide-dependent, Dec.-Aug., 4 hours, $75 pp, min. age 15) paddles through the offshore caves, ocean conditions permitting. This tour is for experienced kayakers only.

Cave Camping at Diamante Waterfall

One of the most extraordinary overnight experiences you can have in Costa Rica is **cave camping** at **Diamante Waterfall,** immediately east of Dominical. **Pacific Journeys** (2.5 km south of Road 243, Tinamaste, tel. 506/2266-1717, www.pacific journeyscr.com, 8am-5pm Mon.-Fri., $159 adults, $80 children 0-6) guides you on this two-day adventure that features a challenging hike (3 km

beach cave at Playa Ventanas

one-way) to the 183-meter waterfall's highest point and an overnight stay in an open-air rock crevice—nicknamed Casa de Piedra, the Rock House—at the side of the cascade. Also included are exploration of an organic garden and three healthy vegetarian meals. Nature doesn't get any closer; you'll fall asleep to the sound of the water's soothing thunder while tucked away in a natural stone cave under a starry sky. For your convenience and comfort, the cave (which sleeps up to 25 people) is equipped with toilets, showers, and raised platform beds. Sleeping bags, pads, liners, and pillows are provided. You can even add rappelling down the waterfall ($70 pp) to your once-in-a-lifetime stay.

BEACHES

You don't need a tour guide to enjoy the beaches in the park. Pack plenty of sunscreen because the unshaded beaches are piping hot. Hold on to your ticket; you can use it to enter any of the ranger stations over the course of the day.

PLAYA UVITA

Wide, sun-soaked, and bare, **Playa Uvita** is four kilometers from its eastern end to its western tip, where you will find its intriguing natural feature: a **whale-tail-shaped sandbar**

COSTA BALLENA FOOD

NAME	LOCATION
★ Café Mono Congo	Main St., 100 m west of Hwy. 34, Dominical
★ Fuego Brew Company	Sesame St., Dominical
★ Los Laureles Restaurant	400 m northeast of Hwy. 34, Uvita
★ Exotica	main street in Ojochal, 1 km northeast of Hwy. 34
★ Citrus	200 m east of Hwy. 34, Ojochal
★ Kua Kua Restaurant	Three Sixty Boutique Hotel, Ojochal
Café Ensueño	75 m north of the main street in Dominical, beside the Cool Vibes Beach Hostel

that extends one kilometer into the Pacific Ocean, with its stretch of sand running perpendicular to the shore. It's referred to by Ticos as **Paso de Moisés** (Moses's Step). Stroll out to the end for a surreal experience. When you've gone as far as you can, turn around and take in the view: You're almost surrounded by water. You'll see layer upon layer of mountains that gleam in multiple shades of green, plus waves that roll in to your left and to your right. For the best experience, visit the beach at low tide; the sandbar disappears into the ocean at other times of day.

Access is via the park's main entrance at Bahía. A short two-minute walk on an unnamed, 50-meter trail departs from the entrance and leads through forest. Where the trail ends at the sand is the beach's midpoint, which also represents the divide between Playa Uvita and the eastern half of the beach, which locals call **Playa Colonia.**

PLAYA DOMINICAL

Dominical's principal beach is **Playa Dominical.** From Rio Barú in the north, the beach fronts the entire town for one kilometer, then continues south for another kilometer along undeveloped coastline. Most of the beach's visitors come to surf, so they don't mind that the dark gray sand is often awash with debris and not ideal for sunbathing. And, of course, where there's great surf, swimming conditions are usually dangerous. Watch yourself in the water here, as riptides reign supreme.

CONTACT INFO	FOOD	PRICE
tel. 506/6312-8766, www. cafemonocongo.com	café with vegetarian and vegan options	$3-10
tel. 506/8373-0635, www.fuegobrew.com	brewpub	$9-24
tel. 506/2743-8008	pub grub	$7-13
tel. 506/2786-5050, www.restoexotica. wordpress.com	international	$11-36
tel. 506/2786-5175, www. citrusrestaurante.com	French-inspired international	$15-26
tel. 506/2100-9206, www. hotelthreesixty.com	international	$15-21
tel. 506/2787-0282	Costa Rican	$4-8

FOOD

The food in Ojochal is a delight, both in quality and variety. Here, you can get first-class food—Costa Rican favorites, international specialties, and fusion cuisine—skillfully prepared and beautifully presented. If you're stationed in Ojochal, you'll love having a few great restaurants nearby, but even if you plan to stay elsewhere along the central Pacific coast, Ojochal is worth a road trip for lunch or dinner. To enjoy a gourmet meal in the community is to literally taste the destination's leading contribution to the region, a rich culinary experience that shouldn't be missed. Prices are comparable to standard entrées served in popular tourist towns around the country. Reservations for all restaurants are recommended.

STANDOUTS
Café Mono Congo
Main St., 100 m west of Hwy. 34, Dominical, tel. 506/6312-8766, www. cafemonocongo.com, 7am-5pm daily, $3-10

Start the day off right with one of several sweet and savory breakfast options—many vegetarian and vegan—at **Café Mono Congo.** Wash it down with coffee, tea, kombucha, cold-pressed juice, gingerade, or a smoothie, such as my preferred drink, the Banana-Espresso Wake Up, a blend of coffee, banana, and cacao. To satisfy midday hunger, you cannot go wrong with a fresh wrap or burrito with a fruit-topped smoothie bowl or gluten-free chocolate brownie for dessert. Built on the southern bank of Rio Barú, the café has a river view that is almost as delightful as the staff is friendly.

COSTA BALLENA LODGING

NAME	LOCATION
★ Vista Ballena	1.5 km north of Hwy. 34, 2 km north of Uvita
★ La Cusinga Lodge	450 m west of Hwy. 34, 4.5 km south of Uvita
MAVI Surf Hotel	200 m north of the main street in Dominical, up the road from Cafe Ensueño

Fuego Brew Company

Sesame St., Dominical, tel. 506/8373-0635, www.fuegobrew. com, 11:30am-10:30pm daily, $9-24

Dinner and drinks are great at the two-story, al fresco, treehouse-like **Fuego Brew Company.** Draped in a mix of bohemian and beer-themed decor, the upscale restaurant and bar stays true to Dominical's vibe while bringing a touch of class. The place serves more appetizers than entrées, likely so you'll have room to down glasses of their nine kinds of craft beer. The brewery and taproom are on the bottom floor; the restaurant and bar are on the top.

Los Laureles Restaurant

400 m northeast of Hwy. 34, Uvita, tel. 506/2743-8008, 11:30am-8:30pm Mon.-Sat., $7-13

You can grab pub grub like quesadillas, wraps, nachos, tacos, wings, chili fries, and more at the casual and homey **Los Laureles Restaurant.** Surrounded by natural flora, this small, open-air restaurant has a few tables scattered under a wood roof with fans. It's clean and well-kept, and run by a hospitable and appreciative family who provides great customer service.

Exotica

main street in Ojochal, 1 km northeast of Hwy. 34, tel. 506/2786-5050, www.restoexotica.wordpress.com, 5pm-10pm Mon.-Sat., $11-36

There are too many great choices in Ojochal to name them all, but at the top of the list is **Exotica.** Softly lit with candles and lanterns, the intimate spot is perfect for a date night. Beef, chicken, and fish orders surpass the ordinary and feature flavors and cooking styles from countries around the world. Even the cocktails are a step up from most. Don't leave without indulging in the restaurant's sweet and slightly spicy chocolate cake, the Devil's Fork.

Citrus

200 m east of Hwy. 34, Ojochal, tel. 506/2786-5175, www.citrus restaurante.com, noon-9pm Mon.-Fri., $15-26

People gush over **Citrus,** which serves high-quality dishes from a menu that is French-inspired but spans a variety of international cuisines. The restaurant offers a fine-dining experience in a quaint and sophisticated courtyard with a laid-back, family-friendly vibe. The unique and eclectic decor includes funky artwork, a quirky chandelier, pendant lights, and banquette seating.

Kua Kua Restaurant

Three Sixty Boutique Hotel, Ojochal, tel. 506/2100-9206, www.

CONTACT INFO	OPTIONS	PRICE
tel. 506/2743-8150, www.vistaballenahotel.com	hotel rooms in three buildings	$179 s/d
tel. 506/2770-2549, www.lacusingalodge.com	rustic cabins	$229 s/d
tel. 506/2787-0429, www.mavi-surf.com	motel rooms	$135 s/d

hotelthreesixty.com, noon-9pm by reservation only, $15-21

The **Kua Kua Restaurant** is one of the newest restaurants to augment Ojochal's gastronomic scene. The small menu offers a few fresh lunch options, 13 exquisite dinner entrées, several tasty tapas, and delectable desserts like sugary homemade churros. The superior-quality food is matched by an excellent view. Visit during the day or just before sunset so you can take in the sight of an endless ocean and a lush rainforest canopy while dining on the open-air patio perched on the side of a mountain. The restaurant is best reached in a 4x4 vehicle.

LODGING

STANDOUTS
Vista Ballena
1.5 km north of Hwy. 34, 2 km north of Uvita, tel. 506/2743-8150, www.vistaballenahotel.com, $179 s/d

What's most impressive about **Vista Ballena** is its panoramic view. From high up in the quiet and remote hills north of Uvita, this hotel overlooks the Pacific Ocean, the national park, and the famed whale-tail sandbar from each of its 20 rooms. The hotel is three separate buildings spread vertically on a hillside. The top building provides a reception, restaurant, and lounge area complete with a two-tier infinity pool. In the bottom two buildings are fresh and modern rooms (for 1-4 people) with rich, dark-wood furniture, air-conditioning, television, and a balcony with an outdoor sitting area perfect for taking in the view.

La Cusinga Lodge
450 m west of Hwy. 34, 4.5 km south of Uvita, tel. 506/2770-2549, www.lacusingalodge.com, $229 s/d

With some downtime in Uvita, you can easily pass a day in a rocking chair on the open-air deck at **La Cusinga Lodge,** gazing at the forest and the sea. The tranquil ecolodge encourages relaxation at its yoga pavilion, restaurant, and lounge area, and invites exploration of nature through on-site trails. Ten simple, rustic, all-wood cabins aim to bring the outdoors in and unite with the jungle, not overpower it.

INFORMATION AND SERVICES

Hospital Max Terán Valls (Hwy. 34, 650 m northwest of the Quepos airport, tel. 506/2774-9500, 24 hours daily) serves most of the central Pacific coast's communities. It's in Quepos, a 40-kilometer drive northwest of Dominical. The closest hospital to the south is **Hospital de Osa Tomás Casas Casajús** (Hwy. 34, just west of Ciudad Cortés, tel. 506/2786-8148, 24 hours daily) in Ciudad Cortés, a 30-kilometer drive southeast of Uvita.

Banco de Costa Rica (Centro Comercial Plaza Pacifica, Hwy. 34, tel. 506/2442-7700, 9am-4pm Mon.-Fri.) has an **ATM** (5am-midnight daily). It's on Highway 34, just east of the turnoff to Dominical. On Dominical's main road are a few **supermarkets** and a **police station** (tel. 506/2787-0406, 24 hours daily).

Uvita also has a **police station** (off Calle Uvita, 700 m northeast of Hwy. 34, tel. 506/2743-8538, 24 hours daily). Nearby is the community's **clinic, Ebais Uvita** (Calle Uvita, 75 m northeast of Hwy. 34, tel. 506/2743-8170, 7am-4pm Mon.-Thurs., 7am-3pm Fri.).

A few **pharmacies,** including **Farmacia Ibarra** (tel. 506/2743-8460, 8am-7pm Mon.-Sat.), **banks,** and **supermarkets** huddle around the entrance to Uvita on Highway 34 near Río Uvita. Additional supermarkets can be found in Bahía.

The closest **gas station** to Dominical is three kilometers northwest of town on Highway 34. There is also a gas station near Uvita. It's on Highway 34, northwest of Río Uvita and the turnoff to the beach.

TRANSPORTATION AND TOURS

Getting There

Car

There are two ways to get to Dominical from downtown **San José.** The easiest and fastest trip parallels the coast on Highway 34 and enters Dominical from the northwest. This **coastal route** is a 210-kilometer drive via Highway 27 and Highway 34 that takes a little over three hours. The alternate trip departs east from San José via Highway 2, climbing steeply over mountains and cutting through clouds at Cerro de la Muerte

(Hill of Death). It then descends through the city of San Isidro de El General and enters Dominical via Road 243 from the northeast. This **mountain route** is a 170-kilometer, 3.5-hour drive—though it takes longer when cloud cover slows traffic.

From downtown **Liberia,** Dominical is a 295-kilometer drive via Highway 1, Highway 23, Highway 27, and Highway 34 that takes just over four hours. From **Uvita,** it's an 18-kilometer, 15-minute drive northwest on Highway 34. From **Quepos,** Dominical is a 40-kilometer, 30-minute drive north on Road 235 and southeast on Highway 34.

From **Dominical,** it's an 18-kilometer, 15-minute drive down the coast to reach **Uvita. Ojochal** is a 16-kilometer, 15-minute drive from Uvita and a 35-kilometer, 30-minute drive from Dominical, all via Highway 34.

Bus

To reach Dominical or Uvita by **bus,** catch one from **San José** (6am and 3pm daily, 5-5.5 hours, $8-9.50) or **Quepos** (multiple times 5:30am-5:30pm daily, 1-2 hours, $3). You can also travel between Dominical and Uvita by bus (multiple times 4:45am-7pm daily, 20 minutes, $1.50-2.50). Buses end their run in Dominical next to the office for the Instituto Costarricense de Electricidad, the government-run electrical company. In Uvita, they drop off passengers alongside Highway 34, 100 meters east of the turn-off to town.

Private Transfer and Shared Shuttle Services

Desafio Adventure Company (tel. 506/2479-0020, www.desafiocostarica.com) offers **private transfer services** to Dominical with free Wi-Fi on board their vehicles. Prices average around $246 from San José, $129 from Quepos and Manuel Antonio, $308 from La Fortuna, and $277 from Monteverde.

Grayline Costa Rica (tel. 506/2220-2126, www.graylinecostarica.com) offers daily **shared shuttle services** to Dominical and Uvita from San José, Manuel Antonio, La Fortuna, Monteverde, Tamarindo, Brasilito, and Playa Flamingo. One-way services range $47-98 per person. Most shuttles offer drop-offs at Dominical, Uvita, and Bahía hotels.

the black sand beach of Bahía Drake

BAHÍA DRAKE

Costa Rica is known for its biodiversity, and no region provides such a concentrated dose as the Osa Peninsula. Way down in the southern part of the country, amid pristine primary and secondary forest, silent mountains, and unfrequented coastline, is a rugged wilderness. Wildlife and marine life, including many of the country's rarest species, are all around: along the tucked-away trails that lead through protected land areas, around the trees that tower over restaurant tables, and in the waters of the ocean. A kaleidoscope of ecosystems decorates the landscape and invites up-close exploration.

Bahía Drake (Drake Bay), in the northwest corner of the Osa Peninsula, is the most visited area in the region, but you won't feel like you've stationed yourself in an overly popular place when you visit. Development, in the form of low-key establishments and rustic all-inclusive ecolodges, is spread out along 25 kilometers of coastline. This area offers seclusion and sublime privacy. Get a feel for the area by visiting the rainforest-backed Bahía Drake, exploring underwater at the Isla del Caño Biological Reserve, and trekking through Corcovado National Park.

coast of Isla del Caño

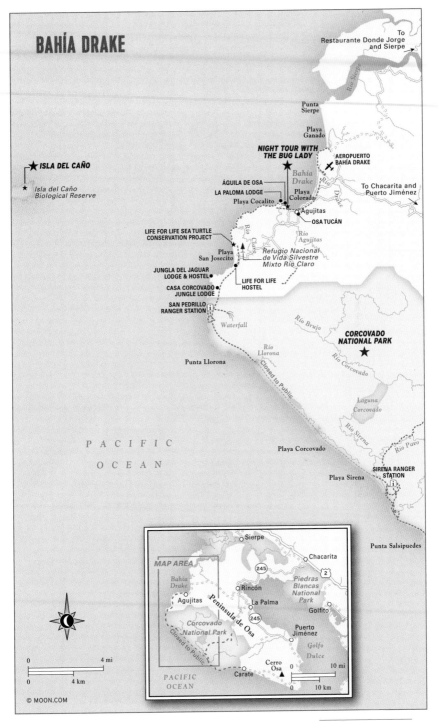

BAHÍA DRAKE

To Restaurante Donde Jorge and Sierpe

Punta Sierpe

Playa Ganado

ISLA DEL CAÑO

Isla del Caño Biological Reserve

NIGHT TOUR WITH THE BUG LADY

Bahía Drake

AEROPUERTO BAHÍA DRAKE

To Chacarita and Puerto Jiménez

ÁGUILA DE OSA
LA PALOMA LODGE
Playa Cocalito
Playa Colorada
Agujitas
OSA TUCÁN

LIFE FOR LIFE SEA TURTLE CONSERVATION PROJECT

Río Agujitas

Río Claro

Playa San Josecito

Refugio Nacional de Vida Silvestre Mixto Río Claro

JUNGLA DEL JAGUAR LODGE & HOSTEL

LIFE FOR LIFE HOSTEL

CASA CORCOVADO JUNGLE LODGE

SAN PEDRILLO RANGER STATION

Waterfall

Río Brujo

CORCOVADO NATIONAL PARK

Río Corcovado

Punta Llorona

Río Llorona

Laguna Corcovado

Closed to Public

PACIFIC OCEAN

Playa Corcovado

Río Sirena

Río Pavo

SIRENA RANGER STATION

Playa Sirena

Punta Salsipuedes

Sierpe

Chacarita

245

2

MAP AREA

Bahía Drake

Rincón

Piedras Blancas National Park

Agujitas

La Palma

Golfito

Península de Osa

Puerto Jiménez

Corcovado National Park

Golfo Dulce

245

Closed to Public

Cerro Osa

PACIFIC OCEAN

Carate

0   4 mi

0   4 km

0   10 mi

0   10 km

© MOON.COM

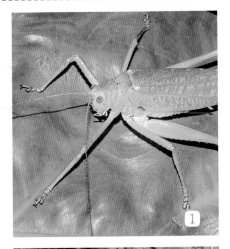

TOP 3

⭐ **1. NIGHT TOUR WITH THE BUG LADY:** Search for creepy-crawlies after dark (page 227).

⭐ **2. SNORKEL OR DIVE AT ISLA DEL CAÑO:** There's a good chance you'll spot sea turtles, dolphins, and maybe even sharks (page 227).

⭐ **3. HIKE IN CORCOVADO NATIONAL PARK:** On a wilderness expedition into Costa Rica's wildest park, you may encounter some of the rarest wildlife species in the country—and the world (page 228).

BEST 5 DAYS IN BAHÍA DRAKE

DAY 1

Embark on a **3-day hiking expedition** to remote, biodiverse **Corcovado National Park.** Boat transportation and some meals are included with the experience. A trained tour guide will accompany you on each hike.

In the early morning, ride the tour boat that travels from Bahía Drake to the park's **Sirena Sector,** then check in at the **Sirena ranger station** in the heart of the park, where you'll sleep over the next two nights. Spend the late morning and the afternoon traversing **nature trails** to spot birds and other wildlife.

DAY 2

Wake up before sunrise for the 5am **guided hike** to see and hear the park transition from night to day. Dedicate the rest of the day to hiking less trodden nature trails that weave through the park's interior and the natural habitats of rare wildlife, including **jungle cats** and **tapirs.**

DAY 3

In the morning, take one last **hike** in the park. Snap photographs of the park's **abundant flora and fauna** before returning to the ranger station and checking out midday. Return via tour boat to Bahía Drake and spend the rest of the day relaxing.

DAY 4

Set out on a full-day **snorkeling** or **diving** excursion to the **Isla del Caño Biological Reserve,** a protected island encircled by abundant marine life. Keep an eye out for breaching **whales** during the boat trip to the island. Once you arrive, you'll search for colorful **fish, turtles, rays,** and **sharks** at notable dive sites. Lunch is included with the tour.

DAY 5

Take the day to explore the **Sendero Costero** (Coastal Trail) south of Bahía Drake at your own pace, stopping to swim or relax at **Playa Cocalito** along the way. Walk farther to see **Playa San Josecito,** considered the prettiest beach in the area. Return to Bahía Drake before nightfall so you can shift your focus to nocturnal wildlife with the help of the **Bug Lady** on her guided **Night Tour.**

Corcovado National Park

PLANNING YOUR TIME

Best Bases

Many hotels and resorts along the coast southwest of Bahía Drake include room and board, making them ideal home bases. (The village of Agujitas is only reachable via a hike or boat ride from most accommodations, so it's possible you'll never set foot in the village.) Tour operators typically provide pickups (usually by boat), so you can access the region's top attractions from your accommodation with ease.

It's less common to stay directly in Agujitas. If you do, consider the village your home base, and expect complimentary tour transportation to be provided to and from Playa Colorada.

Weather

December to April is considered the dry season and May to November the wet season. Annual rainfall amounts in the region are high, so it's more accurate to describe these periods as the sunny-with-sporadic-rain season and the soaked season. Temperatures average 75-79°F. Humid, densely forested areas can feel like saunas.

Connect with...

To minimize lengthy cross-country travel, combine your visit to Bahía Drake with time spent just up the coast in the Manuel Antonio and Costa Ballena region. Despite its distance from Bahía Drake, the La Fortuna and Monteverde region is often coupled with visits to the destination to create a vacation that's rich in nature exploration.

The most common way to reach Bahía Drake is via a combination of ground transportation (provided by a shared shuttle service, private transfer service, or rental car) and boat transportation.

coral snake in Corcovado National Park (left); ocelot (right)

HIGHLIGHTS

★ SNORKELING AND DIVING AT ISLA DEL CAÑO

tel. 506/8946-7134, www.sinac.go.cr, 7am-3pm daily, $15 adults, $5 children 2-12

About 24 kilometers off the coast of Bahía Drake, abundant marine life congregates in the nearly 15,000 acres of waters that surround the tiny 800-acre, rainforest-filled island, protected as the **Isla del Caño Biological Reserve** (Reserva Biológica Isla del Caño). Once an Indigenous burial ground, the uninhabited island remains largely undeveloped, except for a small ranger station on its northwest side that welcomes visitors on organized day tours. The region's best snorkeling and scuba diving experiences take place at the reserve. Humpback whales frequent the area from December to March and July to October. There's a good chance you'll see one playing in the waves while you're boating to and from the island.

Shallow inlets and offshore reefs are great spots for snorkeling, and year-round visibility in the area makes it easy to spot sharks, rays, eels, octopuses, sea turtles, and dolphins during open-water dives. Snorkeling and scuba diving tours to the reserve are commonly operated out of Bahía Drake and the gateway town of Sierpe.

The reserve has several dive sites, some with paradisiacal sandy bottoms. You can swim through an arch at **El Arco;** encounter whitetip sharks at the **Cueva del Tiburón, Paraíso,** and **El Barco** (the site of a washed-away shipwreck); and spot colorful coral at the **Coral Gardens.** Discuss the various options with your chosen tour provider when you book. Visibility is optimal between December and April (10-15 meters). Dive depths range from 15 to 25 meters.

La Perla del Sur

just south of Road 223, Sierpe, tel. 506/2788-1082, www.laperladelsur. cr, 6am-9pm daily; snorkeling and diving tours 8am daily, 8.5 hours, $150 pp for 2 tanks, $80 pp for snorkeling

Tour opportunities are seemingly endless and are offered by hotels and tour outfitters alike. A good option is **La Perla del Sur,** which runs snorkeling and diving tours out of Sierpe. Expect to pay $80-85 per person for a snorkel tour or $125-135 per person for a two-tank dive. Both experiences typically last seven hours and begin around 7am-7:30am.

Getting There

The reserve is accessible by boat only. Guided snorkeling and scuba diving excursions depart from (and return to) Bahía Drake and Sierpe.

★ THE NIGHT TOUR WITH THE BUG LADY

tel. 506/8701-7356, www.thenight tour.com, 7:30pm daily, 2.5-3 hours, $40 pp

The **Night Tour** run by biologist Tracie Stice, also known as the **Bug Lady,** and photographer and naturalist guide Gianfranco Gómez is the best of its kind in the region. The duo leads a leisurely hike through the dark night of Bahía Drake's biodiverse forest, on a search for rare and photogenic insects, frogs, spiders, snakes, bats, and nocturnal animals. Stice and Gómez relate facts and stories that they've collected over decades of exploration and offer witty commentary, elevating the tour experience.

Reservations are required. Contact Stice and Gómez directly to avoid accidentally booking a different night tour through an area operator or hotel. If you stay at an accommodation in Agujitas, the tour meeting place is the hotel Jinetes de Osa (at the west end of Playa Colorada). Pickups at hotels near Jinetes de Osa can also be arranged. Have Stice and Gómez confirm your meeting place and time when you book your tour. Headlamps are provided for use during the tour. Bring your own light if you plan to walk to and from the meeting place; you'll need it to navigate the route after dark. Closed-toe footwear is mandatory.

★ CORCOVADO NATIONAL PARK

tel. 506/2735-5036, www.sinac.go.cr, 7am-4pm daily, $15 adults, $5 children 2-12

Extraordinary biodiversity, vast primary forest, dense vegetation, and trails that go deep into remote wilderness make **Corcovado National Park** (Parque Nacional Corcovado) a bucket list experience for any big-hike adventurer or avid nature lover. Covering over 100,000 acres, the protected land and marine area occupies much of the Osa Peninsula's inland region, as well as a 40-kilometer stretch of its western coastline and is the primary attraction in Costa Rica's south end. It's a mélange of ecosystems; visits here often lead to surprise encounters with some of the rarest wildlife species you can see in the country—and the world. Sea turtles nest on the shores of the park's perimeter. Bull sharks and crocodiles invade the area's rivers and swamps. Nearly 400 species of birds fill the forest's canopy. More than 70 varieties of reptiles, 45 types of amphibians, and a whopping 8,000 species of insects traverse the park. Tapirs, monkeys, peccaries, anteaters, agoutis, ever-elusive jungle cats, and other mammals roam freely.

The park has six sectors. The most visited are the **San Pedrillo Sector** (on the northwest side of the park near Bahía Drake), the **La Leona Sector** (on the southwest side of the park), and the **Sirena Sector** (on the west side of the park). **Los Patos Sector** (on the northeast side of the park) and **El Tigre Sector** (on the east side of the park) are less frequented. **Los Planes Sector** (on the north side of the park near Bahía Drake) is closed to the public indefinitely.

Self-guided exploration is not permitted. The region's certified tour operators and agencies, many of which are based in Sierpe and Bahía Drake, run **guided day tours** and **overnight expeditions** through several areas in the park. Tour guides can also be reserved through area accommodations. Visits to the El Tigre Sector are handled separately and best arranged through the nonprofit **Corcovado el Tigre** (in the village of Dos Brazos, tel. 506/8691-4545, www.corcovadoeltigre.com).

Planning Your Time

It can be tough to choose a Corcovado experience. With **one day** to tour the park, visit either the San Pedrillo Sector or the Sirena Sector from Bahía Drake on a **boat tour.** Not only is the experience relatively affordable and easy to arrange

hiking In the jungle of Corcovado National Park

through most tour operators and hotels, but you'll also be able to set foot in the park (sign the guest book at the ranger station to record your presence), snap memorable photos, likely lay your eyes on some wildlife you've never seen, and be back in Bahía Drake reminiscing about the day long before sundown. Expect to pay roughly $85 per person for a tour of the San Pedrillo Sector and $95-125 per person for a tour of the Sirena Sector; both tours begin around 6:30am and last approximately eight hours. With **2-3 days** to spend in the area and ample energy, book a multiday Corcovado package. You're bound to see abundant wildlife, not to mention a variety of the park's elevations, throughout the epic journey. Overnight stays take place at the Sirena ranger station in the thick of the park's wilderness.

Surcos Tours
Puerto Jiménez, tel. 506/2735-5355, www.surcostours.com, 7am-6pm Mon.-Sat., 8am-4pm Sun., 2-day package $240 pp, 3-day package $415 pp
Respected operator **Surcos Tours** offers several multiday itineraries that suit a variety of interests, timelines, departure locations, and budgets. Though the outfitter is based in Puerto Jiménez, on the east side of the peninsula, they offer tours to travelers in Bahía Drake.

La Perla del Sur
just south of Road 223, Sierpe, tel. 506/2788-1082, www.laperladelsur. cr, 6am-9pm daily, $80 pp for the San Pedrillo Sector, $100 pp for the Sirena Sector
La Perla del Sur offers full-day park tours from Sierpe, which typically depart at 8am and return at 4:30pm.

Hiking
An intertwined system of nature trails weaves throughout the park and connects several ranger stations. Dress and pack for high humidity, scorching sun, and torrential rain. Closed-toe shoes or boots, socks, insect repellent, canteens, sunscreen, a hat, a poncho or jacket, a small towel, a flashlight, and a basic first aid kit are must-haves. If you plan to stay overnight in the park, bring an alarm clock; morning hikes are scheduled as early as 4:30am. Hiking at night is not permitted in any sector of the park.

Before you even get into the park, a 14-kilometer **unnamed trail** referred to by locals as the **Sendero Costero** (Coastal Trail) connects the village of Agujitas to the San Pedrillo ranger station in Corcovado National Park. A great way to spend a free day in Bahía Drake is to explore the first seven kilometers of this trail. It begins near Agujitas and offers a moderate, 2.5-hour, forested hike alongside the Pacific Ocean to Playa San Josecito. The trailhead, marked by a rickety wood suspension bridge, is at the west end of Playa Colorada, an approximate 20-minute walk from Agujitas center. You won't enter the park by doing this section of the trail.

The **San Pedrillo Sector** operates as its own individual corner of the park. Five trails totaling 12.5 kilometers are accessible beyond a **ranger station** and offer treks of easy-to-moderate difficulty alongside Río Pargo, through primary and secondary forest, and to a series of **small waterfalls.** You can tour this sector via organized **day trips** that depart from and return to Bahía Drake, an approximately 30-minute boat ride. Day tours typically start between 6am and 7am, last eight hours, and cost $80-90 per person.

The **Sirena Sector** is the heart of the park, and its **ranger station** is the home base of overnight visitors. Twenty kilometers of trails are spread out over eight routes around the station. Most trails offer prime wildlife-spotting opportunities. Guided **day tours** (expect to pay $95-125 pp from Bahía Drake or $100 pp from Sierpe) and guided **multiday excursions** (roughly $335 pp for a 2-day package from Bahía Drake) visit the sector daily. Tucked away in the forest, a one-kilometer hike leads to the ranger station along a trail that begins at the shore. From Bahía Drake, it's a one-hour boat ride to the trailhead.

La Leona and **Los Patos Sectors** are most often toured by hikers on their way to (or coming from) the Sirena Sector. Connecting to the ranger station at Sirena are a 16.5-kilometer **beach trail** that begins at La Leona ranger station, and a 20-kilometer **forest trail** that departs beyond Los Patos ranger station. The flat path through La Leona traces much of the coast and is a sweaty endeavor on sunny days, but occasional tree-shaded passage provides temporary relief. In contrast, the narrow, partly downhill trail (or partly uphill, if hiked from Sirena) that departs from Los Patos connects the area's highlands to the lowlands of the Corcovado basin. Both trails require river crossings, sometimes waist-deep. The Los Patos Sector also offers a second trail, a challenging three-kilometer hike that rewards brave trekkers with a waterfall, but it is unfrequented.

Practicalities

Overnight stays ($30 pp) inside the park are permitted for 1-4 nights at the **Sirena ranger station.** The open-air, solar-powered, dormitory-style accommodation has enough beds to sleep 70 tired souls, and it supplies linens, mosquito nets, potable water, and rented lockers ($4). Meals ($20-25 adults, children 3-12 half-price) are surprisingly gourmet versions of typical Costa Rican dishes. Vegetarian and gluten-free choices can be provided with advance notice. Outside food of any kind is not permitted at the station.

Meals and overnight stays at the Sirena ranger station require reservations. Most tour operators, agencies, and hotels that sell multi-day guided park excursions include the cost of room and board in their tour rates and handle reservation arrangements on behalf of travelers. Direct booking is not sanctioned by the Costa Rican government, so you'll need one of these businesses to book your stay for you.

Getting There

Corcovado isn't a national park you can drive to leisurely. To reach most ranger stations, you'll need time, energy (some entrances are hike-in only), and a flexible itinerary that allows you to work around park permit availability and transportation schedules. Fortunately, outfitter-led day trips are the norm, and tour operators, agencies, and hotels handle most logistics, such as transportation arrangements. You can get to the park by booking a day tour or multiday package through a certified provider.

To get to the **San Pedrillo ranger station,** take one of the boats that depart from Bahía Drake and the dock in Sierpe. Arrivals, here and at the Sirena ranger station, are normally wet landings, meaning you'll step off the boat several meters from the shoreline and wade through water to get to the mainland.

To get to the La Leona ranger station, road access is permitted as far as Carate following a rugged two-hour drive (weather, vehicle, potholes, and river crossings permitting) from Puerto Jiménez. From Carate, also reachable via a charter flight into the community's airstrip, it's a 3.5-kilometer walk along the beach to the ranger station. Without a vehicle, you can hitch a ride on a flatbed truck that commutes between Puerto Jiménez and Carate daily (6am and 1:30pm). The slow ride, which makes stops along the way and is dubbed the *colectivo,* departs from the corner with the hardware store (100 m west of Road 245, just south of the bus station) and costs $10 per person. If you plan to stay in Matapalo, the truck passes through that area

approximately one hour post-departure from Puerto Jiménez. La Leona ranger station can also be accessed on foot via a 16.5-kilometer trail that departs from the Sirena ranger station.

Set in the park's interior, the Sirena ranger station is only accessible by boat (mainly from Bahía Drake, Puerto Jiménez, or the dock in Sierpe), by charter flight (the station has a small airstrip), or on foot (via trails from the La Leona and Los Patos sectors).

You'll need a reliable 4x4 vehicle, a wild sense of adventure, and luck that brings good weather to reach Los Patos ranger station. The road to the station, which cuts south from the village of La Palma, is virtually impassable much of the year when rain swells the road's numerous river crossings. The only other way in is to hike the 15-kilometer road. The Los Patos ranger station can also be accessed on foot via a 20-kilometer trail that departs from the Sirena ranger station.

BEACHES

PLAYA COCALITO

Less than a half-hour walk down the coast from the south end of Playa Colorada is **Playa Cocalito,** Bahía Drake's most accessible swimming beach. Playa Cocalito has crystalline (albeit sometimes wave-filled) waters that are great for wading. The short and narrow beach is also quiet and just barely escapes Bahía Drake's lush forest, where monkeys can sometimes be seen playing in the trees that tower over the sand.

PLAYA SAN JOSECITO

The prettiest beach in the area is **Playa San Josecito.** This remote beach with a *Castaway* feel is backed by a tall hill, has several bright-green palms spread out across light, gray-tinged sand, and features rocky islets near the shore. The calm waters between the islets and the sand are great for snorkeling. It can get busy midday, as the beach is a popular spot to enjoy a picnic lunch.

It's a seven-kilometer, 2.5-hour hike to Playa San Josecito from Agujitas along the Sendero Costero.

Alternatively, you can reach Playa San Josecito via a 15-minute **boat ride** from Playa Colorada. Boats moored in Bahía Drake depart each morning to transport travelers on guided day tours to Corcovado National Park and Isla del Caño; when there's a seat to spare, you can hitch a ride to Playa San Josecito on one of these boats for around $10 per person. During the high season, when there may not be extra seats available, or during the low season, when fewer boats operate collective services, you can hire a private boat (budget $100 per group) to take you to the beach. Boat transportation can be arranged through Henar Cespedes, who operates the tourist information center **Osa Tucán** (25 m south of Mar y Bosque, tel. 506/8529-6750, 1pm-9pm daily) in Agujitas.

FOOD

There aren't many restaurants in Agujitas. Most visitors come to the region with a prepurchased package that includes daily meals.

STANDOUTS
Restaurante Donde Jorge
south of Road 223, Sierpe, tel. 506/2788-1082, 6am-9pm daily, $4-10
In Sierpe, I've never left **Restaurante Donde Jorge** disappointed.

The flavorful but not-too-oily *arroz con vegetales* (rice with vegetables) is my go-to dish. Other large helpings that sell for a reasonable price include fish plates and fast food like hamburgers and sandwiches. Enjoy your pick at the open-air restaurant as you watch local captains ready their boats by the riverbank. Sierpe is an hourlong boat ride from Bahía Drake.

Restaurante Donde Jorge

BAHÍA DRAKE LODGING

NAME	LOCATION
★ La Paloma Lodge	500 m northwest of the beach at Playa Colorada, Agujitas
★ Casa Corcovado Jungle Lodge	just north of the San Pedrillo ranger station, Corcovado National Park
★ Life For Life Hostel	8 km down the coast from Agujitas
Hotel Margarita	400 m south of the beach at Playa Colorada, Agujitas

LODGING

Many travelers favor the waterfront accommodations southwest of the village along the coast. Stays at most of these spots are sold as all-inclusive two- or three-night packages that include a private room and three daily meals (dining options outside of Agujitas are scarce). In some cases, local tours and round-trip boat transportation from Sierpe—or combined ground and boat transportation from other locations, such as Palmar or San José—are included.

STANDOUTS
La Paloma Lodge
500 m northwest of the beach at Playa Colorada, tel. 506/2239-0954, www.lapalomalodge.com, 3-night package $1,120 s, $2,300 d, all-inclusive, 3-night minimum
The 11 clifftop rooms and bungalow-style ranchos that form **La Paloma Lodge** are utterly relaxing and exquisitely furnished. Each offers a touch of luxury with orthopedic beds, air-conditioning, in-room seating areas, gleaming hardwood floors, and wall-to-wall windows that take in the area's lush surroundings

and ocean views. The hotel's superb service is second to none in the area. Guided tours of Corcovado National Park and the Isla del Caño Biological Reserve are included in the package rates.

Casa Corcovado Jungle Lodge
just north of the San Pedrillo ranger station, tel. 506/2256-3181, www.casacorcovado.com, 2-night package $794 s, $1,361 d, all-inclusive, 2-night minimum
Adjacent to Corcovado National Park, the **Casa Corcovado Jungle Lodge** is Bahía Drake's most upscale and environmentally sustainable accommodation. It's also the farthest hotel from Agujitas. Staying here means having a room with a romantic canopy bed and roofless outdoor shower. Guests have access to a 170-acre property with tropical gardens and nature trails as well as two swimming pools, a restaurant, a bar, a spectacular sunset viewpoint, and a waterfront boathouse. The lodge is perched atop a hill that overlooks the ocean. A steep road separates it from the beach. To get

CONTACT INFO	OPTIONS	PRICE
tel. 506/2239-0954, www. lapalomalodge.com	rooms and bungalow-style ranchos	3-night package $1,120 s, $2,300 d, all-inclusive
tel. 506/2256-3181, www. casacorcovado.com	hotel rooms	2-night package $794 s, $1,361 d, all-inclusive
tel. 506/8450-7198, www. lifeforlifehosteldrakebay. com	shared and private rooms	dorm $55 pp, private $165 s, $130 d
tel. 506/6176-3735	hotel rooms	$180 s/d

here, you'll take a tractor provided by the hotel.

Life For Life Hostel
tel. 506/8450-7198, www.lifeforlife hosteldrakebay.com, dorm $55 pp, private $65 s, $130 d

Escape to a distant part of the Osa Peninsula at the modest **Life For Life Hostel,** eight kilometers down the coast from Agujitas. Each room has bunk beds and one queen bed and can be booked as shared or private accommodations. Owner Ricardo (nicknamed "Clavito") is a long-time local and passionate naturalist, who also operates the **Life For Life Sea Turtle Conservation Project** from beaches around Punta Río Claro, a half-hour walk up the coast. Proceeds from overnight stays, as well as **nature tours** ($20-50 pp) that Ricardo runs in the area, buy protection for the marine species. Three authentic daily meals and the use of snorkeling gear—perfect for exploring nearby Playa San Josecito—are included in the room rate.

INFORMATION AND SERVICES

Agujitas has a **police station** (just south of Playa Colorada, tel. 506/2775-0300, 24 hours daily), a **clinic** named **Ebais Bahía Drake** (just south of Playa Colorada, tel. 506/2775-1975, 7am-5pm Mon. and Wed.-Fri.); a mini **pharmacy** called **Macrobiótica Hidalgo** (on the main road in Agujitas, tel. 506/2775-0909, 9am-7pm Mon.-Fri., 9am-6pm Sat.); and a few **supermarkets.** There are no banks or ATMs in Bahía Drake, so bring as much cash to the area as you plan to spend, plus a little extra in case of unforeseen expenses.

TRANSPORTATION AND TOURS

Getting There

Boat

Bahía Drake is one of the few destinations in Costa Rica where visitors don't typically arrive in a vehicle. Most travelers arrive via a one-hour **boat ride** from Sierpe. The roughly 40-kilometer journey, which begins calmly along Río Sierpe and gradually increases in speed to battle the raging ocean at the river's mouth, can be fun if you're up for an exhilarating ride. Skip the experience if you have a fear of small boats or the open ocean. Boats should be equipped with life jackets—don't board one that isn't.

Public **boats** offer drop-offs at hotels around Bahía Drake and at Playa Colorada; choose the latter if you're headed to Agujitas. Boats depart twice daily (11:30am and 3:30pm) from the main dock in Sierpe, at the south end of the village in front of Restaurante Donde Jorge (south of Road 223). The restaurant is owned by local tour operator **La Perla del Sur** (tel. 506/2788-1082, www.laperladelsur.cr, 6am-9pm daily), one of a few Sierpe-based companies to offer boat service to Bahía Drake. La Perla boasts skillful captains and coordinated, on-time service.

Expect to pay around $15-20 per person for transport to Playa Colorada and upward of $30 per person for destinations as far away as the Casa Corcovado Jungle Lodge. Reservations are not required. Wet landings, which require you to climb off the boat a short distance from the shore and wade through water toward the beach, are common. Wear shorts or quick-dry pants and secure footwear in preparation. If you drive yourself to Sierpe, you can leave your vehicle in the parking lot at La Perla del Sur for $6 per night. Be sure to lock the doors and remove any valuables.

Many of the area accommodations will handle boat travel arrangements and costs. Some accommodations use private docks, boats, and captains. Be sure to confirm the departure location, time, and the boat captain's contact information with your chosen hotel. Regardless of whether you travel via public or private boat, verify whether there's a luggage weight limit. Some vessels permit only 25 pounds of luggage per passenger.

Air

The quickest way to get to Bahía Drake is to fly. The **Aeropuerto Bahía Drake** (Bahía Drake Airport, DRK) is six kilometers north of Agujitas. **SANSA Airlines** (tel. 506/2290-4100, www.flysansa.com) offers direct flights to Bahía Drake from San José daily. The flight time from San José is approximately 40 minutes.

Car

There are two ways to get to Agujitas from **San José.** Via the **coastal route** (Hwy. 27, Hwy. 34, Hwy. 2, Road 245, and the unnamed dirt road that leads to Agujitas), Bahía Drake is a 375-kilometer drive southeast from downtown San José that takes roughly 6 hours. Via the **mountain route,** which begins on Highway 2, continues to Highway 34 (via Road 243), returns to Highway 2, follows Road 245, and ends on the unnamed dirt road that leads to Agujitas, it's a 335-kilometer, 6.5-hour drive southeast from downtown San José.

From downtown **Liberia,** Agujitas is a 460-kilometer drive southeast via Highway 1, Highway 23, Highway 27, Highway 34, Highway 2, and Road 245 that takes a little over 7.5 hours.

There is no gas station in Agujitas. Be sure to fill up the tank in **Chacarita** (there's a gas station on the corner of Highway 2 and Road 235) so you have enough fuel to get to Agujitas and back, roughly a 150-kilometer journey round-trip. The turnoff onto the unnamed dirt road that leads to Agujitas is at the hamlet of Rincón, roughly 45 kilometers south of Chacarita.

Visitors without a rental vehicle can catch a ride on the local *colectivo* that commutes between Agujitas and **La Palma** (from La Palma: 11:30am and 4pm Mon.-Sat., 2 hours, $3; from Agujitas: 4am and 1pm Mon.-Sat., 2 hours, $3), a village on the eastern side of the peninsula. La Palma can be reached by hopping on any bus that travels to or from Puerto Jiménez; buses travel through La Palma. Be aware that if you're staying at an accommodation outside of Agujitas, you'll likely need to hitch a boat ride from Playa Colorada to your hotel after the *colectivo* drops you off in the village.

Getting Around

Rough terrain in the area makes cycling around Bahía Drake a chore. Walking is the primary mode of getting around the village. Boat transportation, best arranged through your chosen accommodation, is the most common form of transport between Agujitas and areas of interest around the bay.

resplendent quetzal

WILDLIFE GUIDE

National parks, biological reserves, and wildlife refuges account for more than a quarter of Costa Rica's landmass. Dispersed throughout these areas are more than half a million species of mammals, birds, reptiles, amphibians, insects, and other living creatures, making it one of the most biologically diverse places on earth. Immerse yourself in the habitats of some of the world's most precious and distinctive species. You'll need to keep your eyes open, but spotting wildlife here is nearly guaranteed.

LAND MAMMALS

SLOTHS

If there is one type of animal that draws wildlife-lovers to Costa Rica more than any other, it is the **sloth** (*perezoso*). Sloths live much of their life in the same area, making it easy for experienced tour guides to know exactly where to find them. If you're exploring Costa Rica's forests on your own, look for the cute creatures in **cecropia trees,** identifiable by their whitewashed bark and large fans of lime-green leaves.

Of Costa Rica's two sloth species, you're more likely to come across a **three-toed sloth.** The species has distinctive dark markings around the eyes like a racoon. Less commonly spotted are **two-toed sloths,** which have a more pronounced, pig-like nose. Rather confusingly, both species have three toes on each "foot." It's their "hands" that show the difference: Three-toed sloths have three "fingers" on each hand and the two-toed sloth has two.

Where to See Them

Fortunately, the sloths, which spend most of their time sleeping or hanging upside down from treetop branches, can be seen all over the country, but especially within **Manuel Antonio National Park.** Rescued sloths reside at several wildlife centers including **Selvatura Park** in Monteverde and the **Jaguar Rescue Center** on the Caribbean coast.

MONKEYS

Monkeys are everywhere in the country, but the **Osa Peninsula** and the **southern Pacific coast** are the only parts of Costa Rica where all four monkey species reside.

The most commonly spotted species is the social (and sometimes aggressive) **white-headed capuchin monkey,** colloquially referred to as white-faced monkeys or *cara blancas* in Spanish. Of the four monkey species that reside in Costa Rica,

two-toed sloth (top); mantled howler monkey (bottom)

white-faced monkeys are the only ones that descend from the trees to forage on the forest floor, so encounters can be at close range.

Large, all-black **mantled howler monkeys,** referred to by many tour guides as congos, also abound in Costa Rica. You may not see them as often as you hear their startling, loud, low-toned roar, which can be heard up to nearly five kilometers away.

Encounters with lanky and agile **Geoffroy's spider monkeys,** also known as Central American spider monkeys, are less frequent but not rare.

Most exotic-looking—and the smallest of the bunch—are **red-backed squirrel monkeys,** also called Central American squirrel monkeys or mono tití monkeys, which have a cinnamon-colored body and a white- and dark-gray face.

Where to See Them

Capuchin monkeys frequent popular parks and beaches on a mission to steal travelers' food. Keep watch over your belongings—especially in **Manuel Antonio National Park** (on the Pacific coast) and **Cahuita National Park** (on the Caribbean coast)—or they'll be gone before you know it.

Look and listen for troops of the territorial howler monkeys in the **treetop canopy**—they rarely frequent the forest floor. Countrywide, sightings are common during **forest hikes,** during **hanging bridge tours,** and on **safari float tours.**

Spider monkeys can be seen in several natural areas around the country. I've had the best luck spotting the brown-bodied creatures around **wetlands,** including **Caño Negro Wildlife Refuge.**

Red-backed squirrel monkeys are best spotted in **Manuel Antonio National Park** (on the Pacific coast) or **Corcovado National Park** (on the Osa Peninsula).

TAPIRS

The largest animal in Costa Rica's forests, the **Baird's tapir** (*danta*) is roughly two meters long and weighs anywhere between 150 and 350 kilograms. This gray, short-haired tapir, sporting a wiggly nose not unlike a miniature elephant's trunk,

Baird's tapir (top); margay (bottom)

helps regenerate Costa Rica's green zones through seed redistribution as it moves about the land.

Where to See Them

Tapirs are difficult to see, although they course throughout several of the country's national parks, including **Corcovado National Park** (on the Osa Peninsula).

WILD CATS

Costa Rica is home to six species of wild cats. The king of Costa Rica's jungle is the **jaguar,** which can grow to be 1.5 meters long and 0.75 meter tall and weigh over 90 kilograms. It's also the most elusive mammal. Many devoted naturalist tour guides spend much of their life hoping to see one in the wild and never do, but the few who have seen a jaguar tell marvelous tales of the beautiful creature's sleek look and cunning, predatory ways. Jaguars require a forested territory large enough for them to roam and hunt.

One of the biggest wild cat species in the country, second only to the jaguar, is the **puma** (also known as a mountain lion, *león de montaña*). The big cat is easily recognizable by its short, smooth, and solid light-brown coat.

The most striking feline of the bunch is the **ocelot** (*ocelote* or *manigordo*), which is spotted like a jaguar but is roughly half its size and has notably large paws. Also spotted, and sometimes mistaken for small ocelots, are **margays** (*cauceles*) and **oncillas** (*tigrillos*). The margay weighs just under five kilograms and has a long tail that can extend almost 50 centimeters beyond its body. The oncilla, sometimes referred to as the little spotted cat, weighs between 1.5 and 3 kilograms, looks like a kitten, and is the smallest wild cat in Costa Rica's animal kingdom.

Weasel-like in appearance and slightly smaller than an ocelot is the **jaguarundi** (*león breñero*), which resembles a long and slender house cat. Jaguarundis can be

---

puma

grayish-brown, reddish-brown, or black in color.

Where to See Them
The majority of Costa Rica's wild cats are nocturnal. Your best chance of encountering one is during a **night tour,** though sightings are extremely rare. Sightings of jaguars most commonly occur in **Corcovado National Park** (on the Osa Peninsula). Recent years have seen the closure of public beaches in some protected land areas where jaguars have been spotted swiping turtle eggs and cracking the shells of sea turtles with their teeth. The other five species of wild cats inhabit many of the same remote, undeveloped spaces in Corcovado National Park. They've also been spotted in the **Monteverde Cloud Forest Biological Reserve.**

COATIMUNDIS, KINKAJOUS, AND OLINGOS
Relatively easy to see in Costa Rica are **coatimundis** ("coatis" for short, or *pizotes*), which resemble racoons but have a long, white nose and a slender tail. In less traveled areas, the animals are timid and will wander away when approached. In popular destinations, coatis turn out in droves, especially around **roadsides,** and are accustomed to getting attention from travelers.

Tougher to spot than coatis are other, less social members of the racoon (Procyonidae) family, including **kinkajous** (*martillas*) and **olingos** (*olingos*). These species are similar in appearance (though kinkajous are reddish-brown in color and olingos are grayish-brown); they have a thick, short coat, a long and flexible tail, and an elongated body like a ferret.

coatimundi

Where to See Them
I've always had the best luck seeing groups of coatimundis around **La Fortuna,** at **Místico Park** and the **Arenal Observatory Lodge.**

PECCARIES
Essentially wild pigs, **peccaries** (*saínos*) roam about heavily in natural areas around the country. They traipse through the forest in search of food, rustling leaves and branches. If the noise doesn't give them away, you can identify their recent presence by taking note of messy or muddy tracks, or by catching a whiff of their hog-like smell.

Two peccary species inhabit Costa Rica—**white-lipped peccaries,** which typically appear in groups and can be aggressive but are the more difficult species to spot, and **collared peccaries,** which are generally smaller, nonaggressive, and encountered in forests on their own

Where to See Them
Groups of white-lipped peccaries have been spotted in **Corcovado National Park** on the Osa Peninsula.

agouti (left); white-tailed deer (right)

AGOUTIS AND PACAS

As you trek through Costa Rica's national parks, you may spot a small rodent crossing the trail. If the critter's body resembles a large rat and is brown with a tinge of yellow, orange, or red, it is likely an **agouti** (*agutí*, nicknamed a *guatusa*). You'll regularly come across them within natural areas as they eat fruits and seeds off the **forest floor.** They move quietly about the ground but can scurry when startled.

Small rodents encountered during **night tours** are most likely nocturnal **pacas** (*tepezcuintles*), which are slightly larger than agoutis. They are brown in color and usually have white markings on both sides of their body that resemble the spots on a deer or the stripe on a chipmunk.

Where to See Them

Agoutis and pacas can be seen all over the country, including within **Carara National Park** on the central Pacific coast.

DEER

Declared a national symbol of Costa Rica in 1995, the **white-tailed deer** (*venado*) is most commonly seen in **lowland areas,** as well as along the central Pacific and northern Caribbean coasts. More challenging to see is the **Central American red brocket deer,** which is slightly smaller, reddish-brown in color, and prefers mountain highland areas in remote sections of the central Pacific coastal region and the southern inland area.

MARINE LIFE

SEA TURTLES

Costa Rica's beaches host five types of nesting **sea turtles** (*tortugas marinas*)—six if you count **Atlantic green sea turtles** and **Pacific green sea turtles** separately. Though sightings are never guaranteed, sea turtles are best witnessed during **turtle nesting tours,** which are highly regulated, guided excursions at popular nesting beaches that typically run at **night.** With a lot of luck, you can spot sea turtles, mainly olive ridleys and leatherbacks (as well as the occasional hawksbill), swimming in the clear, open water of the Pacific Ocean while you participate in a snorkeling, scuba diving, stand-up paddling, or sailing excursion.

Where to See Them

Sea turtles can appear on any beach along Costa Rica's Caribbean and Pacific coasts at any time of year.

DOLPHINS AND WHALES

Costa Rica's **Pacific coast** is a known mating site for **humpback whales** (*ballenas*), which migrate to the region from the north (Dec.-Mar.) and the south (July-Oct.). A few species of **dolphins** (*delfines*), including **bottlenose dolphins, spinner dolphins,** and **spotted dolphins,** can be seen playing in the Pacific Ocean year-round.

Where to See Them

Boat tours and sailing tours along the coast provide the best spotting opportunities, especially those that tour the waters of **Isla del Caño Biological Reserve** (off the coast at Bahía Drake) and **Marino Ballena National Park.**

SHARKS AND RAYS

Potential sightings of **sharks** (*tiburones*) and **rays** (*rayas*) draw in scores of scuba divers to Costa Rica each year. A reputable dive operator can help keep the encounters safe,

humpback whales (top); southern stingray (bottom)

especially run-ins with bull sharks, which have a reputation for being aggressive. Attacks on humans by any species of shark in Costa Rica are rare.

FISH

The waters of the **Pacific Ocean** and the **Caribbean Sea** are full of an extensive list of **fish** (*peces*). Tropical and colorful varieties, including species of **parrotfish,** **puffer fish,** and **butterfly fish,** can make appearances during snorkel and dive trips.

Sportfishing expeditions reel in big fish like **marlins, sailfish, wahoos, snappers, roosterfish, dorado,** and **tuna.** Expeditions most commonly depart from destinations along the **Pacific coast,** including Playas del Coco and **Tamarindo** (both along the northern Pacific coast).

BIRDS

TOUCANS AND ARACARIS

If you're lucky, you'll get the chance to see a beautiful **toucan** (*tucán*) or **aracari** (a member of the toucan family, nicknamed a *piti*) in the wild. If not, plenty of **wildlife rescue centers** have resident varieties, including Alajuela's **Rescate Wildlife Rescue Center,** which houses the first toucan in Costa Rica to receive a prosthetic beak. Toucans are loved for their unique and sometimes colorful bill. You'll often hear the birds' boisterous, loud calls before you spot them high up in the canopy or soaring between trees.

Where to See Them

The **chestnut-mandibled toucan** makes a sweet, high-pitched sound; the bird is best seen in low elevations along the **Caribbean coast** and **central and southern Pacific coasts,** and on the **Osa Peninsula.** The **keel-billed toucan,** sometimes referred to as the rainbow-billed toucan, has a rougher and slightly lower-pitched caw. Keel-billed toucans are commonly spotted only in the northern half of the country, including around the **northern Pacific coast,** the **Nicoya Peninsula,** and the **Caribbean region.**

Two similar-looking species of aracaris, the **fiery-billed aracari** (seen around the **central and southern Pacific coast** and the **Osa Peninsula**) and the **collared aracari** (seen around **Guanacaste,** the **northern Pacific coast,** the **Nicoya Peninsula,** and the **Caribbean region**), can be found in Costa Rica and are best identified by their beak color. Fiery-billed aracaris have red on their beak. Keep watch for toucans and aracaris in the sky after rain

keel-billed toucan

scarlet macaws

showers; they tend to shy away from the sun and are most active when there is cloud cover.

MACAWS AND PARROTS

Talkative, lime-green **parrots** (*loras*) and loud-squawking **macaws** (*lapas*) are some of Costa Rica's most exotic birds. Parrots are found along both coasts, usually at low elevations. Macaws are monogamous and almost always seen in pairs.

Where to See Them

Look for red, yellow, and blue **scarlet macaws** along the Pacific coast, primarily on the **Nicoya Peninsula** and on the **Osa Peninsula**. Seek out tough-to-find **great green macaws** around **Manzanillo** (in the southern Caribbean region). You'll have the best chance of spotting either type in *almendro* trees; macaws enjoy their almonds.

QUETZALS AND OTHER TROGONS

Ten species of **trogons** (*trogones*) reside in Costa Rica, but the one every bird-watcher longs to see is the **resplendent quetzal.** Although female quetzals resemble most other trogons in appearance, males wow viewers with their unique colorful plumage and long tail feathers. Named after the Spanish verb *tragar* (to swallow), trogons are known for swallowing fruits whole and redistributing seeds around the forest upon regurgitation.

Where to See Them

While trogons can be seen all over Costa Rica, quetzals stick to **cloud forest ecosystems.** If you're lucky, you might spot one in the many nature reserves that blanket the

Monteverde vicinity. They're often seen feeding on small avocados in *aguacatillo* trees.

BIRDS OF PREY

Costa Rica has several varieties of birds of prey, including **hawks** (*gavilanes*), **vultures** (*zopilotes*), and **eagles** (*águilas*). The **harpy eagle,** one of the most sought-after birds in the country, is spotted so rarely that some people believe the species no longer resides here.

Where to See Them

If harpy eagles are still in the country, you'll likely only see them on the **Osa Peninsula** or in the **southern inland region.** A few types of **caracaras** (a kind of falcon) are a common sight throughout the country. Most are spotted mid-flight or perched on tall tree branches while they scope out their prey.

FLYCATCHERS

More than 70 species of flycatchers (nicknamed *pechos amarillos*) call Costa Rica home. Most have brown or olive-green backs and a yellow-tinged chest. You're bound to see at least one **social flycatcher, boat-billed flycatcher,** or **great kiskadee** resting on cables and fences or visiting feeders at tourist attractions and accommodations **across the country.** The three species are nearly identical. Experienced birders search the Pacific side of the country high and low to view a **scissor-tailed flycatcher** or a rare **fork-tailed flycatcher,** both of which stand out from other family members with their long tails.

Where to See Them

Scissor-tailed flycatchers inhabit the **entire Pacific coast.** Fork-tailed

Montezuma oropendola (left); hummingbird (right)

flycatchers are mainly seen in the **southern Pacific region.**

HUMMINGBIRDS
The most delicate birds you'll come across are tiny **hummingbirds** (*colibríes*), which are always a treat to see zigzagging amid natural areas. More than 50 species whiz around Costa Rica. Endemic to Costa Rica and parts of Panama is the rarely seen **fiery-throated hummingbird,** which has a beautiful, rainbow-colored throat.

Where to See Them
You can see many at once at **hummingbird gardens** scattered throughout the country, especially in **cloud forest ecosystems.** The attractions also permit up-close viewing, ideal if you wish to admire the birds' shimmery, jewel-tone bodies.

MOTMOTS
Six species of motmots (nicknamed *pájaros bobos*) can be seen throughout Costa Rica. Except for one species (**Tody motmots**), all are easily identifiable by their long tail, which they sway back and forth like a pendulum when threatened.

Where to See Them
Tody motmots, which can be seen around the **foothills of volcanoes in Guanacaste,** are the smallest of Costa Rica's motmots and have a white breast, olive-green plumage, and a short tail. I've always had good luck getting close to motmots, so they're a good species to aim for if you're into bird photography. The black bands around the eyes and the blue, green, turquoise, and copper coloring add to the bird's striking appearance. Look for nests in holes along **forest banks and walls.**

CURASSOWS AND GUANS
Much like a wild turkey (*pavón*), a **curassow** or a **guan** is a medium-sized bird you might encounter wandering the **forest floor** in most areas of Costa Rica in search of food. They're able to fly, so you may also spot the birds in trees. **Great curassows** are regularly seen in pairs; the male is black and the female is brown. If you come across a set, approach them with caution because they scare easily and are quick to escape into the brush.

SONGBIRDS

Tons of songbirds fill Costa Rica's forests with sweet serenades. Small and colorful **tanagers** (*tangaras; some species are nicknamed *viudas*) can be seen singing from the **tree-top canopy** and hopping around the **forest floor** just about everywhere in the country. The **clay-colored robin** (*yigüirro*), also known as a clay-colored thrush, has been Costa Rica's national bird since 1977. It sings a nearly constant tune between March and June. Locals claim the birds *llaman la lluvia* (call the rain) since their song corresponds with the transition between the dry season and the wet season. Several **warblers** and **orioles** add melodies to the natural symphony. These songbirds can be seen and heard across the country.

One of the most distinct bird-songs you'll hear in Costa Rica, which plays on repeat throughout the **Caribbean region** and **Guanacaste,** is the combined squeak and gobble of the **Montezuma oropendola.** The blackbird species, which is dark brown in color with a yellow-tinged tail and an orange-tipped beak, is a common sight around fruit feeders and in the wild. You may spot their funny-looking nests first, which hang from tree branches and appear as large, grayish-brown woven sacks, that can be up to two meters long.

WATERBIRDS

Costa Rica's countless **wetlands, mangroves, rivers, lakes, lagoons, and beaches** host flocks of waterbirds. Most species come looking for crabs, mollusks, fish, insects, and other foods in and around the water. **Sandpipers** (*andarríos*), **gulls** (*gaviotas*), **herons** and **egrets** (*garzas*), **pelicans** (*pelícanos*), **cormorants** (*cormoranes*), **spoonbills** (*espátulas*), **anhingas** (nicknamed *pato aguja*), **kingfishers** (*martín pescadores*), and **storks** (*cigüeñas*) are common varieties.

REPTILES AND AMPHIBIANS

FROGS

Costa Rica has more than 175 different types of amphibians, the majority of which are frogs (*ranas*). Several are entertaining to look at, such as the **strawberry poison dart frog** (nicknamed the blue-jeans frog given the denim-colored legs that contrast with its bright red body) or various species of **glass frogs,** whose transparent bodies put internal organs on full display. The nonpoisonous **red-eyed tree frog** is arguably the most sought-after, as its striking light-green body, blue legs, orange feet, and beady red eyes—all of which are used to trick predators into thinking it's poisonous—make it a unique sight. Most other frogs have earth-tone bodies that camouflage well with the environment. The majority of Costa Rica's frog species prefer moist environments to dry areas; look for poison dart frogs, glass frogs, tree frogs, and more hopping along wet or humid **nature trails,** sleeping **under leaves,** or depositing eggs in waterlogged bromeliads, usually near small bodies of stagnant water in the **Caribbean region,** the **central**

and southern Pacific coast, and on the **Osa Peninsula.**

GECKOS, IGUANAS, AND LIZARDS

The closest encounter you'll likely have with a lizard is in your hotel room, as tiny **house geckos** are common guests—wanted or not. Some geckos run across walls and ceilings, and others hide behind mirrors and hanging artwork. You'll hear them making clicking sounds every few minutes as they attempt to make a meal out of small flies, worms, and other insects. If you can't direct them out the door, don't fret. They're harmless.

Iguanas (*iguanas*) are also frequent finds in Costa Rica, especially along coastlines where there are plenty of sunny and sandy spots for females to bury their eggs. Black spiny-tailed iguanas and green iguanas can be seen basking in the sun on tree branches.

Lizards (*lagartijas*), of which there are many varieties in Costa Rica, dash across **nature trails** and hurry up **tree trunks.** Arguably the most remarkable species is the **common basilisk,** better known as a Jesus Christ lizard, which escapes land predators by scurrying across the surface of narrow bodies of water on its hind legs.

Where to See Them

Basilisks, along with most other lizards in the country, can be seen near **lowland rivers** and **streams** along the **Pacific coast.**

SNAKES

According to San José's Instituto Clodomiro Picado, the country's leading snake research center, which produces antivenom serums

baby green iguana (top); black spiny-tailed iguana (middle); red-eyed tree frog (bottom)

and exports the products around the world, Costa Rica has 140 species of **snakes** (*serpientes* or *culebras*), but only 23 are considered poisonous (22 species of land snakes and 1 species of sea snake). One of the most aggressive species is the pit viper known as the **fer-de-lance,** but the most poisonous is the **bushmaster.** Many snakes are brown in color and camouflage easily among natural settings; be mindful of where you walk and don't venture off flattened trails into **dense brush.** Other snake varieties are bright green or yellow.

It's worth noting that encountering a poisonous snake in Costa Rica is uncommon. In my many years of traveling throughout Costa Rica, I've only come across a handful in the wild; most were encountered during night tours or nonroutine activities like overnight deep-jungle expeditions. Although snakes can appear anywhere and at any time (carry a flashlight wherever you go at night), Costa Rica's most traveled trails rarely produce daytime snake sightings.

Where to See Them
Look for snakes in **trees** or curled up in **holes.** If you're fearful of snakes, visit forested areas with a knowledgeable and experienced tour guide, or examine them from behind glass walls at one of many **herpetariums** and other snake exhibits in the country.

INSECTS AND ARACHNIDS

BUTTERFLIES AND MOTHS
More than 1,200 species of **butterflies** (*mariposas*) and roughly 8,000 species of **moths** (*polillas* or *mariposas nocturnas*) flutter **all around Costa Rica,** mainly in **natural areas** with plenty of **flowers.**

The most beloved butterfly in the country is the shimmery **blue morpho butterfly.** You're most likely to catch a glimpse of it up-close when it rests on plants or feeders to drink the juice of fermented fruit. With the blue side of its wings closed while it consumes the liquid, the butterfly displays a striking brown design with several circles meant to mimic eyes. The blue morpho is often misidentified as the **magnificent owl butterfly,** which displays similar brown markings on one side of its wings and an iridescent purple—not blue—hue on the other.

Where to See Them
To see them in abundance, visit one of the country's many **butterfly gardens,** which protect and breed several species within enclosed habitats.

ANTS
The tiny **leaf-cutter ants** (*hormigas*) you'll see marching across **nature trails** and up **tree trunks** in virtually every outdoor area in the country are wildly fascinating. If you plan to participate in a guided nature tour anywhere in the country, ask your tour guide about the ants' behavior. In short, the strong critters carry bits of leaves and other debris (sometimes 2-3 times their own weight) across forests to underground colonies,

some of which consist of millions of ants. They later feed off the fungus of the decomposing materials. Colonies are overseen by queen ants, which run an impressively organized and smart operation. Watch out for the hardworking insects whenever you embark on forest treks to avoid stepping on their ingenious system.

SPIDERS AND SCORPIONS

Costa Rica has all kinds of **spiders** (*arañas*), from small varieties not unlike the ones you're used to shooing out of your home, to large **tarantulas** and plenty of weird-looking ones in between. A few are poisonous, including the ***Phoneutria boliviensis*** (one of the world's most feared spiders), but most are not. A common nonpoisonous variety you're bound to come across is the thin **golden silk orb weaver,** adored by some for its yellow-tinged web. If you're not up for running into one (literally), keep your head up as you walk through **forested areas** and approach exhibit enclosures; webs, often thin and easy to miss, are all around.

Dispelling several myths, findings from 2017 confirm that of Costa Rica's 14 species of **scorpions** (*escorpiones*), none is poisonous. Rarely seen in Costa Rica, the stinging arachnids shouldn't be feared; most hide behind **forest vegetation.**

magnificent owl butterfly (top); leaf-cutter ants (middle); golden silk orb weaver (bottom)

beach in Manzanillo

ESSENTIALS

TRANSPORTATION

AIRPORTS

Juan Santamaría International Airport (SJO, Aeropuerto Internacional Juan Santamaría, tel. 506/2437-2400, http://sjoairport.com) is located just outside of Alajuela city, an approximate 20-minute drive northwest of the capital, San José. Choose this airport if you plan to begin your trip in La Fortuna and Monteverde, the central and southern Pacific, the Osa Peninsula, or the Caribbean coast.

Daniel Oduber Quirós International Airport (LIR, Aeropuerto Internacional Daniel Oduber Quirós, tel. 506/2666-9600, http://lircr.com) is just west of Liberia, in the northwest corner of the country. Choose this airport if you plan to begin your trip in Tamarindo in Guanacaste and continue south into the Nicoya Peninsula. (If you plan to focus on the Nicoya Peninsula, you can choose either LIR or SJO.)

Several popular destinations have domestic airports, and a few remote areas provide private landing strips. On the western edge of San José is the **Tobías Bolaños International Airport** (SYQ, Aeropuerto Internacional Tobías Bolaños). Though it's technically an international airport, it operates primarily as a domestic one. It used to be the country's most visited small-scale airport but has dwindled in popularity since losing the well-known local flight provider Nature Air in 2018. **SANSA Airlines,** which operates out of Aeropuerto Internacional Juan Santamaría, is the best provider for in-country flights.

Domestic flights offer several advantages and disadvantages. They can be more or less expensive than other modes of transportation, but there's no question they save a ton of time, especially getting to and from the distant Osa Peninsula and southern Pacific region. Environmentally conscious travelers can (and should) be concerned about the carbon output of each flight; however, especially given that most planes seat only 12 people. SANSA Airlines claims its fleet is fuel efficient; its partnership with the **Fondo Nacional de Financiamiento Forestal** (National Fund for Forest Financing, FONAFIFO, www.fonafifo.go.cr)—which helps protect primary forest on the Osa Peninsula—helps offset carbon dioxide emissions.

If money is no concern, **charter flights** can be arranged through providers like SANSA Airlines.

ORGANIZED TOUR TRANSPORTATION

For travelers looking to maximize their time and minimize the cost and hassle of arranging separate transportation services and tours, **city-to-city transportation-inclusive tours** are a helpful tool. This form of transportation, sometimes referred to as an **Adventure Connection** or **post-tour onward transportation,** allows you to move between destinations while participating in an activity along the way. How it works: You'll get picked up in one city in the morning, participate in an adventure or nature tour (like white-water rafting) during the day, and get dropped off in a different city in the afternoon or evening. You choose the route and the tour from a list of available options, and the tour operator coordinates the rest. Lunch and sometimes breakfast are included.

Trailblazer tour operators that offer this service include **Exploradores Outdoors** (offices in San José and Puerto Viejo de Talamanca, tel. 506/2222-6262, www.exploradoresoutdoors.com) and **Desafio Adventure Company** (Road 702, 1.5 km south of Road 142, La Fortuna, tel. 506/2479-0020, www.desafiocostarica.com). The most common destinations selected as tour start or end locations are San José, Alajuela, La Fortuna, Monteverde, Tortuguero, Turrialba, Puerto Viejo de Sarapiquí, Manuel Antonio, Jacó, Sámara, Nosara, Puerto Viejo de Talamanca, Cahuita, and beaches along Guanacaste's northern Pacific coast.

FAST FACTS

- Costa Rica utilizes the **metric system.**

- The **electrical system** uses the same 110- to 120-volt, 60-hertz sockets found in the United States and Canada. Newer accommodations provide at least one three-prong connector per room, but sometimes only in the bathroom. Older properties may only have two-prong sockets.

- **Costa Rica time** is six hours earlier than Greenwich Mean Time. The country shares the **Central Time Zone** with the United States and Canada but does not observe Daylight Saving Time.

- **Business hours** vary significantly by business type and region. Some establishments are closed or open late on Sundays. **Government offices** typically operate 8am-5pm Monday-Friday, give or take an hour. **Police stations** and **hospitals** are open 24 hours daily. Businesses in touristed areas offer extended hours and are usually open on weekends. **Tourism operations,** including adventure and nature tours and transportation services, operate every day of the year, including holidays.

- Travel agencies and tour operators are available in nearly every corner of the country. The government-run **Instituto Costarricense de Turismo** (Costa Rican Institute of Tourism, ICT, Avenida Central, between Calle 1 and Calle 3, tel. 506/2222-1090, www.ict.go.cr, 8am-5pm Mon.-Fri.) and the private organization **Canatur** (National Chamber of Tourism, tel. 506/2234-6222, www.canatur.org, 8am-5pm Mon.-Fri.), both based in San José, are Costa Rica's leading tourism organizations.

- **Maps** are provided by most vehicle rental agencies, tourism offices, and even some hotels free of charge. The ICT website **Essential Costa Rica** (www.visitcostarica.com) offers maps as free downloadable PDFs. **Google Maps** also permits downloads for offline use.

PRIVATE TRANSFER SERVICE

A great option for families, private transfer services can transport you and your travel companions between destinations in air-conditioned tourist vans typically built for 8-12 occupants. Modern services include complimentary onboard Wi-Fi. Included in the cost, which may be $75-400 each way, is the driver's service and your choice of pick-up time. Some service providers apply a surcharge for departures between 7pm and 7am. Brief stops along the way, typically up to one hour, are permitted. Longer stops require extra payment to cover the driver's time. If you're headed to a remote location, this service type may be the only possible means of transport.

SHARED SHUTTLE SERVICE

Shared shuttle services, which operate vehicles similar to those used by private transfer services, are a form of public transportation. They're also one of the most popular ways to get around Costa Rica. Van seats are reserved on an individual basis and are priced per person per way ($19-125); some service providers offer reduced rates (typically half price) to child travelers. Connecting the most popular tourist destinations around the country, the services run according to set schedules and typically offer one or two departure times daily per route. A scheduled bathroom stop is provided along the way.

RENTAL CAR

Nearly all car rental agencies require renters to be at least 25 years of age and have a valid driver's license in their home country as well as a credit card. Rent a vehicle if you feel confident driving abroad, are familiar with Costa Rica's driving laws, and you have access to a reliable GPS system for navigational support. In most areas of the country where Wi-Fi signal is decent, you can get away with using Google Maps on devices like cell phones, laptops, and tablets. If you're unsure whether you need a **4x4 vehicle,** rent one anyway. Road trips to beaches and attractions, as well as entrances to some accommodations, lead down rugged roads that are a far cry from paved highways. Routes in backroad areas can be steep, rocky, or overrun with flooded rivers. Some roads become impassable during the green (wet) season.

Mapache Rent-A-Car (offices in San José, Alajuela, Liberia, and La Fortuna de San Carlos, tel. 506/2586-6300, www.mapache.com, hours vary by office) offers transparent price quotes and is one of few **sustainable** vehicle rental agencies in the country. Through water recycling, material composting, and practically turning its head office in San José into a greenhouse, it earned the highest ranking of the Certificación para la Sostenibilidad Turística (Certification of Sustainable Tourism, CST).

Gas Stations

Most gas stations around the country do not offer self-service pumps or English-speaking attendants. When an employee approaches your window, say *"Lleno, por favor, regular,"* which translates to "Full, please, regular," assuming you want standard unleaded fuel. Payment is typically accepted in cash (colones or US dollars) or by credit card. In remote areas, gas stations are few and far between, and it helps to know where they are before getting on the road. Always keep your tank above the halfway mark, filling up wherever you can, so you're less likely to find yourself strapped for gas if you end up in an area without fuel.

Parking

Downtown San José has several public parking lots. In destinations outside of the capital, secure places to park are practically nonexistent beyond the confines of private properties such as accommodations, tour offices, and restaurants. Locals often park vehicles haphazardly along the sides of streets and at the back of beaches. Several beaches have an unofficial watchman who promises to keep an eye on vehicles for tips. I usually pay $1-2 for every hour of parking time. No matter where you park, always lock your vehicle and never leave belongings in plain sight.

Traffic Regulations

You must be at least 21 years of age and have a valid driver's license from your home country and passport to drive in Costa Rica. The ***policía de tránsito*** (transit police), who typically ride in navy-blue pickup trucks, are responsible for traffic enforcement. You must abide by the speed limit (generally 80 kilometers per hour on highways and 60 kilometers per hour on other roads), wear a seat belt when driving, and be able to provide your license, passport, and vehicle documentation if asked.

Officers with radar guns hide along highway edges; locals typically alert one another of their presence with a quick flash of the high beams. Speed cameras, mainly around the Central Valley and Highlands, provide added vigilance. If you receive a ticket, you can pay the fine through your rental agency, which will handle the necessary

CAR RENTAL INSURANCE

Driving around Costa Rica can be freeing, but car rental insurance is a tangled issue. Not only is there a ton of fine print to deal with, but surprise charges not disclosed at the time of reservation can be downright frustrating. Before you travel, and even before you reserve a car for your trip, be sure to review this information.

There are two types of car rental insurance in Costa Rica. As mandated by the Instituto Nacional de Seguros (INS, National Insurance Institute), the first type, commonly cited as **SLI insurance** (also known as **TPL insurance**), must be acquired in Costa Rica. Typically purchased through the rental agency, this insurance provides coverage for damage caused to other drivers and their vehicle. The second type, which provides **limited coverage** for damage caused to you and your rental car (according to a set deductible), can be acquired from providers outside of Costa Rica, such as credit card companies in your home country. It's important to note that there's no universal term for either type of insurance, so you may see other names used.

Most rental agencies require renters to purchase both types of insurance. Many rental agencies will require you to supply proof that the second type of insurance was acquired elsewhere, usually in the form of a letter from the insurance provider.

Not all rental agencies include the cost of both insurance types in their quotes. Some agencies market the two insurance types together and automatically include the combined insurance cost in their quotes. If you're able to provide proof of partial insurance acquired elsewhere, the quote can then be reduced to reflect the cost of SLI insurance only.

Other rental agencies opt to include only SLI insurance in their quotes, which helps them appear less expensive than competitors. If you choose one of these companies and you haven't arranged partial insurance from home, you'll likely learn when you pick up your car that astronomical fees have been added to your bill to cover the second type of insurance. Almost always, this type of rental will end up costing more than one of the seemingly more expensive agencies. When comparing quotes, don't be swayed by low costs. If a price seems too good to be true, it likely is.

Additional insurance is available for purchase. Most rental agencies sell **extra insurance** that can broaden coverage for damage caused to you and your rental car, as well as lower the deductible amount (typically to $0). Although beneficial, extra insurance is optional.

Supplemental fees (some mandatory and others optional) can increase your rental price. Confirm with your chosen agency whether a license plate fee, additional driver fee, roadside assistance fee, smoke damage fee, cleaning fee, airport fee, pickup fee, drop-off/delivery fee, late return fee, refueling fee, green/environmental fee, and/or sales tax have been or will be applied to your quote. Some supplemental fees apply per day and others are one-time charges.

CROSSING FLOODED ROADS AND RIVERS

My favorite way to explore Costa Rica is by car. I love the flexibility and the opportunities to explore the extraordinary. But there's nothing worse than setting off on an exciting journey only to turn a corner and be confronted by a flooded road or a swollen river. You can't go over it, you can't go under it, and you can't go around it. Unless you turn back, you must go through it. Before you hold your breath and plunge in, make sure you know the following information.

- Having a **4x4 vehicle with high clearance** is a must, not only to best avoid flooding the engine but also to ensure that water doesn't enter through low side doors.

- Rental agencies **do not cover damage** to vehicles as a result of river crossings. Admitting that you crossed a river (even when no damage is caused) can jeopardize your insurance.

- A dirty river (marked by opaque, brown water) can be a sign that the water came from a mountain. Rainfall at higher elevations increases the likelihood of **flash floods** at lower elevations. These can engulf rivers (and vehicles) at any moment. Although still dangerous, clear and still water is the least risky to enter. Don't attempt to cross a river if it is moving swiftly; you could get swept away. If you misread river currents, flash floods can be deadly.

- Your best chance for success is to **shadow another driver,** ideally

paperwork. In the rental agreement fine print, some agencies require you to notify them immediately after you receive the ticket.

Accidents and Breakdowns

In the event of an accident, Costa Rican law dictates that you must not move your vehicle. It can be tempting to do so if you're holding up traffic (now you can appreciate why road accidents in Costa Rica cause such awful delays), but the scene of the accident will be treated much like the scene of a crime, and evidence cannot be tampered with.

First and foremost, call 911 if you or anyone else has been injured. Next, phone your vehicle rental agency (many will provide a 24-hour emergency line) as well as the traffic accident report line

of the **Instituto Nacional de Seguros** (National Insurance Institute, INS, 1-800-800-8000). If you have a camera or cell phone, take photos of the scene and all vehicles involved for your own records; then wait for assistance to arrive.

BUS

Costa Rican buses are known for being crowded and having windows that slide open just a crack; bumpy roads mean rides aren't always comfortable. However, there are plenty of routes, and buses are generally punctual.

Most passengers are Ticos, so ticket prices are inexpensive, making buses a great option for travelers on a tight budget. To make the most of your time, hop on a bus marked *directo* (direct), which should provide nonstop service or a local driver who knows the area well. Watch how other vehicles proceed and follow the same course. If no one else is around, look for entrance and exit tracks. Sometimes the best route proceeds through the water on an angle and doesn't follow a straight and obvious path.

- It's smart to **prepare for the worst.** Don't attempt to cross a river if you don't have access to a phone and a reliable signal to call for help in case of an emergency. In remote areas of the country where river crossings are most common, it can be hours (or longer) before you meet other people.

- Don't forget to assess the area for **dangerous wildlife.** I wouldn't want to stall a vehicle in the middle of a river with a crocodile on its bank, would you?

- Avoid crossing a river **after dark** when it's next to impossible to assess water depth, condition, and current, not to mention roadblocks and other hazards. Stranding yourself anywhere at nighttime is never safe.

If and when you're good to go (make sure your windows are down and your doors are unlocked), drive slowly but steadily through the water. Don't stop halfway in and don't gun the vehicle to create unnecessary and potentially engine-drowning waves. When you make it across, give yourself a pat on the back for journeying through the jungle like a pro—but don't make it a habit. Each crossing is different, and river conditions can change instantaneously. You can never fully predict what lies ahead.

make only one or two quick stops along the way.

Travel around Costa Rica by bus sometimes requires connections, and these may call for a walk or taxi ride between bus stations. Plan out your routes before you travel to avoid ending up at the wrong destination or spending more time and money than necessary getting to where you need to be. Check and double-check destination names carefully. Beware of similar names, like Puerto Viejo de Talamanca and Puerto Viejo de Sarapiquí; these two places are 200 kilometers apart!

Prepare yourself for the unexpected. Every bus, operator, and route is different. In some cases, usually for longer routes, you'll be riding in a comfortable air-conditioned bus with your luggage tucked away in a storage compartment below the vehicle. In others, you'll be sandwiched between your neighbor and a humidity-drenched window with your belongings stacked on your lap. Sometimes you can arrive at a station, prepurchase a ticket with an assigned seat number, and board the bus when it's time to go. For another route, after purchasing a general ticket, you may need to join a line by the bus's front door and claim a seat on a first-come, first-served basis. If you can, arrive at bus stations at least an hour before departure so you have time to sort out logistics and wait in line if necessary. Keep some small denomination colones handy; several bus stations charge a fee (typically between 200 and 500 colones) to use the bathroom.

TAXI

Taxis serve all major cities and popular tourist areas in Costa Rica. They're a good way to get around towns and cities but aren't the most economical mode of transportation between destinations.

Most **official taxis** are red and display a yellow triangle with a black number on the door. **Official airport taxis** are the exception—they're orange. Most taxi drivers do not speak English, but simply saying the name of your destination is sufficient. You can also ask, *"¿Por favor, me puede llevar a...?"* ("Please, can you take me to...?"), filling in the name of your destination. Plan to pay the exact fare in colones to avoid losing money on a poor exchange rate. Many *taxistas* (taxi drivers) do not carry change. Unofficial taxi drivers, known as *piratas*, are everywhere, but unless you know and trust the driver (as locals often do), they're best avoided. The going rate for an official taxi is 660 colones (approximately US$1.10) for the first kilometer and 615 colones (roughly US$1) for every kilometer thereafter.

Like taxis, **tuk-tuks** (motorized rickshaws) can chauffer you around town. They are unofficial but widely used, especially in some beach towns, and in some areas, they are the only option for getting around. They're primarily used for in-town transportation and, while drivers determine the rates, they are usually slightly cheaper than taxis.

BOAT, FERRY, AND WATER TAXI

Alternatives to ground transportation are boat, ferry, and water taxi rides. Common crossings take place over the Golfo de Nicoya, the Golfo Dulce, and Lago Arenal. Most ferries are large and can carry vehicles on board. Boats and water taxis are significantly smaller; some resemble safari boats, and others look like speedboats. Each service runs according to set schedules and is priced per person per way.

GOLF CART, ATV, AND BIKE

Golf carts (gas or electric) and ATVs (for one or two people) are available to rent, mainly in beach towns. Both require presentation of a valid driver's license. You must be at least 18 years of age to drive a golf cart, and at least 16 years old to drive an ATV. All vehicles should be plated and insured. Be forewarned: ATVs are full of pep and have been known to leave speedy drivers banged up and bruised. For your own safety and the safety of others, please drive slowly. A golf cart or ATV rental should cost $55-100 per day.

You can rent a bike in most tourist towns. Destinations with rugged terrain and bike parks typically offer a selection of mountain bikes. Coastal communities have rows of beach cruisers. Some places have tandem bikes and electric road bikes. Expect to pay $10-60 per day for a bike, depending on the type.

VISAS AND OFFICIALDOM

Many countries, including the United States and Canada, detail entrance requirements to Costa Rica on their own government websites. However, the official source of Costa Rica entry regulations is the **Dirección General de Migración y Extranjería** (General Directorate of Migration and Immigration, www.migracion.go.cr). Up-to-date entry requirements are posted on the department's website.

DOCUMENTS AND REQUIREMENTS
Entry

Entry into Costa Rica requires presentation of a signed, legible, and unexpired **passport** with enough space to receive official stamps. Although you may not be asked to provide this documentation, legally you must come to Costa Rica prepared to provide **proof of intent to exit** before your entry stamp expires; most entry stamps are valid for 90 days. A prepurchased onward flight or bus ticket to another country qualifies as proof of your intent to depart Costa Rica, as does a cruise ship vacation confirmation if you plan to arrive and leave by boat. You must also be able to show that you have **access to at least $300** ($100 for each potential 30-day stay within the standard 90-day access period) to support you during your visit.

Your country of origin determines whether you need a **visa** to enter Costa Rica, as well as whether your passport must be valid for a minimum of one day, three months, or six months. More than 60 countries, including the United States and Canada, are awarded the one-day validity period and do not need a visa. Countries that must abide by the three-month validity period do not require a visa. Countries that must have a passport valid for six months also require a visa to enter Costa Rica. See the website of La Dirección General de Migración y Extranjería for lists of countries that form the various groups.

Minors traveling on their own to Costa Rica must have both a valid passport and **written authorization** to travel from their parents or legal guardians.

In addition to passport requirements, travelers from several African and South American countries must provide proof of **yellow fever vaccination** in order to enter Costa Rica. This requirement could also apply to other nationals who have recently traveled to the flagged countries. A list of the flagged countries can be obtained from the World Health Organization's website (www.who.int) or by calling La Dirección General de Migración y Extranjería (tel. 506/2299-8100). According to some foreign health organizations, vaccinations that protect against hepatitis A, hepatitis B, typhoid, and rabies are suggested but not mandatory. Make sure your routine vaccinations are up to date.

Departure

In order to leave Costa Rica by air, you must pay the **departure tax** ($29 pp). Most airlines incorporate the cost of the tax into the price of their flights. Double-check your airfare's fine print—the charge is usually noted in the price breakdown—to determine if the tax has already been paid. If not, you'll need to pay it at the airport's departure tax desk prior to approaching the airline counter. Some hotels and vehicle rental agencies can pay the tax for you in advance if you'd prefer to save the time and hassle the day you fly.

FOREIGN EMBASSIES

Most foreign embassies are in San José. The **U.S. Embassy** (just north of Road 104, 1.5 km northwest of the Parque Metropolitano La Sabana, tel. 506/2519-2000, https://cr.usembassy.gov, 8am-4:30pm Mon.-Fri.), the **Canadian Embassy** (just east of Road 177, on the south side of Parque Metropolitano La Sabana, tel. 506/2242-4400, www.canadainternational.gc.ca/costa_rica, 8am-4pm Mon.-Thurs., 7:30am-1pm Fri.), and the **British Embassy** (corner of Paseo Colón and Calle 38, tel. 506/2258-2025, www.gov.uk/world/organisations/british-embassy-in-costa-rica, 8am-4pm Mon.-Thurs., 8am-1pm Fri.) are all on the west side of the city.

RECREATION

Costa Rica is an adventure destination. Enjoy two or three of these adrenaline-pumping experiences—or ideally as many as your itinerary, budget, and energy level permit—and you'll understand why. Most activities require **advance reservations.**

Your safety is never fully guaranteed. Accidents can and do happen, sometimes because of a negligent tour operator and other times due to unforeseen events. Select your tour operators carefully; at minimum, stick to those recommended in this book. Many won't allow people with health conditions, those recovering from an operation, or pregnant women to participate in activities out of concern for participants' well-being.

CORONAVIRUS IN COSTA RICA

Costa Rica's government was praised for its swift, stern, and steady response to the coronavirus pandemic, which saw early border, business, beach, and school closures; driving and social gathering restrictions; and face mask mandates. At the time of writing in 2021, much of Costa Rica was beginning to stabilize. The vital, hard-hit tourism industry remains significantly impacted by international travel restrictions, but the situation is constantly evolving.

Now more than ever, Moon encourages its readers to be courteous and ethical in their travel. We ask travelers to be respectful to residents, and mindful of the situation in their chosen destinations when planning their trips.

BEFORE YOU GO

- Check local websites (listed below) for **local restrictions** and the overall health status of the destination and your point of origin. If you're traveling to or from an area that is currently a COVID-19 hot spot, you may want to reconsider your trip.

- Moon encourages travelers to **get vaccinated** if your health status allows, and to take a coronavirus test with enough time to receive your results before your departure if possible. Some destinations may require proof of vaccination or a negative COVID test result before arrival, along with other tests and potentially a self-quarantine period once you've arrived. Check local requirements and factor these into your plans. If your airline or home country requires negative test results, you can get tested in Costa Rica prior to your return.

- Check with your **airline** and the **health authorities** for **updated travel requirements.** Some airlines may be taking more steps than others to help you travel safely, such as limited occupancy; check their websites for more information before buying your ticket. Consider an early or late flight to limit exposure. Flights may be more infrequent, with increased cancellations.

- Pack **hand sanitizer,** a **thermometer,** and plenty of **face masks,** at least one fresh (or freshly washed) mask for each day, or more if you plan to engage in activities that will get the mask wet or sweaty like hiking, canyoneering, and white-water rafting. Consider packing snacks, bottled water, a cooler, or anything else you might need to limit the number of stops along your route.

Be prepared for possible closures and reduced services over the course of your travels.

- **Expect some disruptions.** Events may be postponed or canceled, and some tours and venues may require reservations, enforce limits on the number of guests, have hours of operation different from the ones listed, or be closed entirely. Verify with tour operators which guided excursions are available and whether any aspects of their tour experience cannot be provided during this time.

- **Assess the risk** of entering crowded spaces, joining tours, and taking public transit.

RESOURCES

If you experience COVID-19 symptoms while in Costa Rica, call the nation's **coronavirus hotline** (dial 1322; English-speaking representatives are provided) or 911 in case of an emergency. For additional coronavirus information, see the following websites.

- **Ministerio de Salud** (www.ministeriodesalud.go.cr): The website for Costa Rica's Ministry of Health provides the health status of the nation and breaks down coronavirus case counts by region.

- **Essential Costa Rica** (www.visitcostarica.com): The online presence of the Costa Rican Institute of Tourism lists coronavirus-specific entry requirements for Costa Rica visitors. It also provides the names, locations, and contact details for labs that perform coronavirus testing.

- *Tico Times* (https://ticotimes.net): This online English-language newspaper documents life and travel in Costa Rica during the coronavirus era.

HELPFUL PHRASES

- mask: *mascarilla*
- hand sanitizer: *desinfectante de manos*
- thermometer: *termómetro*
- Do you sell masks?: *¿Vende mascarillas?*
- Do you sell hand sanitizer?: *¿Vende desinfectante de manos?*
- to-go/takeaway: *para llevar*
- Do you have outside seating?: *¿Tiene asientos al aire libre?*

HIKING

Nature trails in government-regulated or private land areas known as **parques nacionales** (national parks), **reservas biológicas** (biological reserves), or **refugios** (refuges) exist in all regions of Costa Rica. Self-guided exploration is permitted at most, typically without advance reservations, but it's still a good idea to visit these places with a guide. The most obvious benefit is the guide's wealth of experience. Knowing where to walk to avoid stepping on a snake, which trees to look at to see birds and sloths, which insect species produce the sounds you hear, why certain root systems look the way they do, and countless other lessons are what turn ordinary walks into educational journeys and extraordinary wildlife-spotting opportunities. In remote regions, guides are strongly recommended for the navigational support and extra security they provide. **Advance reservations** are almost always required for **guided night hikes** and **guided bird-watching hikes** that take place early in the morning.

Hiking conditions and experiences vary immensely due to Costa Rica's diverse terrain, elevation, weather, and ecosystems. Some hikes are quick walks along paved and sometimes wheelchair-accessible paths. Others are challenging climbs through narrow clearings in the forest. You can feel the coolness of clouds on your cheeks in several areas; in others, you may need to wipe sweat from your brow due to the humidity. Familiarize yourself with trail lengths and levels of difficulty before setting out, to avoid hiking a route that is either too physically intense or not stimulating enough.

ZIP-LINING

A favorite recreational activity of many travelers is zip-lining. After being secured in a harness and connected to a pulley with carabiners, you'll be thrust through the forest or skim the top of it while you glide across thick cables (most routes have 7 to 13 cables). Zip-lining activities are also called **canopy tours** in Costa Rica. This term can apply to any experience in and around the treetop canopy, including **hanging bridge tours.** Most of these tours take place in areas with lush, verdant scenery; the best are in **La Fortuna** and **Monteverde.**

Nearly all zip-line tour operators enforce a **minimum age requirement:** typically, children must be at least 3-8 years old. Some also enforce **maximum weight limits,** which depend on the particular zip line's materials and equipment. Zip-lining requires you to stand atop high platforms and soar above the forest floor. In most cases, once you begin the circuit, there's no turning back. If you have a **fear of heights,** skip zip-lining altogether.

Most commonly, zip-lining tours require participants to **brake manually,** with their hands, which requires you to wear a thick glove and place gentle pressure on the cable to slow yourself down. The process sounds more difficult than it is, but if you're concerned about it, go with a tour operator that uses a handlebar system. With this option, you grasp the handlebars and jostle them back and forth to reduce your speed.

For added thrill, some zip line tours offer **superman cables,** hands-free cables you ride while lying on your stomach in a sling, which deliver the feeling of flying through the air like Superman. Other zip line tours provide freefall experiences, sometimes called **Tarzan swings**, where you jump from a high platform and safely fall or "swing" through the forest before gently landing on the ground. Superman cables and Tarzan swings are typically sold as optional canopy tour add-ons; however, some tour operators automatically include the cost of one or both experiences in their zip line tour rates.

Although zip-line tours take place around the forest, they're hardly wildlife-spotting excursions. While you may get lucky and see birds, butterflies, insects, frogs, monkeys, and maybe even sloths along the way, it's best not to expect any sightings to avoid disappointment.

HANGING BRIDGES

Essentially a calm and quiet nature hike with uphill and downhill sections, this experience allows you to walk through the forest and cross a series of bridges along the way. Most hanging bridge attractions offer a combination of stationary bridges and suspension bridges, the latter typically being the highest and the longest. There's a rush that comes with standing in the middle of a suspension bridge, surrounded by the sights and sounds of the rainforest or the cloud forest. Amid the leafy treetop canopy, you'll have decent bird-watching and wildlife-spotting opportunities. Hanging bridge attractions can be explored with or without a tour guide. Most hanging bridge attractions are family friendly and don't have minimum age limits. The best place for these is in **La Fortuna** or **Monteverde.**

WHITE-WATER RAFTING

White-water rafting tours are among the most exciting adventures you can have in Costa Rica. No previous experience is necessary; however, you should be in good physical condition, be able operate a paddle, feel comfortable around water, and have a thirst for thrills.

Most companies enforce a **minimum age requirement** that varies by river according to the class of the rapids. On average, tours on **Class III** and **IV rivers** (the most common for white-water rafting in Costa Rica) require child participants to be at least 12 years old. **Class II** and **III rivers,** typically rafted only by families with young children, tend to allow kids as young as 6 years old to participate.

The risk of sunburn is high, and the results severe, given the many hours spent on the water. Make sure you apply a waterproof variety of high-SPF sunscreen generously and frequently throughout the day.

Most rafts have a waterproof barrel for storage, and many tour guides carry dry bags as well. Any medication you may need during the day can be stored in the raft. Tour outfitters also provide secure storage for other items that you won't need in the raft, such as a set of dry clothes to change into, a towel, and money.

SURFING, SNORKELING, AND SCUBA DIVING

Scheduling water sports during your trip depends greatly on ocean conditions. Always have your provider confirm the latest conditions to avoid snorkeling or diving when the water visibility is poor or surfing when waves are lackluster.

The long Pacific coast provides breaks for surfers of all skill levels. Lessons are offered in abundance. Surf trips to popular breaks are available to advanced-level riders. Beware of dangerous riptides, rip currents, and undertows.

Scuba diving requires a valid certification through **PADI** (the Professional Association of Diving Instructors). If you don't obtain one before you travel, you can do so through most dive shops in beach communities, assuming you have two full days to commit to the course.

FOOD

TYPICAL DISHES

Costa Ricans consume fruit, meat, rice, and beans multiple times daily in a variety of forms. Literally meaning "spotted rooster" in English, **gallo pinto** (a traditional rice and bean blend) is served each morning. In addition to *gallo pinto,* a typical Costa Rican **desayuno** (breakfast) includes fresh fruit, a tortilla with a slice of cheese, or made-to-order *huevos* (eggs). Eggs can be requested *fritos* (fried), *picados* or *revueltos* (both terms mean scrambled), *tiernos* (over easy), or sometimes *duros* (hard boiled). *Café* (coffee), *té* (tea), *agua* (water), and *jugo* (juice) are commonly served drinks.

Casado (a traditional dish that marries servings of rice and beans on a plate, accompanied by a variety of side dishes) is consumed at **almuerzo** (lunch) and/or **cena** (dinner). *Queso frito* (fried cheese) and *plátano frito* (fried plantain, also called *plátano maduro*) commonly accompany the meal, as does a mix of vegetables, typically including *palmito* (heart of palm). **Bocas** (Costa Rica's take on Spanish tapas) commonly include **gallos** (tortillas topped with cheese, egg, or meat). **Tres leches** (a sweet cake soaked with three kinds of milk and topped with whipped cream) and **flan de coco** (coconut flan) are delectable, must-try desserts.

Costa Rican food in general is flavorful but lightly seasoned. Spices are passed over for herbs, and leafy, dark-green cilantro adds a flavorful zip to most dishes. Although some preparations are bland on their own, vinaigrettes, oils, and homemade salsas like *pico de gallo* (diced tomato, pepper, onion, and pineapple mixed with cilantro and lemon juice) enhance the flavors of most foods. Many tables are topped with a bottle of **Salsa Lizano,** the preferred condiment of most Costa Ricans. Adding a few drops of the potent liquid to your meal will give it a tangy, peppery punch.

During holidays or special events, **tamales, *chicharrones*** (fried pork rinds), and **churros** appear on many Costa Rican tables. Sold from carts regularly stationed at beaches and in public parks are **ceviche** (raw seafood or fish marinated in citrus) and **copos** (snow cone-inspired desserts topped with syrup and condensed milk). On the Caribbean coast, Afro-Costa Rican specialties take center stage, including **rondón** (a fish and vegetable coconut-milk soup flavored with Caribbean spices), **patís** (savory turnovers often stuffed with meat, pineapple, or plantain), **pan bon** (a dark sweet bread), and **coconut rice and beans.**

DIETARY RESTRICTIONS

Over the last decade, Costa Rican cooking has shifted toward worldwide culinary trends. Most chefs and waitstaff are conscious of gluten-free diets, as well as what vegetarians and vegans will and won't eat. Organic fruit, vegetable, and coffee plantations dot the country, making for fabulous farm-to-table meals at health-conscious restaurants and accommodations.

Being a **vegetarian** in Costa Rica isn't difficult. Some dishes, like *arroz con vegetales* (rice with vegetables), are naturally vegetarian, and others can be made so simply by asking for the serving without meat or fish. Since Costa Rica's bean-based diet is packed with protein, you shouldn't need to supplement your meals. If you're a **pescatarian,** you'll find yourself surrounded by variety, as many menus include meat and fish plates equally. Not surprisingly, the best fish and seafood in the country are served along the coasts.

Vegans may struggle to find meal options at most run-of-the-mill restaurants. But every day it seems a new little café, diner, or high-end restaurant has popped up with the purpose of catering to vegans. Seek out these specialty eateries and you'll find a fantastic repertoire of creative, innovative, and delicious meals worth eating more than once.

If you avoid **gluten,** it is best to have restaurant waitstaff confirm which menu items contain it. Recipes vary across establishments, so treating meals on a case-by-case basis is the smartest approach. Gluten-free cooking is one of the more recent trends to hit Costa Rica, and not all restaurants have caught up with suitable menu options. A select few have opted to be 100 percent gluten-free.

DRINKS

On humid days, you can quench your thirst with nonalcoholic **batidos** (smoothies) made to order with fresh tropical fruits including *banano* (banana), *piña* (pineapple), *mora* (blackberry), mango, and papaya. The drinks can be made with milk or water. If you're up for something different, give the local delicacy *cas* (guava) a go, or try a glass of **agua de tamarindo** (juice produced from tamarind pulp). **Pipa fría** (cold coconut water) is typically consumed directly from the coconut and is sold all over Costa Rica, generally on beaches, in markets, and at roadside stands. Locally produced alcoholic drinks include **Imperial** and **Pilsen beer, Ron Centenario rum,** and **Cacique guaro** (sugarcane liquor).

By a landslide, **café** (coffee) wins as the most beloved drink in the nation. It's consumed morning, noon, and night. Some restaurants and attractions like coffee plantations and roasteries prepare the beverage traditionally and tableside in a *chorreador* (a wood device equipped with a cloth filter used to brew coffee).

RESTAURANTS

Inexpensive **sodas** (traditional Costa Rican family restaurants) are much more than restaurants; they're authentic establishments, popular gathering places, and sources of the best Costa Rican cuisine. Often found in city centers or markets frequented by locals, these informal establishments, which are sometimes open-air structures filled with picnic tables, are bursting with unassuming character. Menus feature Costa Rican staples, usually with a few pasta or sandwich options thrown in. Several offer **small buffet bars**— usually in the back, near the kitchen—where you can try an assortment of traditional foods. The best spots will top off your visit with a small, complimentary bowl of *arroz con leche* (rice pudding). With hundreds of *sodas* all over Costa Rica (even small towns typically have more than one), you can dine at many throughout your trip if you're looking to save money, indulge in the local cuisine, and feel what it's like to live like a Tico.

If you grow tired of eating at *sodas*, there's no shortage of tourism-oriented restaurants that will happily accept your business. Fine dining isn't the norm in Costa Rica, but several fantastic options exist. Expect a warm or romantic ambience, top-notch service, and enjoyable food and drinks; leave your black-tie attire at home.

ACCOMMODATIONS

Costa Rica offers an immense selection of accommodation types. The types, however, are difficult to define, due to the fluid use of terminology across the industry. Keep in mind that similar hotels may describe themselves in completely different ways. Likewise, two accommodations that couldn't be more different may label themselves as the same kind of establishment—for example, a resort. Use the categories here as a guide, but also recognize that many places don't fall neatly into one.

Lodging prices are determined by many factors, including reputation, location, size, style, room amenities, on-site facilities, travel season, and inclusions (such as meals). **Prices vary significantly within each category.** Hostels, the least expensive lodging option, offer beds in shared rooms as low as $10 per person, but I've seen private rooms in a hostel go for more than $150 a night. A room at a hotel might cost $50 per night in a rural area during the low season but $200 per night at a popular destination during the high season. Adding to the confusion, some resorts cost less than some rustic lodges. Don't make presumptions about cost or quality based on accommodation type.

When selecting your accommodation, **prioritize location.** Accommodations can be in downtown cores where noise may be an issue; on the outskirts of town and a taxi ride, walk, or drive to dining options; down a poorly maintained road; in sketchy areas you may prefer to avoid; or even in areas only accessible by small plane or boat. They may also fall outside of common tour excursion pickup zones, which means you'll end up paying surcharges to tour operators for pickups and drop-offs every time you wish to participate in a guided activity. Find accommodations with desirable locations first, according to your interests, needs, and comfort level, before narrowing the choices according to secondary factors like price, style, and ambience.

Be aware that the sewage lines below some accommodations in the country don't process toilet paper well. Most places will ask that you deposit paper into waste bins.

Cama (bed) sizes may be written in English, Spanish, or a combination of the two languages, as is the case with "*cama* king" and "*cama* queen." A double bed or a full-size bed is called either a "*cama doble*" or a "*cama matrimonial.*" A pair of twin beds or single-size beds is called "*dos camas individuales.*"

Sometimes, rooms are named for their capacity. You may see rooms advertised as the following types: *habitación individual* or *habitación sencilla* (room for 1 person), *habitación doble* (room for 2 people), *habitación triple* (room for 3 people), *habitación cuádruple* (room for 4 people), and *habitación familiar* (room for 4 or more people).

HOSTELS

Hostels in Costa Rica are not unlike hostels elsewhere in the world. Each typically offers a few dormitories—capacity ranges from 4 to 16 people—and many provide women-only rooms. Most are outfitted with bunk beds, but a few offer single beds. Bathrooms are typically *compartido* (shared), as are kitchens and common areas.

Although nearly all hostels cater to young travelers, the ambience in hostels varies significantly. Some have game rooms, television lounges, swimming pools, and a vibrant social atmosphere, while others have libraries or reading nooks and a calmer vibe. Almost all

offer a handful of private rooms (for 1 to 4 people) with private bathrooms.

HOTELS

Hotels range from small and informal buildings to modern high-rises, some with 5 individually styled rooms and others with 100 nearly identical suites. Many resemble one- or two-story motels. Most others comprise multiple structures separated from one another by paved paths or nature trails. Sometimes these structures are called **cabinas** or **cabañas** (both mean cabins), **bungalows, villas,** or **casitas** (little houses). The five terms are used interchangeably. All but a few hotels in Costa Rica provide rooms with *baños privados* (private bathrooms).

BED-AND-BREAKFASTS

Many B&Bs in Costa Rica are no different from hotels. Many strive to provide guests with the quintessential homey, service-oriented experience that differentiates B&Bs from other accommodations, but others simply use the name. If you plan to stay at a B&B, research the accommodation thoroughly to determine the type of experience you'll have.

RANCHES AND LODGES

If you plan to stay at a ranch or lodge, expect accommodations that are rustic in design and decor. Although hotels built as *cabinas, cabañas,* bungalows, villas, and casitas often provide a similar look and feel, ranches and lodges are almost always bucolic. Sometimes they're set on farms and offer a slew of rural activities from horseback riding to cow milking. It's worth noting, however, that these kinds of experiences aren't limited to ranches and lodges; many hotels and resorts (as well as theme parks and small-scale attractions) operate similar activities.

RESORTS

Where Costa Rican accommodations really play it loose is with the term "resort." In most cases, the word refers to a high-quality accommodation, but I've come across several that are mid-range hotels at best. Always research resort options before you select one, and don't rule out small properties; sometimes they're the most intimate and provide the best service.

Most resorts are not **all-inclusive,** meaning that three daily meals and beverages are not automatically included. However, several all-inclusive resorts do exist, especially in Guanacaste (which is home to many of the country's most exclusive accommodations) and in the Osa Peninsula and southern Pacific region (where remoteness and a lack of dining establishments require meals to be provided).

An **eco-resort,** an unregulated title some accommodations bestow upon themselves, is an accommodation that engages in environmentally friendly practices. Not necessarily high-quality accommodations, eco-resorts may be small, family-run hotels, woodsy lodges, or high-end contemporary resorts. Some eco-resorts have earned a **Certificación para la Sostenibilidad Turística** (Certification of Sustainable Tourism). The program is a good starting point for finding green businesses in Costa Rica, but don't dismiss an eco-resort (or any Costa Rican business) if it doesn't have the CST. There are plenty of sustainable properties worth your consideration that aren't part of the program.

VACATION HOME RENTALS

With the rise of companies like **Airbnb** (www.airbnb.com), **VRBO** (www.vrbo.com), and **FlipKey** (www.flipkey.com), it has never been easier to find a house to crash at throughout your Costa Rica travels. But the option isn't always safe, especially if you plan to travel alone or to remote areas. If you like the idea of having a large space to spread out in and an opportunity to cook your own meals, you'll find many hotels offer both. **Apartotels,** hotels outfitted with apartment-style rooms, may be exactly what you're looking for.

HEALTH AND SAFETY

HEALTH

Potential health hazards are ubiquitous in Costa Rica, but most won't cause a problem if you pay attention and take normal precautions. Pack a basic first aid kit so you can treat minor cuts, scrapes, burns, stings, bites, and sprains. Cleanse and disinfect your hands often, especially after visiting areas where wildlife is present. If you fall ill or suffer a major injury (severe bleeding, bruising, vomiting, or having a high fever are clear indicators), seek medical attention immediately.

In most developed areas of the country where tourism is present (except for the Caribbean), tap water is considered safe to drink and is consumed by locals. Bottled water is preferred by most travelers and is widely available for purchase at grocery stores and restaurants.

Diseases and Common Ailments

Dengue, chikungunya, malaria, and the **Zika virus** are the most pressing health concerns for visitors. However, cases of each are rare. Travelers are more likely to encounter episodes of **traveler's diarrhea,** which can be treated with over-the-counter medications or by letting it run its course. Most of the time, the upset is caused by a sudden change of diet; eating or drinking lots of fresh tropical fruit can bring it on too. Don't let yourself get dehydrated; drink water regularly.

Bites, Stings, and Sun Exposure

There's no shortage of bugs, bees, spiders, scorpions, and snakes in the forests, and there's little you can do after you've been bitten or stung by one—apart from waiting out the itch or burn or seeking medical care. Travel proactively. Use waterproof sunscreen and a strong insect repellent. Some people swear by Avon's Skin So Soft line, which has a few bug guard options. Others prefer products with DEET. Regardless of which product you purchase, buy it in a spray bottle (not an aerosol) so it's suited for air travel.

Use mosquito nets whenever they're provided with accommodations. Shake out shoes, towels, and clothes, especially items that have been left outside, before putting them on or packing them away. Check under beds and tables and in baths and showers for surprise guests. Keep unscreened windows closed as often as you can. Limit time spent around swampy areas or walking around at night. Avoid being out in the sun for long periods of time to prevent sunstroke. If you have open wounds, keep them fully covered while you're active during the day to help prevent infection.

MEDICAL CARE

In the event of an emergency, call 911. Ambulances can also be reached by phoning 128 or the central office of the Cruz Roja (Red Cross, tel. 506/2542-5000, www.cruzroja.or.cr), which has several stations around the country. Serious illnesses and injuries should be treated at the *emergencias* (emergencies) department of a hospital. The majority of hospitals in Costa Rica have one.

If you're far from a hospital, you can visit a clinic. Some are small, informal public clinics, and others are top-of-the-line private medical centers. Nearly every town has at least one clinic, typically an *ebais* overseen by the government-run Caja Costarricense de Seguro Social (Costa Rican Social Security Fund, CCSS or simply the Caja, www.ccss.sa.cr). The CCSS also oversees public hospitals. Several private hospitals dot the nation and are known for providing the highest level of medical care in Costa Rica.

For non-urgent concerns, some large hotels have on-call medical professionals on retainer. Most towns have at least one pharmacy (cities typically have many) stocked with run-of-the-mill items including medications for headaches, stomachaches, muscle soreness, itch relief, and countless other conditions. Pharmacies also carry a range of contraceptives. A surprising number of pharmacies in touristy areas have English-speaking staff.

SAFETY

When common sense is exercised, traveling throughout Costa Rica is generally safe. Travelers should be extra alert in San José and cities around the Central Valley. These areas account for roughly 70 percent of all victim-based crimes in Costa Rica); the Caribbean accounts for an additional 10 percent. Always keep your wits about you wherever you go.

In case of an emergency, it's easiest to call 911, which will connect you to the police for assistance. If you're a victim of a crime, you can contact the tourist police (tel. 506/2286-1473), who typically have English-speaking staff, and/or the Organismo de Investigación Judicial (Judicial Investigation Agency, OIJ, tel. 506/2295-3000, https://sitiooij. poder-judicial.go.cr/), Costa Rica's central crime investigation unit. For assistance with less pressing matters, you can ask for help from accommodation or restaurant staff, vehicle rental agencies, or tourism companies. Most Ticos are willing to lend a helping hand.

If you need to reach the fire department, dial 118, or call the regular emergency dispatch via 911 and ask for the *bomberos* (firefighters).

Police

Costa Rica has two police forces that operate under different divisions of the government. Under the watch of the Ministerio de Obras Públicas y Transportes (Ministry of Public Works and Transportation, MOPT), the *policía de tránsito* (transit police) oversee transportation-related matters that pertain to permissions and licenses, driving laws, and parking infractions.

They usually wear uniforms with white shirts and vests (typically with *Tránsito* on them) and drive navy-blue pickup trucks or motorcycles. You'll see them along the sides of roads and highways with their radars ready to catch speeders.

Under the umbrella of the **Ministerio de Seguridad Pública** (Ministry of Public Security, MSP), the *fuerza pública* (public force) maintains public safety in Costa Rica. Divisions of the group include border police, coast guards, and tourist police, the last of which have English-speaking officers to best assist travelers when problems arise. Officers of the *fuerza pública* usually wear navy-blue uniforms and vests (with *Policía* on them) and drive white pickup trucks, motorcycles, or sedans.

Police stations, open 24 hours daily, are scattered throughout the country. Most cities and large towns have one, but they're noticeably absent from several beachside communities.

Robbery and Theft

Countrywide, theft is a problem. Instances usually occur in the form of **pickpocketing** or theft of possessions left in or on unattended areas like beaches, parked vehicles, and bus storage compartments. To minimize risk, use hotel safes whenever provided, hide your camera equipment while sightseeing, and don't wear jewelry. Always keep your eyes on your luggage, especially at bus stations and airports, and keep your cash concealed; divide cash and hide it in various pockets across your body and belongings. Travel with a copy of your passport and important documents so you have backups in the event the originals are stolen. Better yet, email yourself electronic copies so there's always a copy to retrieve if needed.

Assault

Episodes of assault against travelers, especially violent assault, are rare, but they do happen. Some of the most unfortunate incidents are the result of opportunistic nighttime attacks. There are actions you can take to lower your risk of becoming a target. Being vigilant at night is a must. After dark, don't withdraw money at ATMs, drive (if possible), or hang out on the beach or in any city park.

There is safety in numbers; travel with others whenever possible and stick to areas where people are regularly present. If you are a solo traveler—and especially if you're traveling during the low season, when many towns become desolate—visit popular destinations. If you decide to go out at night alone, especially to drink, you're an easy target.

Water and Beach Safety

Dangerous riptides, rip currents, and undertows exist off the shores of many beaches along both coasts. Do yourself a favor and research how to get out of a riptide before you travel. Most beaches in Costa Rica are not staffed with lifeguards, but an increasing number have signposts that issue stern warnings. Abide by them! Costa Rica's open water claims far too many lives every year; it's one of the leading causes of accidental deaths in the nation. You may be a strong swimmer, but you're no match for the ocean.

Extreme caution should also be exercised around waterfalls and swimming holes, which are often surrounded by jagged rocks that make it easy to slip. Don't climb up the side of a waterfall, swim near the base of a powerful cascade, or jump from the top unless accompanied by a tour outfitter who has appropriately scouted out hazards and measured pool depth. Always keep young children and weak swimmers within arm's reach near oceans, lakes, rivers, streams, waterfalls, swimming holes, hot springs, and hotel pools.

As silly as it may sound, don't station yourself directly under the tall palms that back many of Costa Rica's beaches. Coconuts have been known to fall, and they can cause significant damage when dropped from great heights. Pick a shady spot elsewhere

TRAVEL SMARTLY AND SAFELY

Maintaining awareness of your surroundings while you travel can save your life. Vacationing in Costa Rica is exciting, and it's easy to get caught up in the thrill. When you vow to leave your troubles behind on vacation, you may detach yourself from other realities too. Try to maintain a clear head, even while it's pumped full of adrenaline and clouded by the chaos of travel. At the very least, these suggestions should help you become a more conscious and prepared traveler.

Don't sacrifice safety for selfies. Accidents and sometimes deaths have occurred as a result of people taking selfies. Remember, your trip is just a trip! No Instagram-worthy photo of you in a risky place or position is worth your life.

Trust your instincts. Your gut knows when something is wrong. If you're unsure about an experience, such as the safety of a vehicle or an activity, the remoteness of a town, the qualifications of a tour guide, the preparation of a meal, or the condition of a back-road route, don't take the chance.

Remain cautious when befriending strangers. Ticos are friendly and sociable people. Making a friend or two is common, and it isn't a bad idea so long as you keep your willingness to trust others in check. Exercise caution if a stranger invites you out, whether to a bar, the beach, or their home, especially at night.

Be (and stay) organized. Balance relaxation with organization. You can be lazy on vacation; just don't forget to monitor your belongings and watch where you walk. When you let your guard down, someone (with sticky fingers and their eyes on your stuff) or something (like a fallen tree limb you could easily trip over) could make your travel experience miserable.

Plan the details too. Beyond the time you've put into choosing accommodations, securing transportation, and reserving tours, consider other details that will contribute to your travel experience. Estimate travel times between destinations so you can plan stops for snacks. Schedule ample sleep and rest each day to avoid physical exhaustion. Review restaurant menus online ahead of time.

if you can. If you can't, lie under palm fronds as far away from the center of the tree as possible.

Getting Lost

Occasionally, hikers get lost in wooded areas because they either accidentally veered off course or chose to explore an area where access is not permitted. Most of Costa Rica's national parks, biological reserves, and wildlife refuges provide well-marked trails that are easy to follow. It's not difficult to stick to the paths, but it's always a good idea to take a photo of the attraction's map when you enter or take a hard copy if one exists. Some attractions are notorious for having untended trails. In these cases, having a tour guide who knows the area well is a must.

TRAVEL TIPS

SALUTATIONS AND ETIQUETTE

The most common greeting in Costa Rica is *"Hola"* ("Hello"), followed by either *"Buenos días"* ("Good morning"), *"Buenas tardes"* ("Good afternoon"), *"Buenas noches"* ("Good evening"), or *"¿Cómo está?"* ("How are you?"). Shaking hands takes place in the workplace. Kissing on one cheek is common among family members and close friends. Use of either is rare within tourism settings.

Costa Ricans practice most of the same rules of etiquette that the majority of North Americans are accustomed to. Act politely, don't dress provocatively around religious centers and during homestays, and give up your seat on the bus if you see an elderly person or a parent with a child standing in the aisle.

Many Costa Ricans value humility; off-putting behavior typically receives a wry expression of *"¡Qué humilde!"* ("How humble!"). Costa Rican culture also prioritizes relationships with family and friends over money. This means that rude behavior, typically with respect to showing off money, isn't well received. Bartering for lower prices is viewed as tacky, as is waving around cash or acting entitled.

Outside the realm of tourism, Costa Rica's laid-back *pura vida* attitude contributes to a general lack of urgency across personal and business affairs. **Tico time,** a phrase describing the slow pace at which things tend to progress, is a reality in Costa Rica. Be patient if service is slow. Within the tourism industry (which is partially driven by expat business owners), operations from guided tours to transportation services run like clockwork on set schedules.

MONEY

The local currency in Costa Rica is the colón (pronounced coh-lohn). The plural form is colones (pronounced coh-loh-nays). Bills are offered in denominations of 20,000 (orange), 10,000 (green), 5,000 (yellow), 2,000 (blue), and 1,000 (red). *Mil* (one thousand) is written on each. Gold-colored coins come in denominations of 500, 100, 50, 25, 10, and 5. Common monetary terms and phrases are: *dinero* (money), *plata* (a slang term for money used to imply cash), and *en efectivo* (to pay in cash).

Prices in Costa Rica appear in U.S. dollars or colones. Costa Rica uses a period instead of a comma in depicting numbers of 1,000 or greater. For example, if items in a shop are priced in colones, the price might appear as 10.000. This figure is equivalent to 10,000 colones. To make things even more complicated for U.S. and Canadian visitors, the symbol for colón (₡) is similar to the symbol that the United States and Canada use for cent (¢).

In popular tourist destinations, U.S. dollars are accepted by most businesses including accommodations, tour operators, transportation service providers, restaurants, souvenir stores, grocery stores, pharmacies, and gas stations. The majority will not accept Canadian dollars, euros, or other currencies unless their owner has a connection to the foreign country. Businesses in non-touristy towns and remote areas prefer payment in colones. Most establishments won't accept bills greater than US$20, so be sure to bring money in low denominations.

If you don't want to pay in cash, credit card payments (with Visa, Mastercard, and, in fewer cases, American Express and Discover) are accepted by most establishments. If you have two cards, bring both to Costa Rica, in case the *cajero automático* (ATM) eats one, you lose one, or one gets stolen. Your card provider may charge fees if you use a credit card in the country, including one fee for out-of-country purchases and another for foreign exchange when charges are processed in colones. If you plan to visit ATMs often throughout your trip—only taking out small increments of money every few days of travel—you'll get hit with hefty service fees. To avoid paying unnecessary fees, travel with as

PACKING LIST

- Quick-dry clothing
- Multiple swimming suits
- Non-terrycloth towels (microfiber cloths are thin, light, and super absorbent
- Pocket handkerchief, bandana, or other small cloth (for humid forests)
- Sunscreen and insect repellent (more expensive in Costa Rica)
- Sunglasses with clips or bands to secure them during activities
- Flip-flops and/or sandals with arch supports that are suitable for sand
- Walking shoes
- Hiking boots or trail runners (no open toes or slits; some wilderness attractions deny entry to anyone without closed shoes)
- Long pants and long-sleeved shirt (for forests and adventure activities like zip-lining and canyoneering)
- Binoculars
- Camouflage clothing (for bird-watching or wildlife-spotting)
- Waterproof rain jacket or poncho (umbrellas are impractical in dense forests and during adventure tours)
- Waterproof case or bag big enough to carry your phone, identification, and money
- Flashlight and/or headlamp (it's dark by 6pm in Costa Rica)
- Anti-nausea medication (helpful while traversing curving, mountainous roads)
- Backpack (with waterproof rain cover)

much cash as you'll spend throughout your trip. If doing so makes you nervous, rely on ATMs and credit cards, and consider the extra fees payment for your peace of mind.

Payment Requests

Although Costa Rica is a popular tourist destination, many businesses are behind the times with respect to payment options. Payment policies vary across companies. Some will ask you to sign a **credit card authorization form** in order to guarantee bookings. This gives them permission to charge your credit card in the event of a last-minute cancellation or if you're a no-show. Some companies don't use credit card processing machines and only accept payment in cash.

Nearly every business will accept payment via **international wire transfer** (note that there's a transfer fee associated with this method), but only a small fraction of businesses will collect payment via convenient online tools like **PayPal.** A handful, including many water sports outfitters and vehicle rental agencies, need a copy of your identification.

Tax

In 2019, a 13 percent **value-added tax** (VAT) was introduced. The mandatory VAT applies to all tourism services; however, businesses are not required to charge the full 13 percent until 2023. Depending on when you travel to Costa Rica and the companies you use, you could be charged up to 13 percent VAT on arrangements for your trip. Because the tax rate is at the discretion of each business, you may pay different rates across companies.

Many tour operators, hotels, and transportation service providers automatically factor the VAT into their published rates, but several do not. Have each company you book through confirm whether tax is included in their rates. If tax isn't included, inquire about the tax rate so you know exactly how much VAT you'll be expected to pay.

Restaurants have long charged Costa Rica's original sales tax (also 13 percent), so most are unaffected by the VAT. Look for the phrase *impuesto de ventas incluido* (sales tax included, IVI) on websites and menus to learn whether the cost of food and drinks includes tax. Be aware that many restaurants also impose a 10 percent service fee (an automatic gratuity) separate from sales tax. Restaurants might include one charge but not the other, so keep your eyes open for both.

Double taxation—charging 13 percent VAT and 13 percent sales tax—is illegal. You should only ever pay one tax, never both.

Currency Exchange

The currency exchange rate hovers around US$1 to 700 colones. Always know the going rate to avoid losing money when making purchases. It helps to have a small conversion chart in your back pocket while you shop: 2,000 colones is roughly $3.50, 5,000 colones is roughly $8.50, and so on. Some businesses insist on applying their own exchange rates if you want to pay in U.S. dollars, which, not surprisingly, lean in their favor.

Money can be exchanged at airport counters, banks, and some hotels. No matter where you go in the country, if you pay for an item in U.S. dollars, you'll likely receive change in colones. You'll collect the currency over the course of your trip, so there's no need to convert all your money before you travel.

Tipping

Tipping isn't common among locals. But since many foreigners, mainly Americans and Canadians, are accustomed to awarding gratuities at home, tipping has made its way to Costa Rica and is now an expectation in the tourism industry. If the level of service you receive warrants a tip, don't hesitate to give one.

Tour guides earn the highest amount, ranging around $5-10 per person per guide for short excursions and $5-15 per person per guide for full-day adventures. In most cases, tips can be handed directly to your tour guide. Some attractions provide tip boxes, and pooled tips are then divided among the staff.

Some restaurants charge an automatic 10 percent gratuity called the *impuesto de servicio* (service tax). In general, *sodas* don't do so, but tourist-geared establishments do. Look to the menu or waitstaff for confirmation. For exceptional service, a tip of up to 20 percent (including the automatic gratuity) is appropriate.

It's also kind to give a few dollars to hotel porters and to leave the same amount on your night table (sometimes an envelope is provided) for hotel housekeeping staff. Taxi drivers aren't usually tipped, but you can round up the fare if you like. You can also give a few dollars to private transfer service and shared shuttle service drivers, as well as boat and water taxi captains, as a thank you for providing safe travel.

PHONES

Telephone numbers in Costa Rica have eight digits. Most landlines begin with 2, and most cell phone numbers begin with 8. Many landline numbers correspond with geographical regions. For example, most landlines around La Fortuna begin with 2479, landlines around Manuel Antonio begin with 2777, and so on. Newer number assignments, which aren't yet common in the country, can start with 3, 4, 5, 6, or 7. Costa Rica's country code is 506, which does not need to be dialed when making local calls.

It's smart to have access to a cell phone in Costa Rica for navigational and emergency purposes. Unless your phone provider offers a phenomenal deal on international calling and data usage, you'll want to purchase a service plan in Costa Rica to avoid astronomical long distance and roaming fees. There are several Costa Rican providers to choose from, but I've found **Kölbi** (www.kolbi.cr) to be the most reliable. Kölbi has offices (named Tienda Kölbi or Agencia ICE) in popular destinations such as San José, Liberia, Alajuela, La Fortuna, Monteverde, Sámara, Nosara, Jacó, Quepos, Dominical, and Uvita. Conveniently, competitor **Claro** (www.claro.cr) has a small desk near baggage claim at the Aeropuerto Internacional Juan Santamaría. Through either provider you can buy service and a SIM card ($4-20, depending on the quantity of data).

Your phone must be unlocked (not tethered to one particular service provider) to work in Costa Rica. Before leaving home, contact your service provider to confirm whether your phone is locked, and if it is, ask about unlocking it. Hold on to the casing of the SIM card and the paperwork you receive; the documents contain codes and numbers you'll need to activate and reload the service. SIM cards can be reloaded at most grocery stores in Costa Rica. Although cell and Internet service works well in most areas of the country, signal strength weakens as you venture into remote areas; this is the case regardless of which provider you choose.

The free smartphone application **WhatsApp** is used widely in Costa Rica. With an Internet connection, you can place phone calls, send text and voice messages, and transfer photos and videos over the app for free. Many tourism businesses have WhatsApp-equipped cell phones so you can call or message them. Look for the WhatsApp logo on a business's website to determine if the company uses the application. If you download and install the app on your cell phone prior to coming to Costa Rica, you'll be able to use it within minutes of purchasing and installing a SIM card.

Without a cell phone, you can make calls from phone booths in towns; they're usually in public parks or near street corners. Calling cards can be purchased from telecommunication offices and supermarkets. Several hotels offer free local calls, and some offer free international calling too.

Wireless Internet is readily available in Costa Rica. Most accommodations provide it for free, but service may be limited to common areas like lobbies. Some private transfer service providers and shared shuttle service providers have vehicles equipped with Wi-Fi so you can access the Internet on your personal device while traveling between destinations.

ACCESSIBILITY

Unfortunately, much of Costa Rica is inaccessible to travelers with disabilities. Pothole-ridden roads, broken sidewalks, and unpaved paths make it tough to get around, but doing so isn't impossible. Some taxis, buses (mainly in San José), shared shuttle services, and private transfer services can provide wheelchair-suitable transport if requested in advance. Most modern hotels provide at least one wheelchair-accessible room and wheelchair-accessible facilities; however, many hotel restaurants don't have wheelchair-friendly tables.

PHILANTHROPY FOR TRAVELERS

Ever since my husband and I developed a *fútbol* shoe donation project for underprivileged Costa Rican kids enamored of the sport, I've been a proponent of travel philanthropy. The idea is simple—that a vacation can also be an opportunity to help your intended destination. This is done by bringing items from home to donate during your travels.

a child receiving *fútbol* shoes and gear

The American nonprofit **Pack for a Purpose** (www.packforapurpose. org) offers a great way to get involved. Simply visit the organization's website to learn which Costa Rican companies (mainly hotels) are involved in the project and which common items, ranging from school supplies to lightly used clothing to health products (medication excluded), are on the current wish list. Purchase or collect the items from home, bring them to Costa Rica, and drop them off at a project-approved business. (Note: If you plan to donate items with a combined value of over US$500, you may need to pay an import tax to bring the items into the country.) Of the many accommodations I recommend in this guide, **Águila de Osa** (in Bahía Drake), the **RipJack Inn** (in Playa Grande), and the **Si Como No Resort** (in Manuel Antonio) all participate in Pack for a Purpose.

Carara National Park, Manuel Antonio National Park, and **Cahuita National Park** all offer wheelchair-accessible trails.

Santa Teresa's **Shaka Costa Rica** (on the main road that runs parallel to Playa Santa Teresa, 6.5 km northwest of the intersection at Carmen, tel. 506/2640-1118, www.shakacostarica. com) runs youth surf camps for adventurers in wheelchairs in collaboration with the **Ocean Healing Group** (www. oceanhealinggroup.org). **Playa Blanca** in Cahuita provides wheelchair-accessible paths across the sand, nearly to the water's edge.

Travelers who are **visually impaired** will encounter information written in Braille within **Carara National Park** and **Manuel Antonio National Park.** But even areas of Costa Rica without such placards make great travel destinations. Costa Rica has an invigorating natural soundtrack, rich and earthy smells, and flavorful tastes; it can be enjoyed with all the senses.

WOMEN TRAVELING ALONE

Women traveling alone should be vigilant about where and when they travel. In general, daytime visits to popular destinations and attractions are safe. If you go out at night, stick to recommended establishments and avoid venturing into isolated or non-touristy neighborhoods. Consider joining a guided night tour, such as a pub crawl, to experience the nightlife as part of a group led by a local guide. If you're approached at a bar and asked to dance, it's okay to decline the offer with "*No, gracias.*" Don't accept drinks from strangers. Prearrange a private pickup service for the end of the night through your accommodation or have them confirm the telephone number for the closest official taxi service. Use only official red taxis, as opposed to unlicensed taxis, to move around towns. Never share a ride with people you don't know.

Don't go to a park or the beach at night. Visiting these places, which are typically void of security and poorly lit after dark, can put you at risk of robbery or assault. If possible, stay at known and secure hotels or hostels in town centers, not vacation homes or other accommodation types in the outskirts of an area. Travel during the high season when you're most likely to share accommodations, restaurants, and transportation vehicles with others. If you must travel during the low season, avoid remote areas of the country: These empty during down periods and will leave you feeling like you're on your own. Use shared shuttle services, as opposed to taxis or private transfer services, to best surround yourself with other passengers while traveling long distances through unfamiliar areas.

RACIAL AND CULTURAL DIVERSITY

Generally speaking, Costa Rica is welcoming of people of different races and cultures. But that's not to suggest that racism doesn't exist. Marginalized racial groups, namely Afro-Costa Ricans and Indigenous groups, struggle to attain the same opportunities, positions of power, and resources as non-marginalized Costa Ricans.

Progress toward equality is evident, albeit inconsistent, in Costa Rica. Annual celebrations like Limón's **Carnaval del Caribe** (Caribbean Carnival), a grand display that embraces Afro-Costa Rican culture, and milestones like the government's 2016 ratification of the **Inter-American Convention against Racism, Racial Discrimination, and Related Forms of Intolerance,** a formal denouncement of race-based inequality in Costa Rica, are steps in the right direction. The assimilation of some Indigenous people into mainstream society, and the increased presence of Afro-Costa Ricans in regions outside of the Caribbean are also encouraging trends. Rising xenophobic attitudes toward Nicaraguan immigrants—Costa Rica's largest immigrant group—are very troubling.

Within the tourism sector, international visitors—regardless of their background—are equally appreciated for the income and job opportunities they help generate. Because they're regularly exposed to diverse clientele, tourism business owners and employees tend to be more accepting of unfamiliar customs, values, and norms than the rest of the population. Though rare racist behavior can occur anywhere, it is less likely to at popular tourist destinations.

Religion plays a central role in the lives of many Ticos, most of whom are devout Roman Catholics. Accounts of anti-Semitism, Islamophobic acts, and other forms of religious discrimination are uncommon. Rarely is religion discussed during touristic experiences; however, if the subject is broached by someone you don't know and trust, it's best to keep talk light and minimal to avoid possible offense.

LGBTQ TRAVELERS

Costa Rica isn't as progressive in LGBTQ matters as the United States and Canada. But it's not an intolerant country by any means. Public displays of affection should be kept to a minimum, but this applies to couples of all sexual orientations. Roughly 300,000 LGBTQ travelers visit Costa Rica each year. San José and Quepos/Manuel Antonio have the largest concentration of LGBTQ-run establishments.

Costa Rica is making strides toward inclusion and unity, allowing its citizens the option to alter their name and gender on identification documents. Though still widely underrepresented in positions of power, a few openly gay and lesbian individuals hold political and legislative titles and are no doubt influential in moving the country forward. Arguably, Costa Rica's greatest step toward accepting LGBTQ people was taken in 2020 when the nation became the first in Central America (the sixth country in all of Latin America) to legalize same-sex marriage. Costa Rica also awarded same-sex couples the right to adopt children jointly.

Most tourism businesses in Costa Rica work to provide respectful, safe, and enjoyable experiences for all travelers. Some explicitly state on their website that they're LGBTQ-friendly, but others that don't are equally welcoming. Several travel companies offer tailored vacation packages with LGBTQ travelers in mind. With same-sex marriage now legal, a number have opened up their destination wedding services to couples of all orientations.

Instrumental in creating a more inclusive Costa Rica is the **Cámara de Comercio Diversa de Costa Rica** (Costa Rica Chamber of Diverse Commerce, CCDCR, www.ccdcr.org), an organization that teaches local businesses ways to support the invaluable LGBTQ-traveler demographic. If you would rather use an LGBT-specific travel agency to plan your vacation, **Costa Rica Gay Traveler** (www.costaricagaytraveler.com), based in San José, is a great choice.

Marcha de la Diversidad, also known as **Pride Costa Rica,** is an annual event that draws LGBTQ community members and allies to the streets of downtown San José each June or July. It's marked with a lively, colorful, and musical parade. **Orgullo en la Playa** (Pride on the Beach) is a similar but smaller gathering that takes place in Manuel Antonio around mid-July. Event listings are often documented in **Playita,** Costa Rica's LGBTQ-themed magazine. A free copy is available to download on the website of **Gay Tours Costa Rica** (www.gaytourscr.com), a travel company that specializes in creating tours and getaways for gay travelers.

SENIOR TRAVELERS

Life in the tropics can be hot and humid. Carry plenty of water to ensure you stay hydrated. If you're active at home, you'll love being active in Costa Rica. If you're not, don't overdo it while here. Bring all the medication you'll need from home; you may find having a doctor's note and a medication list eases travel through the airport. Also bring any medical equipment you may need. Although Costa Rica has reliable hospitals, clinics, and pharmacies, they may not carry the items you need or be open or nearby when you need them. Cold temperatures at high elevations can be chilling, so travel with warm clothing if you're headed to the mountains.

TRAVELING WITH CHILDREN

Costa Rica is a family vacation destination. It's also an adventure destination in a tropical jungle. Prepare your children for hot days, winding drives around mountains, and unexpected creepy-crawlies. Insects and small geckos often find their way into accommodations. Pack snacks for long car rides. A few transportation services offer free onboard Wi-Fi to help pass the time, and if you plan to drive yourself around Costa Rica, bring or rent (through your chosen vehicle rental agency) a child car seat. Costa Rican law dictates that children under the age of 12 who are smaller than 1.45 meters (57 inches) must ride in one.

Several tour operators impose minimum age limits for activity participation. Some activities, primarily those that require use of a harness, have additional minimum height and weight limits. Verify with each tour operator in advance to avoid disappointment on the day of your reserved excursions. It's also a good idea to confirm tour durations and any potential difficulties (like uphill treks) in advance to avoid surprises. Many tour operators, accommodations, and shared shuttle service providers offer discounted rates for child travelers or don't charge for them at all. A few restaurants have children's meals.

INDEX

LIST OF MAPS

PHOTO CREDITS

National Parks Travel Guides from Moon

Find your next adventure with Moon Travel Guides

MAP SYMBOLS

═══	Highway	○	City/Town	🅿	Parking Area	⛰	Small Park
═══	Primary Road	◉	State Capital	🆃	Trailhead	▲	Mountain Peak
═══	Secondary Road	⊛	National Capital	🅱	Bike Trailhead		Unique Natural Feature
┄┄┄	Unpaved Road	★	Top 3 Sight	🅰	Camping		
┄┄┄	Trail	🥾	Top Hike	🅿	Picnic Area		Unique Hydro Feature
───	Paved Trail	★	Highlight/Sight	Ⓜ	Mass Transit		
▒▒▒	Pedestrian Walkway	•	Accommodation	✈	Airport	🕊	Waterfall
┄┄┄	Ferry	▼	Restaurant/Bar	✗	Airfield	🎿	Ski Area
▬▬▬	Railroad	■	Other Site	🛐	Place of Worship	⬭	Glacier

CONVERSION TABLES

°C = (°F - 32) / 1.8
°F = (°C x 1.8) + 32
1 inch = 2.54 centimeters (cm)
1 foot = 0.304 meters (m)
1 yard = 0.914 meters
1 mile = 1.6093 kilometers (km)
1 km = 0.6214 miles
1 fathom = 1.8288 m
1 chain = 20.1168 m
1 furlong = 201.168 m
1 acre = 0.4047 hectares
1 sq km = 100 hectares
1 sq mile = 2.59 square km
1 ounce = 28.35 grams
1 pound = 0.4536 kilograms
1 short ton = 0.90718 metric ton
1 short ton = 2,000 pounds
1 long ton = 1.016 metric tons
1 long ton = 2,240 pounds
1 metric ton = 1,000 kilograms
1 quart = 0.94635 liters
1 US gallon = 3.7854 liters
1 Imperial gallon = 4.5459 liters
1 nautical mile = 1.852 km

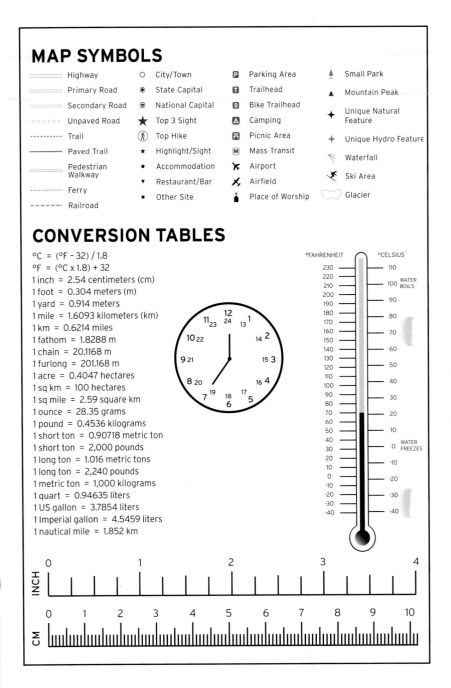

MOON BEST OF COSTA RICA

Avalon Travel
Hachette Book Group
1700 Fourth Street
Berkeley, CA 94710, USA
www.moon.com

Editors: Leah Gordon, Kevin McLain
Acquiring Editor: Nikki Ioakimedes
Copy Editor: Brett Keener
Graphics and Production Coordinator:
Darren Alessi
Cover Design: Marcie Lawrence
Interior Design: Tabitha Lahr
Map Editor: Kat Bennett
Cartographer: John Culp
Foldout Map Cartographer: John Culp
Indexer: Rachel Kuhn

ISBN-13: 9781640497337

Printing History
1st Edition — December 2022
5 4 3 2 1

Front cover photo: tourist rides the
canopy zip line at Sky Adventures
Arenal Park © Jon Arnold Images Ltd /
Alamy Stock Photo
Back cover photos: Keel-billed Toucans
© Ondřej Prosický | Dreamstime.com
(top); Río Celeste, La Fortuna © Chris
Mouyiaris | Dreamstime.com (middle);
tourists on a beach in Manuel Antonio
National Park © Matyas Rehak |
Dreamstime.com (bottom)

Printed in China by RR Donnelley